"... out of the thousands of books that flow by, and the scores that end up as worthy of review, [this book] looked valuable enough to want for myself."

Howard Rheingold, Editor-in-Chief of
The Millennium Whole Earth Catalog
Upon ordering a copy for personal use

"Does this book live up to its pretentious title? Yes, it does, better than any other basic design book I've encountered, ..."

J. Baldwin
The Millennium Whole Earth Catalog

"... both informative and entertaining"

Aletha Solter, author of
Helping Young Children Flourish

"*The Creative Problem Solver's Toolbox* should be issued in every elementary school, to every child who can read, and used as the fundamental textbook for life. The major problems of society could easily be eliminated by the development of thought patterns [this] book generates."

Patricia Aitchison
School Trustee in Alberta, Canada

"It's the creativity book I keep coming back to. It truly is a toolbox. ... easiest and quickest ... crystal clear!"

Sheila Glazov
Leader of creativity workshops

Translated into six languages!

The number-one best-seller among the future-oriented books sold by *The Futurist* magazine

*September/October and November/December 1994 issues of **The Futurist***

"... a lovely and innovative antidote to the kind of linear thinking most of us learned while growing up .... This is a key skill ... for all of us who must design solutions for the challenges of day-to-day life. ... these tools can be applied to any area of life — from inventive to business to personal."

Ilene Rosoff
The WomanSource Catalog & Review

"... the best primer for teaching innovative problem-solving thought techniques published to date. ... an indispensable resource ..."

Dennis P. Eichhorn
Loompanics Unlimited, seller of unusual books

"[This book] has revitalized my outlook on problem solving. I have gained a renewed energy from this book and it has created a fun environment from which I now look forward to each new problem with confidence."

Ken Myers
Transportation Consultant Services

The
Creative Problem Solver's
Toolbox

A Complete Course in the
Art of Creating Solutions
to Problems of Any Kind

By
Richard Fobes

First Edition
ISBN 0-9632221-0-4
Library of Congress Catalog Card Number: 92-80544

Published by:
  Solutions Through Innovation
  PO Box 19003
  Portland, OR 97280-0003

Printed on recycled paper. 1999 printing.

Legal Disclaimer: This book does not offer advice as to whether the reader should implement any of his or her creative ideas. That decision is the reader's responsibility. As explained in the text of the book, creative ideas are not always better than non-creative ideas. Creative problem solving involves being open to creative ideas as additional possibilities, but some possibilities do not deserve to be acted on.

Cover portraits:
  Albert Einstein (see page 306) and Hypatia (see page 309)

Cover artwork:
  Brad Johnson — Front cover panel design and title
    lettering suggestions
  Richard Fobes — Computer artwork, including lettering
    and final portraits traced from initial drawings
  Jana Johnson — Initial drawings of Einstein and Hypatia

Cartoon drawings:
  Jan Reed

Other illustrations:
  Richard Fobes

Pronunciation: Fobes rhymes with *robes*

This book is dedicated to
those who will be living on this planet after us.
May we pass on to them fewer problems than we inherited.

"... life's problems are always new, and defy
all ready-made solutions."

Rudolf Flesch
author of
The Art of Clear Thinking
and *Why Johnny Can't Read*

Welcome to
The Creative Problem Solver's Toolbox

Within these pages you'll learn the valuable thinking tools of creative problem solving. These tools will benefit you whether you use them to solve problems involving employees, employers, children, customers, neighbors, computers, agriculture, warfare, architecture, government, health, finances, feelings, transportation, manufacturing, marketing, or interpersonal relationships.

The tools in this book are brought to life through interesting real-life examples. For instance, you'll read the behind-the-scene stories of how the Braille alphabet and basketball were invented. You'll read the story of a business owner who creatively improved low employee morale by letting his employees choose their own salaries. And, you'll learn how Leonardo da Vinci, who painted *The Mona Lisa* and *The Last Supper*, was able to sketch a crude helicopter 500 years ago!

The tools explained here are specific techniques anyone can learn. And the many examples make it clear how to apply the techniques to real-life problems.

Schools typically don't teach creative problem solving, and other books on the subject are incomplete, simplistic, or abstract. So where did the material in this book come from? The author learned the skills of creative problem solving through a lifetime of creative projects and pursuits, initially motivated by his parent's appreciation of useful creative ideas. After gaining unique insights through careful self-analysis of his thinking process, and after gaining experience teaching these insights in classes and seminars, the author spent five years writing this book to more widely share these valuable tools.

If you doubt the usefulness of the specific techniques inside, flip through the book and read a few of the examples, which are marked with the ◄ symbol in the margin. As you read the examples, consider the benefits you will gain by improving your ability to create effective solutions to whatever problems you face.

If You Don't Have Time To Read This Entire Book

Your Situation	What To Read
You only want to learn a few of the most important tools.	Chapter 2: *Welcoming New Ideas* and Chapter 3: *Reconsidering Your Goals*
You only have time to read a third of the book.	Part One: *The Basic Tools* (chapters 2 through 5)
You tend to have too few creative ideas.	Chapter 4: *Exploring Your Many Alternatives* and Chapter 6: *Thinking In Alternate Ways*
You want to get out of your habitual ways of solving problems.	Chapter 3: *Reconsidering Your Goals*, Chapter 6: *Thinking In Alternate Ways*, and Chapter 7: *Thinking Dimensionally*
You want to improve your skills in implementing your creative ideas.	Chapter 5: *Refining Your Ideas* and Chapter 10: *Taking Action*
You have already learned the basics of creative problem solving and want to learn more advanced skills.	The tools marked with asterisks in the outline on pages 315-321

Your Situation	What To Read
You're already a skilled creative problem solver.	The *Teaching Creative Problem Solving* section at the end of Chapter 11: *Using The Creative Problem Solver's Tools*
You're primarily interested in facilitating group creative problem solving sessions.	The *Conducting Group Problem Solving Sessions* section in Chapter 11: *Using The Creative Problem Solver's Tools* which, in turn, refers to specific chapters of the book
You're only interested in reading the examples of creative solutions of a particular kind, such as marketing, engineering, finding employment, dealing with children, or interpersonal conflicts.	The pages listed in the index under *Examples, types of* for the categories that interest you. The examples in the text are marked with this symbol:

Table of Contents

Refining Your Ideas ——————103

Creative ideas typically arrive in a crude and impractical form, so refinement, which transforms rough new ideas into practical solutions, is essential.

Part Two: The Advanced Tools

The remainder of this book presents the kinds of tools that tend to be more challenging to understand and apply. The division of this book into halves should not be interpreted as an actual gap in the nature of creative problem solving. Instead, you can think of this as a good place to pause after reading Part One.

Thinking In Alternate Ways ———125

Schools heavily emphasize thinking in words and numbers. But there are many other useful ways to think, including thinking visually, thinking in concepts, and using your intuition.

Thinking Dimensionally ———————163

Of course dimensions include quantities such as weight and money that can be measured in numbers. But other dimensions that defy being measured, such as love, risk, and assertiveness, are a part of virtually every real problem. Developing a clear understanding of a problem's dimensions frequently reveals a creative solution.

Understanding Clearly ———— 201

A failure to reach a clear understanding lies at the root of most unsolved problems. Here are tips for seeking out clear understandings that, almost by themselves, make solutions obvious. As a test of your clarity of understanding, do you already understand the main difference between anger and fear?

 ## Considering Your Goals
Some More ——————————— 241

Going beyond the suggestions in Chapter 3, here are some advanced suggestions about clarifying goals.

 ## Taking Action ————————— 247

Once you've created a solution worth acting on, you must prepare to handle the criticisms and resistance your improvement is likely to provoke. Also, there are important attitudes about action that, as a thinker, you may not already know.

 ## Using The Creative Problem
Solver's Tools ———————— 261

Tools sitting unused in a toolbox are of little value. Here are tips for applying the tools to solve specific problems, teaching children how to solve problems creatively, inventing, and avoiding problems that are now heading your way.

 ## Closing The Toolbox ————— 299

The book closes with a brief reminder of a few highlights and a list of suggested sources of additional information about creative problem solving.

Chapter 1

Opening the Toolbox

What is creative problem solving?

The best way to understand creative problem solving is through examples. Here is the first of many such examples.

A bird flew through an open window into a classroom and  then couldn't find its way out. The instructor and students in the room tried to scare it toward the open window, but with no success. Then they tried to catch the bird so they could release it outside, but they couldn't catch it. Fortunately for the terrified bird, the instructor suggested that they leave it alone and think of a better way to help it get back outside. Soon the class came up with a clever and effective solution. They closed the blinds on all the windows except one, which they opened wide, and turned off the lights. Guided by the one source of light in the darkened room, the bird flew out the open window!

This example illustrates that when there's no obvious or known solution to a problem and you're not willing to accept the situation as it is, you must create a new solution. Thus, creative problem solving is the process of creating a solution to a problem.

What kinds of problems can be solved using the tools in this book?

Any problem you're willing to spend time trying to solve. The problems can be big ones, little ones, at work, at home, whatever. To help you appreciate the surprising diversity of problems that can be solved using creative problem solving, here are three examples from three different areas: marketing, employee management, and parenting.

When Xerox Corporation began manufacturing photocopiers, the marketing people were disappointed by poor sales. Faced with the capacity to manufacture more machines than they were selling, the people at Xerox came up with an innovative marketing strategy. Instead of selling the machines, they offered to place their machines in businesses that were willing to pay a few cents for each copy their machine produced. Instead of selling photo*copiers*, they sold photo*copies*. This marketing innovation was so successful that the company came to prefer it over selling their machines. This example demonstrates that traditional approaches are not always the most effective.

Faced with low morale and complaints about inadequate salaries, a small business owner decided to let his employees choose their own salaries and working hours. Very risky, indeed! What happened? The owner's wife was the first to ask for a raise — of $1 an hour. Other employees requested salary increases of $50 to $60 per week. One employee, who had not been an especially good worker, requested an increase of $100 per week; he then came to work early and worked extra hard. Overall, the resulting salaries were slightly above what employees in similar positions elsewhere earned. For the next five years there was no turnover and use of sick leave was extremely low. In other words, the owner's novel way of handling low morale worked. Of course, such an innovation wouldn't be appropriate for many businesses, but it illustrates that there are simple yet unexpected ways to solve very common problems.

A mother had a son who threw temper tantrums: lying on the floor, pounding his fists, kicking his legs, and whining for whatever he wanted. One day while in a supermarket he threw one of his temper tantrums. In a moment of desperation, the mother dropped to the floor, pounded her fists, kicked her feet, and whined, "I wish you'd stop throwing temper tantrums! I can't stand it when you throw temper tantrums!" By this time, the son had stood up. He said in a hushed tone, "Mom, there are people watching! You're embarrassing me!" The mother calmly stood up, brushed off the dust, and said in a clear, calm voice, "That's what you look like when you're throwing a temper tantrum." Sometimes, traditional approaches such as bribing, threatening, ignoring, or giving in seem so natural that we overlook the possibility that something different, such as embarrassment, might work too.

You can probably think of a few situations in your life that you'd like to improve, right? The skills explained in this book can be applied to those situations, whatever they are.

What's the difference between problem solving and *creative* problem solving?

The difference mostly depends on what's meant by the word *problem*. School teachers and textbooks commonly use the word *problem* in the context of math problems and other homework problems. But these are not the kinds of problems this book discusses. It's true that school-assigned problems are problems in the sense that they are challenging to learn how to solve. However, school-assigned problems have only one correct answer that many people already know how to figure out, which is not true for most real-life problems. (The table on page 292 describes additional differences between school-assigned problems and real-life problems.)

In the real world we're faced with problems that, as far as we know, don't have an answer in a book or in someone's mind. If this is the kind of problem a person thinks of when he or she says the word *problem*, then there's no difference between problem solving and creative problem solving. To put it another way, the word *creative* emphasizes that the word *problem* in the phrase *creative problem solving* refers to problems that have not yet been solved — as far as the person knows.

Suppose someone creates a solution and later finds out that someone else created the same solution earlier. Is this still creative problem solving?

Whether you're the first, tenth, or millionth person to create a solution to a problem, you have to go through the creative problem solving process — unless you learn about the solution from someone else. Although being first is important in historical records and patent and copyright disputes, being first is not relevant to the creative problem solving process. All that matters is whether you create the solution yourself or learn the solution from someone else.

If a situation can be improved, yet the situation wouldn't be called a *problem*, can creative problem solving be used to improve the situation?

Definitely. Although the word *problem* has come to be strongly associated with situations that involve discomfort, suffering, or despair, a situation doesn't need to get that bad before creative problem solving can improve the situation.

Whenever you see the word *problem* in this book, translate it to mean any situation in which there's room for improvement — without implying whether or not the existing situation is unacceptable. Unfortunately, the English language lacks a word with this broader meaning. Although the phrase *improvable situation* could be used instead of the word *problem*, doing so would turn the already-awkward phrase *creative problem solving* into the intolerable phrase *creative improvable-situation solving*.

How are inventing and creative problem solving related?

Inventing can be defined as creating new *objects* and *substances* that are useful. Thus, inventing is a special kind of creative problem solving.

How are innovations and inventions related?

All inventions are *innovations*, but there are many innovations that aren't inventions. For example, a new device for heating food would be both an innovation and an invention. However, a new way to resolve divorce disputes would be an innovation but not (in most people's minds) an invention.

The word *innovation* has a much broader meaning than invention. Innovations include not only objects and substances, but strategies, processes, conventions, techniques, methods, ideas, representations, and ways of doing things.

What's the relationship between innovations and creative solutions?

To understand this relationship, consider the situation that existed in banks a few decades ago. Bank customers lined up in front of each teller's window in the same way that customers still line up at supermarket checkout stands. When there wasn't a short line, customers tried to choose a fast-moving line. Sometimes, someone who came in after you and stood in a different line, finished their business and left before you even reached the teller's window — a frustrating experience. From the bank's perspective, it was difficult to close a window during busy times because that would inconvenience the people waiting at that window. Many people regarded the situation as imperfect yet acceptable because they couldn't imagine anything better. Then, a few banks adopted the creative solution of having customers wait in a single line at a sign that said, "Wait here for next available teller." This enabled customers to be served in the order they arrived and enabled tellers to open and close their windows without disrupting the line. Within a few years nearly all banks adopted the same solution. At this point the creative solution became an innovation.

An innovation is a creative solution that's used by people other than the person who created it. In contrast, if someone creates a solution and no one else uses the solution, the creative solution doesn't become an innovation. In other words, whether we call something an innovation or a creative solution partly depends on how many people use it.

Because all innovations begin as creative solutions, the creative problem solver's tools apply to innovating as well as creative problem solving.

The following diagram illustrates the relationship between innovations, inventions, and creative solutions. Specifically, it is a visual reminder that:

- All inventions are innovations, but not all innovations are inventions.
- All innovations began as creative solutions, but not all creative solutions become innovations.

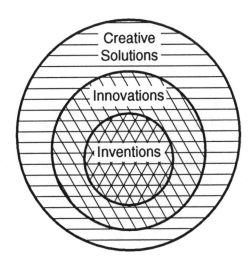

If an innovation remains popular for a long time, it becomes a tradition. For instance, a single waiting line in banks was once an innovation and it's now a tradition. Interestingly, virtually all traditions of today were once innovations. This relationship between tradition and innovation is ironic considering that tradition is commonly regarded as the enemy of innovation.

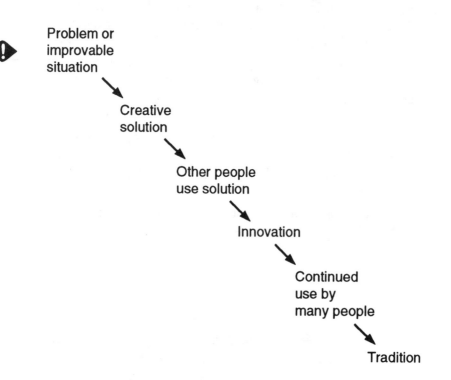

It's obvious that problems are worth solving, but are innovations really needed?

Innovations have the potential to bring about significant advantages, as these past innovations have demonstrated:

- Food preservation techniques have reduced the impact of yearly cycles of scarce food.
- Telephones have removed the limitation of being able to only talk to people standing nearby.
- Money has eliminated the awkwardness of bartering.
- Engines have removed the burden of intense manual labor.

Those of us living today appreciate these and the many other innovations that have advanced civilization to its current level. Similarly, future generations will appreciate innovations that solve large-scale problems such as these:

- No frontiers remain in which our expanding population can settle.

- Acceptable places for dumping garbage are full.

- Non-objects that can easily be copied — such as computer programs, information, recorded music, and video programs — have become important products in our economy, yet existing conventions don't ensure that the people who created them are paid each time such non-objects are copied.

- Large amounts of air and water pollution now cross boundaries that were once adequate for isolating political entities from one another.

These and other problems require that we create new ways to accommodate cultural diversity in confined territories, new ways to deal with garbage, new ways to financially reward people who work hard to create software and video programs that are widely copied, and new ways to ethically resolve conflicts between political entities that are downwind and downriver from one another. In short, innovations are needed.

However, innovations are not necessarily good. This has been proven by past examples of unwise innovations. One example was the medical treatment of putting blood-sucking leeches on a patient's body; it was popular for many decades as a general-purpose cure.

To ensure that unwise innovative ideas are not put into effect, it's important that *all proposed innovations be regarded with suspicion and criticized for their flaws.*

Proposed innovations that are worthwhile can overcome such resistance, using techniques explained later in this book. Fortunately, such techniques work only for well-designed innovations that benefit many people.

How is creative problem solving related to creativity?

The similarity between creative problem solving and creativity depends on which meaning of creativity is intended. Although most people agree that Albert Einstein and Leonardo da Vinci had the kind of creativity we most appreciate, the word creativity is commonly used in ways that emphasize the *newness* of an idea without also implying anything about the *value* of the new idea. Yet it's the value of what Einstein and Leonardo came up with that makes them highly regarded as creative thinkers. Creative problem solving automatically involves value because a creative solution that fails to bring about improvement isn't really a solution.

In this book, creativity and creative problem solving can be thought of as roughly the same if the following considerations are kept in mind:

- The element of value is not forgotten when the word creativity is used.

- Improvement is remembered to be an essential part of creative problem solving.

- The word *problem* is used in its broader meaning as an improvable situation.

Interestingly, this similarity between creativity and creative problem solving means that what's explained in this book can be applied to artistic creations in areas such as composing music, choreographing dances, designing clothes, carving wood, painting, and creating new recipes. However, in order not to stray from the subject of creative problem solving, the examples in this book focus on situations that most people would regard as problems.

How is creative problem solving related to decision making?

A common situation is that of being asked to choose one of several options as the best way to solve a problem. When the decision is difficult, the cause of the difficulty can be that none of the identified options would really solve the problem. If one of the available options were an effective solution, the decision would be easier to make. The ideal way to resolve such a situation would be to create an effective solution to the problem and add that as another option. When that isn't allowed, it's useful to gain a clearer understanding of the issue in hopes that one of the options will stand out as being better, or at least less objectionable, than the others. Because some of the creative problem solver's tools provide ways to more clearly understand a situation, these tools can also be used in decision-making situations.

The presence of a time limit in decision making makes that process very different from creative problem solving. Creative problem solving continues until a solution is created and implemented, however long that takes. Recall that the importance of time was mentioned earlier in pointing out that you must be willing to spend time creating a solution to a problem in order to make use of the tools in this book.

What kinds of things are the tools?

The tools are thinking skills that are explained as techniques. To understand what this means, consider the skill of making a turn on a bicycle. To turn to the *right*, you first turn the wheel momentarily to the *left* and then turn it to the right. The momentary turn to the left tilts you and the bicycle as needed to make the turn. To return to an upright position at the end of the turn, you momentarily turn the wheel *right* by an *extra amount* before turning it back to the straight position. This describes the *technique* you use when you turn while riding a bicycle. You developed the *skill* of bicycle-turning by *using* this *technique* so many times that you now do it unconsciously.

Similarly, the tools in this book are thinking *techniques* that you must *practice using* in order to transform them into thinking *skills*. Just as in bicycle riding, the more practice you get in applying the techniques, the more skilled you become, and the less attention you'll have to devote to applying the thinking skills.

Is it important to do the exercises that appear at the end of the sections of this book?

Ideally, instead of doing the exercises, you should practice applying the techniques to problems of special interest to you. But if you can't figure out how to apply what has been explained in a section, the exercises provide practice opportunities. What's important is that you practice. What you practice on is of less importance.

Where are the answers to the exercises?

In most cases answers to the exercises are not supplied. Here are reasons why:

- The value in doing the exercises is to spend time trying to apply the explained tools. Coming up with an answer that matches someone else's answer is of secondary importance.

- One of the skills of creative problem solving is to arrive at the point of thinking "Oh, now it makes sense!" As long as you remain uncertain about the answer, you have not yet finished the exercise.

- Most of the exercises have more than one correct answer and providing full explanations for each exercise would dramatically increase the length of this book. In some cases, a later section contains part of the answer or explains something that will make it easier to do the earlier exercise.

The few exercises that have suggested answers are clearly identified, and the location of the answer is indicated.

Are there other ways besides doing the exercises to practice applying the tools?

An excellent way to practice is to team up with someone else who has a similar interest in learning creative problem solving. Such teamwork offers advantages that no book can offer.

Is the phrase *he or she* used throughout this book as it has been used above?

No. Here's another limitation in the English language: the absence of a single word that means *he or she*. Because other major languages (such as Chinese) have a single word that refers to a person of an unknown gender, I've used the words *heshe*, *hisher*, *himher*, and *himherself* as placeholders for whatever English words are finally chosen to fit these meanings. (If concatenating words seems radical, keep in mind that words such as workday, worthwhile, carefree, and runaway were created this way.) These new gender-neutral words are used in sentences where the gender is unknown, as in: "If anyone calls, tell himher I'll be back in an hour." Because new words are disruptive, these words are used only when avoiding them would alter the meaning of what's written.

Another limitation in the English language is the lack of a single word that refers to a typical person. The way many linguistically-correct people deal with this problem is to use the word *one*, as in: "One easily recognizes that one period of Picasso's painting is distinctly different from another period." But this sounds snobbish, and it's disruptive when both meanings of the word *one* appear in the same sentence, as they do in the above example. I have chosen to deal with this limitation by referring to you as *you* and to use the second-person (you) present-tense form of conjugation for verbs, as in: "It is what you create, not your efforts to create it, that you should simplify." Although this "imperative" form of verb conjugation sounds bossy to some people, it's not intended that way at all. In fact, the whole point of this book is to make it easier for you to improve your ability to think for yourself so that you won't wait for other people to solve your problems for you. As a final point, some examples begin with "Suppose you..." as if you were involved in the example. This wording is used because of missing English words, not because I'm implying what you have done or should do.

◄SUMMARY►

When you're faced with a problem — or, more broadly, an improvable situation — of any kind, and of any size, you might be able to create a new solution instead of limiting yourself to choosing from traditional alternatives.

If you create a solution to a problem that many people face, share your solution with others, and later find that many people are using what you created, then you've created an innovation.

If someone else creates what they hope will become an innovation and you don't like it, resist it. This resistance ensures that only worthwhile innovations are adopted.

The creative problem solver's tools are techniques that must be applied — to either real situations or exercises — in order to transform them into thinking skills.

This book reveals techniques for creatively solving problems, but it doesn't, and can't, solve your problems for you. You must do the necessary thinking to apply what's explained here.

Part One

The Basic Tools

The following four chapters, 2 through 5, contain the tools that are easier to understand and apply. These tools also are the most crucial ones.

Chapter 2

Welcoming New Ideas

Prompting new creative ideas and welcoming them when they arrive are crucial to creative problem solving.

Looking For Merit In Crude Ideas

Many people don't recognize useful creative ideas when they pop into their minds because the ideas arrive disguised as crude, foolish, and unworkable ideas. A creative person sees through the disguise, refines the idea, and creates a useful solution. An uncreative person sees the same idea, regards it as useless, and tosses it away.

What would you do with the following idea if it popped into your head? Imagine two elevators that are side by side. It occurs to you that by attaching the cables of the two elevators together you could use the weight of a person going down in one elevator to lift another person in the other elevator.

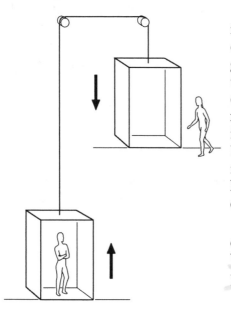

Obviously this idea is impractical for many reasons, one of which is that a person going up wouldn't be willing to wait for someone going down. Because of such flaws, most people would regard the idea as useless and toss it out. But a creative person would recognize that this idea does have value. It would save energy!

This is the "secret" to creating useful solutions. When a creative idea pops into your head, look for its merit.

In my many years of creating solutions, never has a solution popped into my mind in its finished form. Only by recognizing merit in initially crude ideas and refining those ideas have I created useful solutions. The elevator idea was no exception. When it first appeared, I was about to discard it when I remembered my own advice: "Look for merit in *any* idea. Any idea that pops into the mind has *some* merit."

▶ Once you see an idea's advantages (its merit), modify the idea in a way that retains its advantages and removes its disadvantages.

To show that the crude elevator idea can be transformed into a practical solution, let's refine the idea further. Notice that each of the following refinements removes at least one disadvantage without losing any significant advantages.

- Let's replace the person going down with a bag of sand. This arrangement still saves energy but doesn't require the person going up to wait for someone going down.

- The bag of sand might not be heavy enough to lift a large person, so let's use a variable amount of sand instead of sand-bags of a fixed size.

- Pouring sand creates dust in the air, so we can use water instead.

- Automating the loading of water eliminates the need for a person to load the water.

- Using a heavy weight (as is usually done) and a container to hold the water eliminates the need to use a second elevator as a counterbalance.

- Extra water can be used to overcome friction and to get the elevator started.

- We can use the weight of people going down to lift some of the water back up for later use.

At this point we've refined the crude elevator idea into a somewhat practical idea. Specifically, we have an elevator that's partially counterbalanced by a container that holds water, water is poured into the container to lift people, and some water is lifted back up when a heavy load of people goes down. If electrical energy were scarce or expensive, the details of this idea could be worked out to significantly reduce the amount of electricity needed to operate an elevator.

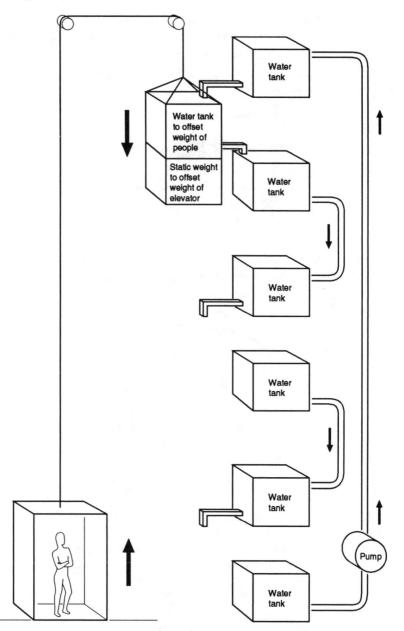

This example illustrates that what begins as a foolish notion can evolve, in little steps, into a practical idea. This is how creative ideas emerge: not *ready to use*, but rather *ready to refine*.

This process of refinement can happen so quickly that the initial idea is quickly forgotten and it can seem, even to the person who created the idea, that the idea arrived in a practical form. Or, the refinement can occur so slowly that it's easy to follow its evolution.

The bicycle is a good example of slow refinement. It began as a seat on two wheels. The rider's feet pushed to make it go and dragged to make it stop.

Later, pedals were added to the front wheel and the front wheel was enlarged so that a comfortable rate of pedaling caused the bicycle to go at a reasonable speed.

Finally, the pedals were connected to the rear wheel with a chain, the front wheel was returned to a practical size, and a brake was added. This is basically the way a one-speed bicycle remains today. By contrast, early bicycles seem crude and almost useless.

In the words of the philosopher and mathematician Alfred Whitehead, "Almost all really new ideas have a certain aspect of foolishness when they are first produced."

Of course, seeing merit must be balanced by an ability to recognize flaws and weaknesses. Otherwise, you'll be tempted to act on ideas that aren't yet fully refined. Tools for recognizing and removing flaws and weaknesses are explained later, in Chapter 5, *Refining Your Ideas*.

◄SUMMARY►

Seeing merit in new ideas is the most important skill of creative problem solving because, without it, you'll toss out creative ideas when they first arrive.

Exercise 1. To improve your ability to see merit in crude ideas, practice seeing merit in seemingly impractical ideas. For example, instead of basing tax rates (the percentage) on the amount of a person's income, consider basing tax rates on the results of spinning a roulette wheel. At first, such an idea seems to have absolutely no merit. Yet, if this idea were actually implemented, what merits would it have? Assume that the roulette wheel has tax rates starting at 0 percent and going up to 50 percent. Here are some possible merits to this otherwise ridiculous idea:

- Some people, that year, would not have to pay any income taxes.
- A rich person and a poor person would have the same odds.
- Some families would become closer by helping out the unlucky ones.
- It would provide a new topic of conversation in social situations.
- Insurance companies would love to offer a new form of insurance: "tax insurance".

Now, here are more seemingly foolish ideas. Some of them have real merit and some of them have merit that's outweighed by disadvantages. Practice seeing merit in these ideas so you can identify whether or not each idea might lead to a practical improvement. More importantly, practice seeing merit here so you can more easily see merit in the ideas that pop up in your mind later.

- Have the person who *receives* a piece of mail pay the postage.
- Earn less, instead of more, money.
- Promote employees randomly instead of doing careful evaluations.
- Move some high school and college subjects into elementary school education.
- Encourage political cartoonists to become politicians.
- Don't fill in the potholes in roads.

If you have trouble seeing merit in any of these (or other) ideas, try looking at the idea not just from your own personal point of view, but from someone else's point of view or from a collective (many people's) point of view.

Looking For Fresh Perspectives

The turning point in solving a problem is typically when a useful insight is reached through an effort to see the situation from a fresh perspective.

Within the Federal Express overnight mail service company, managers were discouraged by the frequent delays in transferring mail between the airplanes that met at night at the central exchange location in Memphis, Tennessee. To keep on schedule, all packages had to be transferred within four hours. The transfer was usually completed barely in time. It was obvious that the employees were not working as fast as they could, but efforts to encourage them to work faster failed. Finally, managers learned that the employees intentionally stretched out the job to earn extra overtime pay. In other words, management had created a pay system that *rewarded slowness*! Once this perspective became clear, a solution was easy to create. The workers were guaranteed pay for a specific number of hours but could leave early if they finished early. Within a month the delays were gone.

When you find yourself thinking "So that's what's been going on!" or "Oh, that's the way it works!", you've succeeded in seeing your situation from a fresh perspective. Frequently, such an insight automatically reveals how to solve the problem.

A fresh perspective is useful in solving any kind of problem. But, the needed fresh perspective can be so hidden that you might never discover it. One mother was discouraged by the trouble her son sometimes caused. In a candid interview the son revealed, "I get what I want by keeping mother thinking I'll be bad. Of course, I have to be bad often enough to convince her that she is not paying me for nothing."

You might discover a needed fresh perspective, yet fail to arrive at a practical solution. In such cases, more than one fresh perspective might be needed.

Consider the relatively low wages paid to teachers and the recognized fact that there is room for improvement in the quality of public education (from kindergarten through high school) in the United States. Teachers' wages are regarded by many non-teachers as acceptable based on the belief that if teachers' wages were too low, people wouldn't choose to become teachers. This reasoning of paying only enough to attract an adequate number of employees works fine for assembly line jobs in which advanced thinking skills don't improve the quality of the manufactured product. But in teaching, exceptional teachers produce better-educated students. Therefore, paying wages that match each teacher's degree of excellence would improve the quality of public education by attracting a larger percentage of excellent teachers to the teaching profession. This fresh perspective points in the general direction of a possible solution: increasing pay for excellent teachers. However, this fresh perspective doesn't reveal a full solution because there appears to be no reliable and fair way to measure excellence. But, by thinking creatively, we arrive at a second fresh perspective: perhaps there's a way to *create* a reliable and fair way to measure excellence. This still isn't a full solution, but it leads us closer to one. Additional fresh perspectives are needed to finish refining this idea for improving the quality of public education. Yet, even in this incomplete stage of refinement, this example illustrates that looking for one fresh perspective might not be enough. It's necessary to continue looking for fresh perspectives until a practical solution emerges.

There are other ways to say *looking for fresh perspectives*. To say *understanding clearly* and *discovering insights* amount to the same thing. What you prefer to call it is up to you. But whatever you call it, be sure to do it.

Now that you know about the need to look for fresh perspectives, you might be wondering, "How do I go about doing that?" Specific techniques are explained in chapters 3 and 4 and chapters 6 through 9 (*Reconsidering Your Goals, Exploring Your Many Alternatives, Thinking In Alternate Ways, Thinking Dimensionally, Understanding Clearly,* and *Considering Your Goals Some More*).

A wise person once said: "No problem can be solved from the same perspective that created it."

◄SUMMARY►

Problems do have solutions, but the solutions aren't always in plain view. To find them, look beneath the surface to reveal a fresh perspective that, almost by itself, makes a solution obvious.

For especially challenging problems, looking for just one fresh perspective might not be enough. Keep looking until you find yourself thinking, "Ah! Now it finally makes sense!"

Specific ways to look for useful fresh perspectives are explained in Chapters 3, 4, and 6 through 9.

Exercise 1. In the United States there are no rules limiting the number of political parties, yet within a few years after a third party becomes popular, one of the three parties fades and the two-party system is restored. Why?

Answering this question requires more than a few seconds of thinking. Remember that you're looking for the fresh perspective that prompts an "Aha!" response. If you need a hint, one contributing cause is implied by an example in the *Imagining Exaggerated Specific Cases To Determine Effects* section.

Exercise 2. Pick a problem of interest to you and spend time and effort looking beneath the surface to understand the situation more clearly. When each new perspective arrives, welcome it by looking for its merit.

Judging Perspectives According To Usefulness

Instead of judging perspectives according to whether they're right or wrong, judge them according to whether they reveal useful solutions.

Often, corporate managers find it necessary to look outside their company to find someone qualified for a key leadership position. On the surface, this situation appears to be due to a lack of qualified candidates within the company. But looking beneath the surface reveals a different perspective. Employees who obediently do what their boss tells them to do are usually promoted more readily than employees who point out weaknesses in their boss's flawed requests. If this tendency is strong, many people with leadership skills leave the company to fill leadership positions in other companies or start their own companies. As a result, middle level managers tend to be *followers* rather than *leaders*. This fresh perspective reveals the following ideas for dealing with a shortage of candidates for a key leadership position:

- Teach leadership skills to managers who lack, yet need, these skills.

- Train managers to distinguish between complainers and people with leadership potential, both of whom readily point out flaws.

- Find out why competent employees quit.

- Encourage the promotion of competent employees who might otherwise be ignored for promotion because of their position. They might not yet have been promoted to the level they deserve.

Because these practical solutions arise from the fresh perspective, does this mean that middle level managers are followers rather than leaders? No!

Just because a perspective reveals practical solutions doesn't mean that the perspective itself is right. Ultimately, what matters is whether you come up with a solution to a problem. How you arrive at the solution doesn't matter (just as it doesn't matter that an initial idea is silly or foolish).

To see this point more clearly, consider the following analogy. Suppose that someone showed the *same object* to three different people and asked them to describe its shape. Suppose their responses were:

- First viewer: "It's square."

- Second viewer: "It's circular."

- Third viewer: "It's triangular."

What would you conclude? You'd probably figure that at least one of them was lying or needed glasses. Yet such an object exists! Depending on which angle it's viewed from, it has the profile of a square, circle, or triangle. To see what it looks like, turn the page. If you still can't imagine what the shape looks like, make a model of it as explained in the first exercise below.

Now that you know what this shape looks like, ask yourself, "Is its shape circular, square, or triangular?" The answer is that each of the descriptions is both true and not true. Each description is simply *one of several possible perspectives.*

Just as there is not one **right** profile that characterizes this tri-shaped object, there is not one **right** way to view middle-level managers in a corporation. They are neither, and yet both, leaders and followers.

◄SUMMARY►

Instead of judging a perspective as **right** or **wrong**, focus on the perspective's *usefulness*. Does the perspective reveal a solution or doesn't it? That's what counts.

Exercise 1. Make a model of the tri-shaped object using the pattern on the next page. Copy the pattern onto a piece of paper, cut out the pieces, and fasten them together with tape. For a larger version, use a photocopier that enlarges. Once you've made the object, look at it from different angles and notice that its profile is square, circular, or triangular depending on which direction you view it from.

Exercise 2. Suppose you've done something that another person doesn't like, and the person's anger is much stronger than would seem appropriate for what you've done. One way to deal with this situation is to imagine that the person's brother, father, sister, or mother is standing behind you and that the person's anger is passing over your shoulders to that family member. You hear the person's words and let most of the anger pass by you. Is this perspective useful? Is it right?

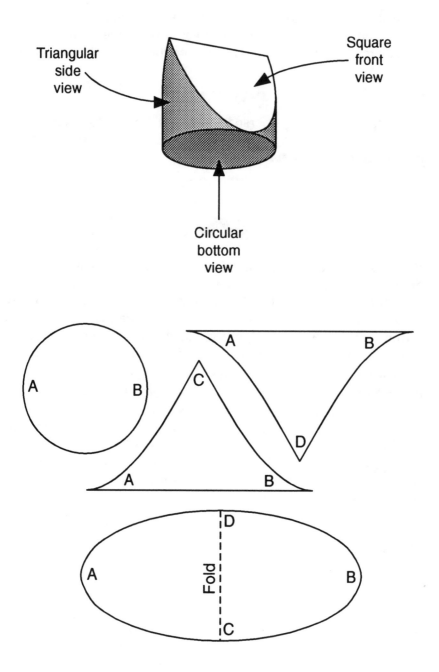

Triangular side view

Square front view

Circular bottom view

Appreciating Humor

It's useful to have a sense of humor as you search for creative solutions.

Imagine that fleas have invaded your carpet. One idea you might think of for getting rid of the fleas is to borrow a neighbor's cat and walk it across your carpet. Without a sense of humor, you would be likely to ignore this idea without realizing the fresh perspective it suggests: there might be something else (that's not alive) that might attract the fleas out of your carpet.

Every idea, even a humorous or silly one, has the potential of leading to a practical idea. Of course, not every idea you think of should be implemented, especially not unethical ones like hurting your neighbor's cat.

There's another reason to appreciate humor. Insights, which are important in creative problem solving, involve a shift in perspective that's similar to the shift in perspective that occurs in humor. The following examples of an insight and a joke demonstrate this similarity.

In the past, architects typically regarded buildings as arrangements of *walls, floors*, and *ceilings*. This perspective certainly makes sense because wall, floors, and ceilings are what workers build and what you see with your eyes and feel with your hands. But buildings can also be regarded as *spaces* whose boundaries are the walls, ceilings, and floors. Spaces are what people move around in, and a space is as important as the boundaries that define it. This shift in perspective has been the basis of numerous innovations in architecture, including some by Frank Lloyd Wright.

Now, compare the above shift in perspective with the shift in perspective in the following joke.

A timid, small-town woman traveled to a conference held in a large city with a high crime rate. Returning from the conference late at night, she entered the hotel elevator to return to her room. Before the elevator doors closed a large man with a fierce looking dog entered the elevator and stood behind her. She was filled with fear and was afraid to turn around. Moments after the elevator started to move, the man said, "Lie down!" Quickly she obeyed. Lying on the elevator floor, she heard him chuckle and say, "Not you. I was talking to my dog!" Notice that the moment of humor is a dramatic and unexpected shift in perspective. Specifically, the meaning of the words "Lie down!" suddenly and unexpectedly shift with the last word of the joke.

The architectural example and the joke illustrate that humor provides an opportunity to experience the same thinking activity that occurs at important moments of insight, namely a dramatic and unexpected shift in perspective. If this logic seems too abstract, then appreciate the fact that both humor and creative problem solving have the same final goal: to make life more enjoyable!

◄SUMMARY►

Humorous ideas are common in creative thinking. Enjoy them! And in addition to being entertained, appreciate that they involve the same kind of shift in perspective that occurs at enlightening moments of insight.

Initially Keeping Your Ideas Confidential

In your early moments of creative excitement, you might be tempted to tell someone else about a promising new idea. But it's worth remembering that many people look for flaws without looking for merit.

To appreciate that something new is typically criticized, regardless of its merit, consider these examples:

- Steve Wozniak's suggestion of making small, relatively inexpensive computers was rejected by his superiors at Hewlett-Packard, a large electronics manufacturing company. To pursue his idea, he quit his job and teamed up with Steve Jobs to start Apple Computer, Inc.

- Along with many other people in the 1500's, one German preacher criticized the innovation of eating with forks, saying, "God would not have given us fingers if He wished us to use such a diabolical instrument."

- The Wright Brothers' airplane was commonly criticized as being a useless, expensive, dangerous toy. Even the leaders of the United States Army initially saw no value in it. (They reconsidered when the French Army expressed interest.)

These examples illustrate that unfavorable criticism doesn't mean that an idea is foolish or unfounded. It simply means that the critic sees little or no merit in the idea.

When a creative idea first occurs to you, it's usually too fragile to withstand criticism, even if the criticism is unfounded. Therefore, consider not sharing a new idea with other people until you've evaluated the idea more carefully. Later, when you're aware of the idea's most obvious strengths and weaknesses, and perhaps after you've partially refined the idea, you'll be ready to ask for suggestions. At that time, criticisms are still likely to arise, but there are ways to handle those criticisms. Until then, consider avoiding unnecessary criticism.

If you plan to claim credit for an idea by revealing it at a time of your choosing, be especially careful not to reveal it in advance. This is especially true for inventions because the first person to patent an invention legally owns it.

Going one step further in terms of privacy, you might not even want to reveal that you're trying to solve a particular problem. Criticism such as "You're foolish to even *attempt* to solve *that* problem!" is also discouraging.

◄SUMMARY►

Instead of censoring your thoughts, keep your ideas private. Other people need never know what silly ideas prompt your creative solutions. Only your final solutions need to be shared.

Writing Down New Ideas

After you've recognized the merit in a creative idea, write down the idea so you won't forget it.

There was a paleontologist who saw a fossilized skeleton of a prehistoric fish embedded in rock. The skeleton was not complete, so he spent lots of time trying to imagine what the missing part of the skeleton looked like. One night he visualized the full skeleton in a dream and woke up excited by his discovery. He went back to sleep looking forward to verifying the accuracy of what he had imagined. Unfortunately, when morning came he was unable to recall the image. A number of nights later in a dream the same image came to him. Again he woke up excited and kept the image in his mind to remember it. Then he went back to sleep. But, again, he was unable to recall it in the morning. After that, he kept paper and pen by his bed in hopes that the image of the fish skeleton would return in his dreams. It did, and this time he drew the image on paper in the dark. In the morning the sketch enabled him to recall the details of the image and he soon verified that it matched the fossilized partial skeleton.

Write down any idea that has potential for leading to a new solution. Creating a useful new idea in your mind accomplishes nothing if you can't later recall your creative insight.

◄SUMMARY►

To avoid forgetting creative ideas, write them down.

Exercise 1. While reading this book has an insight or useful idea popped into your mind? Write it down now.

Exercise 2. Do you have paper and a pen or pencil handy now? If not, get them. Be sure to choose paper and writing implements you like, not what someone else considers **best**. In case you want a suggestion for paper, consider keeping 3-inch by 5-inch pads of paper handy. Notes written on paper that size can be filed in a file box using dividers organized by subject category (instead of alphabetically).

Exercise 3. Put some paper and a pen or pencil within reach of your bed, and anywhere else you spend time.

Reconsidering Your Goals

Goals exist whether or not you're consciously aware of them, and they are often different from what you think or say they are. Even when you know your goals, they can limit your creative problem solving efforts in unexpected and subtle ways.

To open up creative possibilities for solving a problem, become aware of, and clarify, your goals in special ways.

Reconsidering Your Starting Point

A solution can fail to solve the problem as you've defined it and yet solve the problem you really want to solve.

Natural gas is odorless so, in the early days of using natural gas to heat buildings and cook, someone would occasionally light a match without realizing that a gas leak had filled the air with gas. Poof! A definite problem worth solving. Inventors quickly began designing devices that would detect the presence of natural gas in the air and sound an alarm. The designs of these electronic devices were impressive; they even incorporated features to ensure that the device itself didn't generate sparks that could ignite the gas. However, the best solution was not a detection device. Instead, a gas that could be easily smelled was added to the odorless natural gas so that a leak could be detected easily by a human's built-in gas detector, the nose!

A solution that doesn't solve the problem as you've stated it might still solve the problem you really want to solve. So, when you're looking for a solution to a problem, ask yourself, "What am I *really* trying to accomplish?" Then, consider any alternative that accomplishes this goal, even if it doesn't solve the problem as you originally defined it.

Let's look at reconsidering your starting point for a smaller problem. Suppose you're painting a hallway. To reach the ceiling and upper areas of the walls, you use a ladder. But when you reach the adjacent stairwell, you ask yourself, "How can I set up the ladder on the stairs to reach the ceiling above the stairs?" You might consider using boxes to support two feet of the ladder at the same height as the step on which the other two feet rest, but this isn't safe. You might consider shortening two of the ladder's legs to match the unevenness of the stairs, but you don't want to ruin the ladder. Then it occurs to you that maybe setting up a ladder on the steps isn't the way to reach the stairwell ceiling. This is when you reconsider your starting point and realize that, instead, you can extend the handle of the paint roller to reach the high ceiling. Notice that extending the roller handle doesn't solve the problem of setting up a ladder on the stairs, yet it does solve the problem of painting the stairwell ceiling.

◄SUMMARY►

Reconsider your starting point. Do so by ignoring what you've been trying to accomplish and looking at the problem from a broader perspective. A solution can fail to solve the problem as you originally defined it, yet solve the problem you really want solved.

Exercise 1. A frequently suggested invention is to put tiny windshield wipers on eyeglasses to keep a spectacled person's vision clear during rainfall. Someone addicted to mechanical gadgets would attempt to work out the details of such an invention to make it practical. What would you recommend to such an inventor? What other alternatives can you suggest?

Exercise 2. How could you improve the teacher-to-student ratio in a classroom without changing the number of teachers or the number of students? (One possible answer is given on page 311.)

Exercise 3. What have you been trying to accomplish, but without success? What different approaches have you excluded by pursuing a narrowly defined goal?

Reconsidering Your Goals
At Any Time

Rigid goals greatly limit creativity, so increase your creativity by always being open to changing your goals.

Managers of an open-pit copper mine in Utah asked an engineer fresh out of college to find a better way to arrange the railroad tracks used by trains to remove the ore. As the ore was removed from the pit, the railroad tracks had to be relaid to match the pit's new contours and this was very expensive. Although the managers didn't expect the new engineer to succeed, he created a detailed proposal that they later implemented. He convinced them to replace the trains with heavy trucks and use *roads* instead of railroad tracks. An important factor in changing their minds was that he calculated the cost of using trucks and showed it to be less expensive than using railroad trains. Notice that the goal in this example was broadened from creating a less expensive way to move the railroad tracks to creating a less expensive way to remove the ore from the mine.

This example illustrates that being flexible about your goals can open up new possibilities. So, be willing to change your goals at any time.

In a group situation, suggesting that the group's goals be changed or reconsidered is often met with a look that says, "You're joking, right?" Part of the reason reconsidering goals is not welcomed in a group situation is that the group has spent lots of time creating a carefully defined goal. Naturally, they're reluctant to toss aside what it took so long to create. Another reason that groups resist reconsidering goals is that carefully stated goals are frequently used as *limits* to indicate what the leaders, who set the goals, are willing to accept. Sometimes such limits serve a needed function, but such limits also serve as filters that exclude potentially useful solutions.

There's a curse that says, "May you get what you ask for." It's a curse because people commonly ask for what they *think* they want and then find, when they achieve it, "This isn't what I had in mind."

At the beginning of an effort to solve a problem, too little is known to be able to choose a goal wisely. Therefore, at the same time that you're developing a clearer understanding of the problem, spend time developing a clearer understanding of your real goal.

An especially appropriate time to reconsider your goal is when a promising, or even slightly promising, idea arrives but doesn't fit within your goal. When this happens, broaden your goal to include the new solution even if it's not a practical solution. This broadening opens up your thinking to include other, perhaps better, ideas that wouldn't fit within your narrower goal.

In a group situation the possibility of broadening a goal can be encouraged by saying, "Yes, this idea doesn't fit within the goal, but wouldn't it solve the problem?" This draws attention to the fact that, perhaps, solving the problem is more important than fitting within goals.

◄SUMMARY►

Whether you're working individually or as part of a group, be willing to reconsider your goals at any time throughout the creative problem solving process. If you find yourself thinking "This idea has some potential, but it doesn't fit my goals", resist the temptation to toss out the idea. Instead, recognize that there might be something wrong with the goals — regardless of how carefully you chose them.

Converting Negative Goals To Positive Goals

It's usually obvious what you *don't* want, but figuring out what you *do* want can reveal useful, fresh perspectives.

Here are some examples of global goals stated in terms of what we *don't* want. Take time to notice how the portions in italics indicate their negative orientation.

- *Stop* wars.
- *Eliminate* hunger.
- Resolve the drug *problem*.
- Promote *non*-discrimination.

Negative goals amount to pointing somewhere and saying "No, don't go there!", whereas *positive* goals amount to pointing in a different direction and saying "Let's go there!"

Expressing in positive terms where you *do* want to go isn't easy. Consider the first example above: "Stop wars." Transforming this into a positive goal amounts to saying, "Let's have peace." Right? No. Saying "Let's have peace" sounds like a positive goal, but it isn't. Peace is simply the *absence* of war. So, "Let's have peace" translates into "Let's have an absence of war." That's certainly a desirable goal, but not a goal stated in positive terms. Notice that war serves as a way to resolve conflicts. Therefore, to eliminate it, a more mature way of resolving conflicts must be substituted. This reversing of the goal of "stop wars" into something positive reveals that something new must be created — which is unexpected when simply thinking in terms of eliminating warfare. A partially successful attempt to reduce wars has been the creation of the United Nations assembly. Notice that this organization provides a way to use *voting*, instead of war, to resolve many international conflicts.

Because people frequently confuse rebellion with innovation, it's useful to note that rebellion is based on following negative goals whereas innovation is based on following positive goals. Not only is innovation more productive than rebellion, but clearly understanding the final positive goal makes it easier to keep on course in trying to reach the goal. In contrast, when people focus their attention on what they're running away from, they're more likely to run into something unexpected — and undesirable.

◄SUMMARY►

Of course you know what you *don't want*. But do you know what you *do* want? Once you know where you want to go, discovering a way to get there becomes easier.

Exercise 1. Convert the negative goal "Stop drug abuse" into a positive goal.

Exercise 2. Apply this tool to a situation you would like to improve. First, identify the situation you want to improve. Then, write down your goal in whatever way it arises in your mind. If, in any way, the goal indicates what you don't want instead of what you do want, translate the negative goal into a positive goal. Notice what new possibilities arise.

Heading In The Direction
Of An Ideal Solution

Thinking idealistically is a practical way to start designing an effective solution.

Consider August Dvorak's effort to improve on today's keyboard layout. He could have designed an improved keyboard by simply rearranging some of the letters that are awkwardly placed, such as improving the placement of the frequently typed letter *A*, which is now under the weak left little finger. Instead, Dvorak started idealistically by determining how often each letter of the English alphabet is used and evaluating how easily each key location can be reached. Using this information, he assigned the most frequently used letters to the most easily pressed keys and progressively assigned less frequently used letters to less easily pressed keys. Also, he made adjustments to ensure that frequently typed pairs of letters, such as *T* and *H*, *S* and *H*, and *W* and *H*, were not assigned to the same finger. Thus, Dvorak designed his keyboard layout mostly from scratch by pursuing the *ideal* of placing the most frequently typed keys in the most convenient locations. As this example illustrates, once an ideal goal becomes clear, the steps needed to design a solution also become clear.

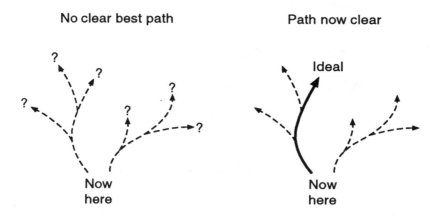

The importance of beginning a design idealistically is fairly obvious for inventions such as keyboards, but it's also very useful in personal situations, such as finding a new job. Instead of beginning a job search by looking in the classified ads, consider beginning by imagining an ideal job. You're probably thinking, "Hey, get realistic! There are no such jobs!" That's true. But the point of beginning idealistically is not to actually try to *reach* the ideal, but to force yourself to more clearly understand what kind of job you *really* want.

Imagining an ideal job isn't as easy as it sounds. Typically, people leap from the realm of jobs they know exist to the realm of unrealistic fantasy, such as somehow getting paid to lie on a sunny tropical beach. But to imagine an ideal *job* requires that you limit yourself to imagining activities that *benefit other people*, which is the basis for getting paid. Yet, within this constraint, there's a tremendous range of creative possibilities.

A beginning point for identifying an ideal job is to identify how you want to benefit others. Do you want to benefit them by operating their equipment, teaching them, managing their activities and resources, creating things for them, or what? Also consider whom you want to benefit: travelers, people with special needs, people wanting information, children, senior citizens?

Another common mistake in imagining an ideal job is to think in *general* terms such as, "I want whatever would be fun and pays well." But to be useful, an ideal must be *specific*. Paradoxically, an ideal should also be *general* enough to encompass a broad range of possibilities. To balance the needs of being both *specific* and *general*, choose a *set of priorities*. How to do this is explained in more detail in the *Pursuing Multiple, Prioritized Goals* section later in this chapter. For now, let's suppose that your set of priorities, starting with the highest priority, looks like this:

- Enough pay to meet basic needs
- Interesting work
- Opportunities to learn
- A balance between working with people and working alone
- A balance between sitting at a desk and moving around
- Additional pay beyond basic needs

Notice that these priorities convey *specific* desires, yet provide *generality* because they don't specify the exact nature of a job.

The order of importance of preferences is what forces you to *balance* your preferences with respect to one another. If earning lots of money is your highest priority, then you probably need to make sacrifices in another area, such as not being as picky about how meaningful your work is. On the other hand, if meaningful work is very important to you, alas, that means you will probably have to make sacrifices in your standard of living. Common sense tells you this, but that's what all the creative problem solving tools lead to: common sense.

When you know what your priorities are, you can identify different kinds of jobs that fit your list of priorities. For instance, teaching or working in an instructional television studio would both fit within the above priorities. Once you know what kind of job you're looking for, you can extend your job search to include places that have such jobs. Specifically, you can write to local businesses and organizations that have jobs of the type you're interested in. Broadening your search in this way improves your chances of finding a job that's closer to your ideal. And if you can't find the job you're looking for, don't forget the possibility of creating such a job — which is an alternative you'll never see in the classified ads.

▶ After you create an ideal, pursue it. Not with the goal of necessarily *reaching* the ideal, but with the goal of giving you a *direction* in which to head.

▶ Although you should clearly identify your ideal, it's wise to be somewhat reserved about sharing an ideal with other people. Many people don't appreciate the value of ideals. In fact, they're often called "useless dreams".

▶ As you create your ideal solution, don't be afraid to *think big*. The purpose of thinking in ideal terms is to expand your awareness of your possibilities. The more ambitious your ideal solution is, the broader your awareness. After all, the word *ideal* implies an absence of limits.

▶ Suppose that, as a parent, you're discouraged that children's television cartoons heavily promote toys and candy. Also, suppose that you and other parents want to find a creative solution to the problem, a solution that isn't as simple as restricting what the children watch on television. It occurs to you that you could make your own cartoons. Certainly this is thinking big. It's highly idealistic and unrealistic. Yet, as you ponder such an ideal, it occurs to you that instead of using drawings, you could have the kids act out a cartoon. That idea leads to the realistic idea of helping your kids put on a play, one that doesn't promote toys and candy. This is how some *small* creative ideas emerge: by thinking *big*.

Creating an *ideal* is not the same as creating a *fantasy*. There are
obvious physical limits to the world we live in. For instance, you
cannot expect to jump into the air and not come down. On the other
hand, there are some limitations that can be overcome. A simple
example is the thought "I could never invent something worthwhile." This belief is a real limitation. However, unlike gravity, it's
a limitation that can be overcome. Therefore, distinguish between
real limitations, which cannot be overcome, and *mental* limitations,
which exist only within people's minds.

◄SUMMARY►

An ideal is like a compass that can keep you from getting lost.
It provides a general direction in which to head as you try to find
your way through the unknown frontiers you're exploring. But
don't confuse an ideal with a fantasy. An ideal is limited to what is
actually possible, whereas a fantasy has no limits.

Exercise 1. From the perspective of a company that writes
computer software, which of the following approaches would be
the most ideal way to overcome the problem of customers
complaining about how difficult their software is to use?

- Offer free classes in how to use their software.
- Supply clear, well-written manuals to accompany the software.
- Make the software easy to use.

Exercise 2. Here's an exercise that provides practice in recognizing
the difference between ideals and fantasies. Arrange the following
limitations in an order that indicates how difficult it would be to
change each limitation.

- The number of hours in a day.
- A boundary between departments in an organization.
- Creating electrical energy without getting it from some other
  form of energy (such as chemical, solar, or nuclear energy).
- A rule that employees arrive at work at 8 a.m. and leave at 5
  p.m.
- Removing a written law that prohibits littering.

(An answer to this exercise appears on page 311.)

Exercise 3. Pick a situation you would like to improve. Then, imagine an ideal solution. Make the ideal specific. Once you know what your ideal is, ask yourself, "How can I get closer to achieving this ideal?"

Pursuing Final, Rather Than Intermediate, Goals

Surprisingly often, people pursue a goal and then, after achieving it, discover they were mistaken in assuming that reaching the goal would automatically cause them to reach what they really wanted. To avoid such a disappointment, distinguish between *intermediate* goals and *final* goals.

The classic example of being disappointed by reaching a goal is the person who achieves wealth, only to discover that money hasn't also brought happiness. Notice that money is always an intermediate goal rather than a final goal because, in itself, money has no value. It has value only to the degree it can be exchanged for something else or used as bait to change people's attitudes or behavior.

To make sure your goal is not an intermediate one, ask yourself, "If I get this, and *absolutely nothing else*, will this make me happy?" As you imagine achieving your goal, you're likely to think, "Of course this will make me happy." But in the image are you also, without realizing it, including some *extra assumptions* beyond your stated goal?

For example, if your goal is to travel to a foreign country, imagine traveling in that foreign country. In addition to seeing the sights, are you *also* imagining yourself enjoying the companionship of fellow travelers? Or, if you're accompanied by family members, are they behaving more agreeably than usual? In addition to the traveling itself, are you also looking forward to the opportunities to tell other people about your vacation after you return? These are the kinds of additional aspects that are frequently, yet unconsciously, added to the image of achieving a goal. They are additions that go beyond the stated goal, which in the case of traveling is simply being in a distant location.

Surprisingly often you'll discover that what you thought was very important is simply an *intermediate* something you thought you had to have to accomplish what you really want. By knowing what your *final* goal is, you can become aware of new alternatives.

For example, to continue with the traveling example, imagine yourself being among new companions, feeling relaxed, and alongside family members behaving more agreeably than usual, but without being in a foreign country. Are you happy in spite of not being in a foreign country? If so, you've discovered that traveling to the foreign country is an *intermediate* goal. The final goal is companionship, relaxation, and the pleasant behavior of others nearby. This insight reveals the following alternatives:

- Instead of going to a foreign country to relax, consider getting a professional massage.

- Instead of going abroad to meet interesting travelers, join a local organization to meet people locally with similar interests. Note that this can include joining an organization devoted to sharing information about foreign countries.

- Instead of going to foreign countries to learn about cultural differences, invite people visiting from foreign countries to stay with you.

Intermediate goals are limiting for these two reasons:

- You've *limited* yourself to a *single path* for getting to a final destination. There might be other paths that also lead to the same destination.

- Reaching the intermediate goal doesn't ensure you'll reach your final goal.

Sometimes there are layers of goals, each one leading, hopefully, to the next layer. In this respect the term *final* is misleading because a final goal, in turn, can be an intermediate goal that leads to yet another final goal. For instance, being healthy is a final goal compared to eating healthy foods, but being healthy is an intermediate goal compared to enjoying life. In other words, final and intermediate are relative, not absolute, terms.

Identifying final goals often involves subtle and surprising issues, so don't expect to identify your final goals in a single thinking session. In major areas such as job or relationships, it can take years to fully identify your final goals. Even then, be willing to re-evaluate your final goals at any time, always looking for goals that deserve to be demoted to intermediate-goal status.

◄SUMMARY►

To increase your awareness of all your alternatives, make sure your goals are not just intermediate goals. Ask yourself, "If I were to achieve this goal and *absolutely nothing else*, would I be happy with the outcome?" Focusing on final goals, instead of only intermediate goals, often reveals other paths that lead to the same destination. Keep in mind that final and intermediate are relative, not absolute, terms.

Exercise 1. In martial arts such as karate and judo the goal is to hurt or disable an attacker. If this hurting or disabling is regarded as an intermediate goal, what is the final goal? (An answer appears on page 311.)

Exercise 2. What characteristics do you look for in people when you want to develop a friendship or relationship? Such characteristics might include facial features, ability to tell a joke, how easily the person gets irritated, or the person's hobbies. Which of the characteristics on your list are necessary for the kind of relationship you want to develop? Which ones are unnecessary? What are your final goals for such a relationship?

Exercise 3. Choose an aspect of your life, such as your work, your social life at work, your social life at home, a specific desire, or a specific project. For this particular area, what is your goal? Assume this goal is an intermediate goal. What is your final goal?

Considering Indirect Approaches

Sometimes an indirect approach makes it possible to achieve what would be difficult, or impossible, to achieve directly.

Henry Fleer tried to talk grocery store owners into selling his product, a new gum he called Chiclets. But the store owners pointed out that they already had too much candy on their shelves; they didn't want more. So, Fleer tried an indirect approach. He offered to give boxes of his gum to store owners who would hand out a free sample package to each customer. The store owners were happy to give away to their customers something the store didn't have to pay for. After trying the gum, many customers asked the grocery store owners where they could buy it. Of course, the store owners were soon buying Chiclets gum.

When you meet resistance, consider trying an indirect approach. Rather than work harder, work smarter.

Perhaps you're thinking that using an indirect *approach* contradicts the earlier recommendation of pursuing final *goals* instead of intermediate goals. But there's no contradiction. Notice that *approaches* and *goals* are different entities. The *goal* provides the long-term *direction*, and the indirect *approach* provides a practical *path* to reach the goal.

Indirect approaches are often overlooked, yet they offer such dramatic advantages that it's worth looking at them in detail.

One manufacturer's canned products needed to be mixed at the retail stores because the contents settled during shipping. Someone came up with the clever idea of putting the cans upside down within the cartons, putting the cartons upside down within the larger shipping containers, and shipping the larger containers upside down. The people receiving the shipments typically turned them right side up, which meant they were turned over each time the next layer of packaging was revealed. This eliminated the need to shake the cans at the stores.

Because an indirect solution can accomplish, with little effort, what would otherwise require a challenging direct approach, it's worth learning several commonly useful kinds of indirect approaches.

- Instead of meeting resistance head on, consider using the principle of *redirection*.

When someone tries to punch someone trained in the martial art of aikido, the intended victim doesn't try to block the punch. Instead, the intended victim *changes the direction* of the punch, such as to one side or the other. This approach takes much less effort than trying to match the strength of the attacker.

• Another indirect approach is the familiar *step-by-step* approach.

When you're pursuing a lofty goal that can't easily be reached in a single step, choose a path of multiple steps. Each step can more easily be reached, and provides a firm footing for the next step.

Suppose you were building a suspension bridge across a river canyon. You know it would be difficult to try to throw a large cable across the canyon. Instead, consider throwing a string across the canyon. What good would a string do? It could be used to pull across a small rope, which, in turn, could be used to pull the cable. Of course, tying the string to a rock and throwing the rock across would get the string across.

• Another indirect approach is the concept of *amplification*.

Some street performers, including jugglers and magicians, have adopted an innovative way to enlarge their audience. In the past, they mainly depended on yelling, whistling, and sounding horns to attract more people. Now, after attracting a small crowd, the performer says, "Now, before I start my act, I want you to help me bring more people over here. So, on the count of three I want you to yell *Ah!* and whistle like there's something really exciting going on here. Here we go ... one, two, three!"

• Finally, there's the indirect approach called *leverage*.

Political parties invest effort influencing where the boundaries between voting districts are placed, because a small advantage in their favor reduces the effort later needed for their candidates to win elections.

◄SUMMARY►

Consider using *indirect approaches* to accomplish more easily what you would otherwise have to struggle to accomplish. The following indirect approaches are especially useful:

- Redirection
- Step-by-step
- Amplification
- Leverage

Being Aware Of Hidden Goals

If you have goals you're not consciously aware of, you might be
tempted to choose a solution that doesn't best solve the problem.

Politicians typically seem reluctant to implement solutions that
will solve problems. This is because solving the problem is not their
only goal. They also want to be reelected. It's when these two goals
conflict that they favor a solution that at least partially satisfies the
people who want the problem solved and minimizes the number of
supporters who are offended. But you don't have to be a politician
to be influenced by hidden goals. It happens to all of us.

Hidden goals aren't only the ones hidden from other people;
they include goals hidden from ourselves.

Below are five common, and influential, goals that are so
familiar they can easily be overlooked:

- Desire to *prove a point.*

    As an example, suppose a car driver makes a right turn
    across the bicycle lane in which you're bicycling. You slow
    down and slap the rear end of the car as it cuts you off, instead
    of getting completely out of the car's way.

- Desire to *hurt,* prompted by *anger.*

    For example, you boycott a store that mails excessive
    numbers of advertisements to lots of people, instead of
    requesting to be taken off its mailing list.

- Desire to *avoid* what prompts *fear.*

    As an example, an architect avoids a creative building
    design because heshe doesn't know how to calculate the size of
    the needed beams and supports. In this case, the architect fears
    being sued or losing referrals because the walls crack or the
    windows break, and fears losing hisher reputation by admitting
    a lack of knowledge.

- Desire to *be appreciated*, due to *low self-esteem*.

    As an example, suppose you favor a clever solution over a conventional solution and ignore the issue of effectiveness because the clever idea is more impressive.

- Desire to *compensate* for feelings of *guilt*. The guilt indicates that in the past you've inflicted hurt or missed an opportunity to help.

    For example, a parent gives a toy to hisher child who wants, but doesn't need, the toy, in order to compensate for spending so much time away from home.

◄SUMMARY►

Desires to prove a point, get revenge, avoid what you fear, satisfy the ego, reduce guilt, and other similar tendencies are, in effect, *goals*. Such goals are just as real, and often more influential, than the ones you think you're following. Once you become aware of such goals, it becomes easier to accomplish what you really want.

Exercise 1. What is the main goal of a medical corporation? How does this goal limit its effort to improve health care?

Exercise 2. Consider your boss or someone with whom you have even a minor conflict. What does this person claim hisher goals to be? What other goals also influence the person's behavior? Is the person aware of these other goals? If so, is the person aware of these goals influencing hisher behavior?

Exercise 3. What goals do you follow without being aware of their influence?

Pursuing Multiple, Prioritized Goals

Splitting up a *single goal* into *multiple specific goals* allows you to make your goals more specific, and therefore, clearer. Deciding the relative *order of importance* of these goals *broadens* your alternatives.

Suppose you're married and your relationship with your
spouse has some rough spots. Obviously, your goal is to improve
the relationship, but this isn't a clear goal.

To make a goal clearer, split it up into separate, specific goals,
and broaden it by putting the specific goals in order of importance.

For example, pretend that this is your prioritized list of specific
goals for improving your relationship:

- Most important: Cuddle up with your spouse more often.

- Medium important: Get your spouse to be on time, so you
  aren't kept waiting.

- Least important: Get your spouse to put the toothpaste cap back
  on the toothpaste tube after using it.

Notice that separating the single goal of improving the relationship
into these multiple goals enables you to state each one more specifically.

Putting your goals into a prioritized list draws attention to the
possibility of creating a solution that meets the most important
goals, without meeting the least important ones.

Of course, a solution that increases the cuddling but doesn't
keep the cap on the toothpaste is a solution worth considering, even
though it doesn't accomplish both goals. This strategy is
commonly stated as, "taking care of big issues and letting little ones
slide."

In visual terms, this strategy is analogous to defining a target in
which the larger areas represent the highest priorities and the
smaller areas represent less important issues, as shown on the next
page. Would it be all that upsetting to score success within the
highest priority area and fail to score success within the less important areas?

Sometimes it's difficult to prioritize. In such a case, it helps to
ask, "Which goal, if it could be met, would make the other goals
worth disregarding — for now?"

Suppose you and your spouse want to choose a vacation spot
and you like both *getting away from crowds* and *participating in
sporting activities*. To determine which goal is more important,
imagine getting one without the other. First, imagine getting away
to an isolated area that has absolutely no opportunities for sporting
activities. Then, imagine going to a very populated area that has
lots of sporting opportunities. Which one appeals to you more?

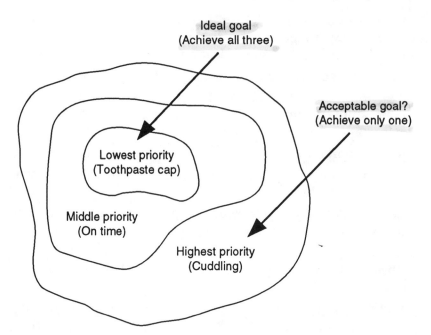

The answer can be more revealing than simply asking, "Which is more important?"

Incidentally, identifying an order of preference is especially useful when trying to resolve conflicts between people. Knowing each person's top priority makes it easier to find a mutually pleasing decision that meets everyone's top priority, even though other preferences aren't met.

Transforming general goals into *specific* goals is an important part of identifying multiple goals.

To illustrate the contrast between a non-specific goal and a specific one, consider what the top managers of the 3M Company did to encourage innovation. Instead of saying "Let's be innovative!", they set the goal of each division earning at least 25 percent of its revenues from products introduced in the previous 5 years. This clearly conveyed what they wanted — without using the abstract term *innovation*.

◄SUMMARY►

A goal can be broadened to include creative solutions by breaking it up into *multiple specific* goals and ranking the multiple goals according to their importance to you. Be willing to consider solutions that meet your most important desires, yet fail to meet less important preferences.

Exercise 1. Identify an important goal in your life that you have not yet been able to achieve. Then, identify other goals that you have placed at a higher priority than the important goal. These account for why you have not yet reached your important goal.

Exercise 2. Choose one area of life, such as food and eating, social activities, vacationing, or working conditions. Identify what's important to you in this area. List your priorities according to their relative importance. Put the most important goals at the top and the least important at the bottom.

Creating Non-Objects

Because our culture emphasizes the importance of objects, we frequently try to solve problems by creating new objects, such as devices, toys, drugs, and machines. We easily overlook the possibility of solving the problem by creating something that isn't an object.

When you need to pour a liquid from a wide-mouthed container into a small-mouthed container, you naturally think of using a funnel. When there's no funnel, you're likely to consider creating a funnel out of available materials. A very different approach is to use a long thin object, such as a spoon handle, to direct the liquid (which follows the spoon handle) into the small-mouthed container, as shown below.

If you didn't know about this technique, then you see the point. Techniques are usually learned by seeing someone do them or by reading about them in a book, which limits the number of people who learn about non-object solutions. In contrast, products that solve the same problem are seen on countless store shelves, window displays, and product catalogs. Innovative *objects* are so important in our economy that they have a special name: inventions. Yet non-object solutions can be just as effective in solving problems, even though they don't have a special name.

What kinds of "things" can non-object solutions be? Possibilities include: techniques, strategies, conventions, processes, systems, representations, spoken and non-spoken languages, words, attitudes, insights, and ways of doing things. Here are some examples of non-objects that have been created to solve problems:

- Waiting in a single line for multiple bank teller windows.
- Agreeing among family members that if someone becomes separated from the others in a large amusement park that the lost person will wait where heshe was last seen by the others.
- Driving on the right side of the road and stopping at stop signs.
- Preventing the spread of infectious disease with a quarantine, in which the diseased person is isolated from others.
- Splashing water on a shower curtain edge to seal it to the shower wall.

Notice that non-object solutions have an important difference from inventions: they can be *copied* easily. In our economic system it's difficult to earn money by creating what other people can copy easily, so large businesses prefer to focus on creating objects. These objects (inventions) are profitable because a business can register the idea with the patent office and sue any other business that makes the object, thus eliminating competition. Although businesses neglect creating non-object solutions, you shouldn't neglect them too. In fact, there's a rich source of creative solutions in the realm of non-objects. Typically, they aren't financially profitable, but they can be quite effective in solving problems.

For a variety of reasons, most of the big problems that remain unsolved require non-object solutions. A classic example of the attempt to solve a social problem with an object-oriented solution is the attempt to end wars by creating the ultimate weapon. This is what the atomic bomb, the hydrogen bomb, and satellite-based defense systems were supposed to do. But social problems are more effectively solved through social innovations, not through physical inventions. For instance, in the case of reducing warfare, the most effective partial solution has been the creation of something non-physical: systems of voting. Specifically, voting can resolve some conflicts that would otherwise be resolved by fighting.

Isaac, when we hired you we expected something better of you than this. This "calculus" thing you've invented — we can't patent it, we can't manufacture it, and the marketing department would have a heck of a time trying to convince people to buy it! Now get back to work and this time, Mr. Newton, come up with something *useful* !

◄SUMMARY►

When creating new solutions, consider creating activities, techniques, strategies, conventions, processes, systems, representations, words, and other "things" that aren't objects. Their potential for solving large-scale and social problems is greater than many people realize.

Exercise 1. Imagine you're a health care professional looking for a new way to improve your patients' back problems. Instead of focusing on object-oriented inventions such as drugs, chairs, pillows, exercise devices, or bad-posture alarms, create one or more non-object solutions.

Exercise 2. Suppose someone special to you (such as a spouse or child) sometimes fails to sense when you would rather be left alone or that this is a bad time to bring up anything potentially irritating. Create a word or phrase you can use to indicate when you're in such a mood.

Considering Pulling Instead Of Pushing

Pulling is frequently more effective than *pushing*.

Some acupuncturists in ancient China were paid by a client as long as the client was well, but payment stopped when the client became ill. This *pulling* arrangement effectively motivated the acupuncturist to heal the patient quickly — to restore his income. In contrast, modern doctors are not financially rewarded for healing patients quickly. In fact, the longer it takes for a patient to get well, the more a doctor gets paid. Competition among doctors, which is form of *pushing*, is what ensures that doctors not take too long to heal patients. Of course, doctors are also pulled by a desire to heal a patient, but this desire is not rewarded financially as it was for the ancient Chinese acupuncturists.

This pull versus push concept is very useful to consider when designing a creative solution because pulling is often better than pushing.

Have you ever noticed that the end post of a fence can be reinforced using either a wire to *pull* the top of the end post or a diagonal post to *push* the top of the end post? Both approaches force the end post in the same direction, but they differ according to which side of the end post something is attached. Notice that using a wire to pull requires less mass to accomplish the same thing that the much heavier diagonal pushing post requires.

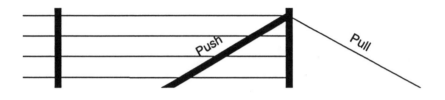

Whereas physically pulling offers the advantage of reduced mass, socially pulling offers the advantage of reduced effort.

Parents learn quickly that rewarding a child's good behavior with a treat, such as ice cream, can be more motivating than discouraging bad behavior with threatened punishment, such as spanking.

When an employee stays home sick, a business loses productivity yet still has to pay the employee (up to a limited time). Naturally, managers focus attention on legitimate ways to discourage employees from using all their sick leave. Commonly unnoticed is the fact that employees who are seldom sick aren't financially rewarded in spite of the productivity they offer. Now, some innovative employers offer *well pay* in addition to *sick pay*. Employees still get paid on days they call in sick, but they get paid even more to the degree they don't use their sick leave.

Whether you're an employer, a parent, or simply someone who spends time interacting with other people, look at where you're pulling and where you're pushing. To pull is to say, in effect, "If you do this for me, then I'll do that for you." In contrast, to push is to say, "If you dare do this, then I'll hurt you by doing that." Which form of motivation is more inviting to you?

Part of the reason pushing is favored is that it takes less thinking effort to *identify* what we *don't want* than what we *do want*. But, extra thinking effort in advance can save lots of effort later because it's easier to *convey* what you *do want* than to convey the many behaviors you *don't want*.

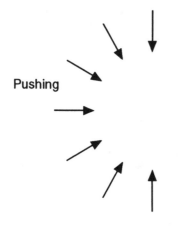

In spite of its advantages, pulling is not always better than pushing. A pulling approach deserves extra consideration not because it's better, but because it's commonly overlooked.

◄SUMMARY►

The next time you're looking for a creative solution, look for ways to attract people, animals, plants, or objects toward what you want, instead of pushing them away from what you don't want. Extra effort invested in figuring out how to pull can reduce the effort needed to bring about the desired change.

Exercise 1. Imagine you supervise employees and one of them usually arrives late at meetings. How can you apply a pulling, rather than pushing, approach to deal with this problem?

Chapter 4

Exploring Your Many Alternatives

An essential part of creative problem solving is seeing beyond one possible solution and exploring the many possibilities that exist.

Following Multiple Ideas

When you seek to solve a problem, look beyond the first obvious choices. That's where you'll find creative solutions.

Suppose you're an employer who's discouraged by an employee's poor performance. The following alternatives easily come to mind:

- Accept the situation as it is, although it's disappointing.
- Complain to the employee and encourage himher to work harder.
- Fire the employee.

These ideas arise easily because they're conventional alternatives. Now, let's look beyond these to other alternatives:

- Find out if working different or fewer hours would improve the employee's efficiency.
- Encourage the employee to take a class to improve a basic skill that's weak, and offer to pay tuition.
- Let the employee know of your dissatisfaction, and don't give a traditional annual raise until hisher performance improves.
- Ask the employee what heshe would do if faced with your problem.

Notice that these alternatives are less obvious and more creative. Thus, a simple way to become aware of creative possibilities is to look beyond the ideas that first pop into your mind.

As already explained in the *Writing Down New Ideas* section, writing down your ideas ensures you won't forget them. In addition, writing down ideas allows you to stay focused on thinking of more ideas instead of getting distracted by remembering your ideas.

Perhaps you're wondering, "How many ideas should I write down?" There's no simple answer to this question. Here are some common-sense considerations:

- The limiting factor is time. How much time do you want to spend looking for a solution you really like?
- The more ideas you've written down, the longer it usually takes to come up with each new idea.
- The most creative ideas usually appear in the middle or end of a list.

As you write down possible solutions, resist the temptation to choose the best one. This premature judging discourages you from looking for yet more solutions.

It's important that you write down all your ideas, including ones you think you won't use. For example, in the poorly-performing employee problem, the idea of denying the employee an annual raise might conflict with a law or a corporate policy, so you might be tempted to exclude it from the list. But don't exclude it.

To help you resist the temptation to not write down ideas you're sure you won't use, here are a few reasons why such "useless" ideas are actually useful:

- In later sections you'll learn how to combine several less-than-great possibilities into a single solution that's better than any of the initial possibilities. The key is to extract *components* of ideas from unused ideas and incorporate the components into the better idea. The result is that the whole "useless" idea is not used, but part of it survives in the chosen solution.
- Because you know you'll use only *one* idea for the chosen solution, it's tempting to try to figure out in advance which ideas are not worth wasting your time on. Such unused ideas can seem to be dead ends. But, no matter how carefully you try, you can't avoid all unused ideas. Nor is there a need to.

A soccer team wouldn't fail to show up for a soccer game just because it's likely to lose. Only hindsight reveals which games will be lost. Also, the effort put into losing games improves the team's performance, and this effort is very *useful* for increasing the chances of winning later games. Similarly, in creative problem solving, only hindsight reveals which ideas become incorporated into the chosen solution. And, effort you put into exploring unused ideas improves your creative problem solving skills.

• The process of refining an idea that turns out to be unused can reveal insights. In turn, the insights can prompt an idea that turns out to be the chosen solution. Again, ideas that are useless as *solutions* are not necessarily useless in the *thinking process*.

Hopefully you now appreciate the importance of writing down silly, impractical, and even unethical ideas. Alas, you'll probably need to experience the usefulness of "useless" ideas before you finally appreciate their value. Ironically, you won't be able to have this experience if you don't write down "useless" ideas.

Attempts to understand the development of successful creative solutions by analyzing other people's creative thinking typically focus little or no attention on "unused" ideas. Instead, the focus of attention is usually on *the* key idea or insight. This kind of hindsight analysis promotes the following *oversimplified linear* (single-line) *sequence of steps* as if it characterized the creative problem solving process:

Oversimplified Linear Sequence

Think ⟶ Idea ⟶ Choose to act on idea ⟶ Implement idea

This linear path is misleading because it implies that only the right idea should be pursued and all the wrong ideas should be ignored. This leads to an attempt to figure out, "Which idea is the right one and which ideas are the wrong ones?" But this question isn't appropriate.

Creative problem solving is actually a branching, rather than a linear, process. The diagram on the next page shows this branching structure for a simple case. In this diagram, as in the one above, time progresses from left to right. The *multiple lines* indicate that *multiple ideas* are being considered. The wavy lines indicate portions of ideas being incorporated into other ideas. Notice that the final implemented idea contains components from ideas that were abandoned. This illustrates how abandoned ideas can contribute to the creation of the chosen solution, even though, as a whole, they're abandoned.

More Realistic Branching Sequence

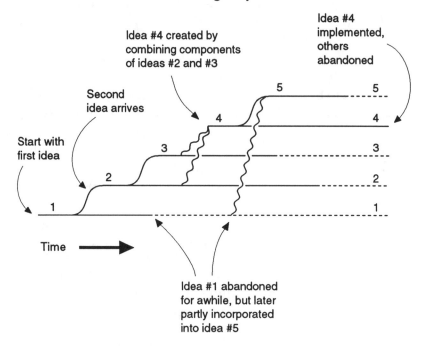

When you find yourself confronted by lots of different ideas, most of which obviously won't be chosen as a solution, recognize that you're doing fine. This is the way creative problem solving works. You must pursue multiple ideas to discover which one — or ones — offer what you're looking for.

Now that you realize you must pursue more than one idea, the question arises, "How can I keep from becoming overwhelmed by too many ideas to pursue?" The key is to *not pursue unpromising ideas*. Unpromising ideas are the ones that don't offer much hope of being refined into usable solutions. However, don't confuse *not pursuing* an idea with *rejecting* the idea! They are quite different. Whereas *rejecting* is deciding to *never again* consider the idea, *not pursuing* is stopping, *at least for now*, your consideration of it.

As a further clarification, choosing not to pursue unpromising ideas happens *throughout* the creative problem solving process, not only at the end of the process when one alternative is chosen.

Not pursuing unpromising ideas is analogous to pruning the branches of a rose bush each year as the bush grows — instead of waiting until it's fully grown to prune it. Just as pruning strengthens the favored branches of a rose bush, pruning ideas enables more of your attention to be focused on the most promising ideas. However, whereas pruned rose branches are killed, pruned ideas lie dormant, ready to be revived if they later appear to offer some value.

Just because you should hold on to the possibility that *any* idea might be the one chosen, doesn't mean you have to thoroughly explore *every* idea. But you usually have to pursue more than one idea.

◄SUMMARY►

When you seek to solve a problem, look beyond the first obvious choices. That's where you'll find the creative ones. The more ideas you explore, the more likely you'll find one you're enthusiastic about.

Recognize that the creative problem solving process is not a sequence of steps along a single path. Instead, possibilities branch out in many directions, all of which, to some extent, should be explored.

Write down all your alternatives, including ones you know you won't act on. Such "useless" ideas contain components that can be incorporated into refined solutions.

Exercise 1. If you've never experienced the creativity that comes from listing possible solutions, try it now. Choose a situation you have a strong desire to improve and list the ideas that occur to you. Remember to see the merit in each idea that pops into your mind. Write down *all* your ideas, even the ones that aren't likely to work. When you think you've run out of ideas, expand the list some more.

If you can't think of any particular situation for this exercise, recall a situation in which someone refused to do something you wanted. What other alternatives might have accomplished what you wanted?

Expanding A Radial Outline
Of Alternatives

A powerful way to expand your awareness of possible solutions is to create and expand a *radial outline* of possible solutions. What's a radial outline? That will be explained after introducing a sample problem that will be used throughout this section.

Suppose you're growing vegetables in a backyard garden. And suppose your neighbors have chickens that wander freely and eat the vegetables in your garden. If your neighbors have ignored your requests to keep their chickens off your property, what could you do? Here are a few possibilities:

- Build a fence.
- Call the animal control department.
- Get a cat.
- Get a dog.

Here's how these ideas can be shown in a radial outline:

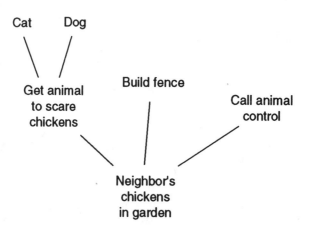

The bottom item in a radial outline is a brief name for the problem to be solved. The possible solutions branch out (radiate) from the main item, similar to the way a tree's branches connect to the trunk of a tree. Related ideas are grouped together within a named category. In this example, getting a cat and getting a dog are grouped within the category of getting an animal to scare the chickens.

It can be useful to think of this outline as a road map (an overhead view) of the roads that stretch out ahead of you. All the roads have some potential for taking you to your goal of solving the problem.

Putting your ideas in a radial outline instead of listing them offers the big advantage of keeping related ideas together in groups. When there are many ideas in the outline, this grouping makes it easier to focus attention on one category or group of ideas at a time.

Now that the sample radial outline has been started, let's expand it with the following two goals in mind:

- Identify specific possible solutions — one of which might be chosen as the final preferred solution.

- Identify new categories — one of which might *contain* the final preferred solution.

When expanding an outline, usually there's not any value in adding an alternative to a category that already has alternatives, if the new alternative doesn't offer *any* advantage over what's already written in that category.

For example, now that we've identified the scaring-the-chickens-with-animals category, it would be easy to expand the outline by adding the names of more animals, such as goats and sheep. But, obviously, it would be pointless to list all such alternatives. Sheep and goats can't do anything better than cats and dogs — assuming you don't make wool sweaters or drink goat's milk. Plus, cats and dogs have advantages over sheep and goats. So, it's appropriate to ignore, at least for now, the idea of getting other animals to scare the chickens.

Suppose it occurs to you that you might be able to scare the chickens with rubber snakes. Unlike a cat or dog, rubber snakes don't require food and attention, so they do offer a significant advantage over the already-listed cat and dog. Therefore, rubber snakes would be added to the outline. (Whether they would have the desired effect is not important for now.) In deciding where in the outline to put the rubber snakes idea, it becomes clear that a broader category can be added, namely scaring the chickens. These additions are shown in the expanded radial outline on the next page.

Another possible way of dealing with the chickens would be to build a moat, in the form of a ditch filled with water. The fact that a moat is similar to a fence reveals a new category: creating a barrier. In turn, this category could prompt the idea of growing dense bushes that act as a barrier. These expansions now make the outline appear as follows:

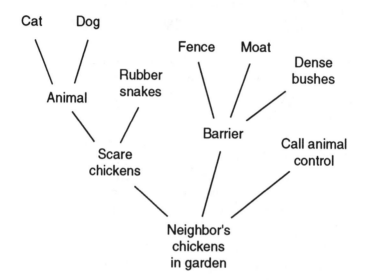

This radial outline makes it clear that all but one of the ideas amount to scaring and obstructing the chickens. This reveals one of the important advantages of putting your alternatives into a radial outline: neglected areas, where there are few ideas, show up clearly. To prompt creative ideas, focus your attention on these neglected areas.

Here are some possible solutions for the chickens-in-the-garden problem that don't fit within the categories identified so far. As you read these ideas, remember to look for advantages in each idea and appreciate humor.

- Grow vegetables that chickens don't like.
- Offer to help your neighbors build a fence around their yard.
- Shoot the chickens.
- Make nests to attract the chickens so you can collect their eggs.
- Invite your neighbors over for chicken dinner.

Notice that inviting your neighbors over for chicken dinner involves the *neighbors* but not the *chickens* (presumably). This distinction reveals two broader categories that weren't apparent before: dealing with the *chickens* and dealing with the *neighbors*. With these additions of ideas and categories, the radial outline now looks like this:

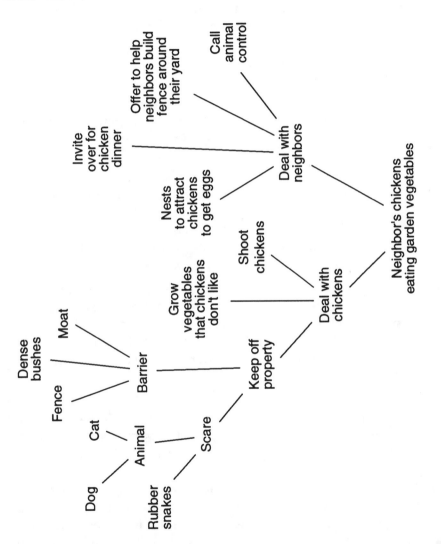

Again, notice that the most creative ideas are in the categories with the fewest ideas. To focus attention on these areas, try to think of ideas that are similar to the ideas in these neglected areas. For example, try to think of ideas similar to the most unusual alternative, which is making nests for the chickens. Because this alternative focuses attention on the fact that the chicken's eggs are worth something, it could prompt the idea of pretending to find eggs in your yard, which might motivate the neighbors to keep their chickens (and eggs) off your property. Notice that this alternative involves less effort than most of the other alternatives and it has a possibility of working. Also, notice how many "useless" ideas arose before this more practical alternative arose.

▶ It's useful to add categories when you recognize them, even when the ideas within them are ones you wouldn't act on. Why? Here are two reasons:

- Grouping ideas into categories reveals where you're focusing most of your attention. This awareness makes it easier to broaden your focus by thinking of ideas within categories that have fewer ideas.

  For example, the categories of putting up a barrier and scaring the chickens, along with the alternative of shooting the chickens, clarify that there's lots of attention on the chickens, but not much attention on the neighbors.

- A category can include a more practical solution along with the impractical solutions that have been recognized so far.

  For example, the not-very-practical idea of making nests to attract the chickens and the somewhat-practical idea of pretending to find eggs in your yard both fit within the same category, namely ideas that involve the chickens' eggs. Any idea that first reveals such a different approach is worth writing down.

▶ Not only is it useful to add a category when you first recognize it, but it's useful to write down the first specific alternative that fits within the category. Why? Because it provides a specific image of an idea within the category, and this image can be used to prompt related ideas.

As an example, consider the idea of dealing with the chicken problem by moving out of the neighborhood. Although you probably wouldn't want to do this, it's worth writing down because it reveals the more general approach of moving. And within this broader category is the possibility of getting the neighbors to move away. For instance, if the neighbors were unemployed and looking for work, you might be able to motivate them to move by finding them a job in a distant city.

The idea of moving also illustrates that an easily-overlooked ◀❗ area for expanding the outline is at the main idea itself. Prior to the idea of moving, the only two categories branching off the main item were dealing with the chickens and dealing with the neighbors. The idea of moving yourself revealed the additional category of moving (either yourself or the neighbors).

If it bothers you to write down alternatives that you know you would never act on, you can mark them in a special way, such as by putting them in parentheses. Then, if someone should look at your radial outline, the parentheses around unethical or impractical ideas indicate that those ideas aren't being considered seriously.

Of course, it's neither necessary nor desirable to simply expand ◀❗ an outline to make it as big as possible. After all, most of the alternatives created that way would be ones you wouldn't use. So, how do you decide how far to expand it? As explained in the previous section, the limiting factor is time, so ask yourself, "How much time do I want to spend looking for a solution I really like?"

It might be confusing to talk about not expanding an outline too far and, at the same time, to expand this chickens-in-the-garden outline beyond what someone would actually do if confronted with this problem. Keep in mind that this extra expansion is being done to *demonstrate* how the expansion can be done, not because you would actually expand an outline this far for a relatively minor problem. With this in mind, look at the expanded radial outline on the next page. Notice how many alternatives there are compared to the few ideas that first came to mind. There are more alternatives than there's room to mention in the text.

Now that you've learned the principles of creating and expanding a radial outline, here are some suggestions for the mechanics of drawing one on paper:

- When you're first drawing radial outlines, consider using a pencil instead of a pen because lots of erasing or crossing out is usually involved.

- If you're using a blank piece of rectangular paper, rotate it so that its left-to-right dimension is longer than its top-to-bottom dimension.

- Write an abbreviated title of the problem near the bottom of the paper.

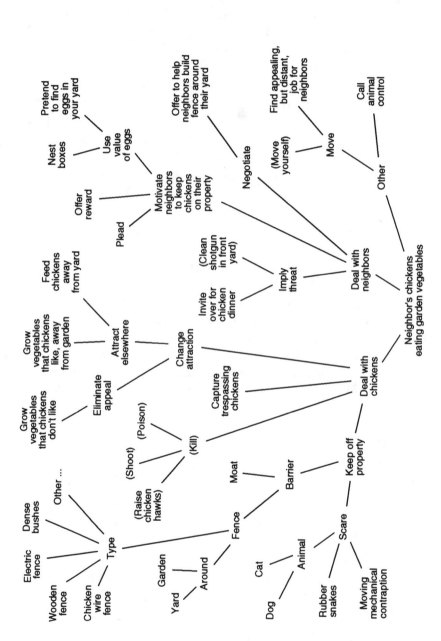

- Leave a little extra space between the title and the bottom edge of the paper. This space is useful if you later realize that the problem, as you've stated it, is actually a category within a broader problem that can be solved without solving your stated problem. In other words, this extra space is useful when you apply what's explained in the *Reconsidering Your Starting Point* section within Chapter 3, *Reconsidering Your Goals*.

- Reserve the areas near the edges for writing last-minute ideas.

- Put specific solutions nearer the edge of the paper and broad categories nearer the main item.

- Put each new idea near the most similar ideas.

Typically, you don't know in advance which category a new idea fits into, so categories are usually inserted into the midst of an outline after specific alternatives have been written. The following two outline segments represent a *before* and *after* view of this process.

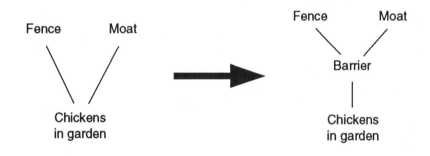

Rest assured that erasing and rewriting are normal when expanding an outline. Such erasing is quite unlike school-oriented tasks where erasing is an indication of a mistake. Also, recognize that sometimes it's necessary to redraw a cluttered outline before expanding it further. (This extra work can be avoided if you create the outline electronically on a computer.)

The outlines in this book were created using a computer to make them look nice. In contrast, drawing an outline by hand while thinking of ideas produces results that are rough and somewhat disorganized. Specifically, such outlines normally include squeezed-in items, lines that curve around other items, and lots of erasures. To emphasize that this is normal, a sample radial outline that simulates the chaos of a freshly-draw outline is shown below. Such chaos emphasizes that a radial outline is a thinking tool, not something for other people to admire.

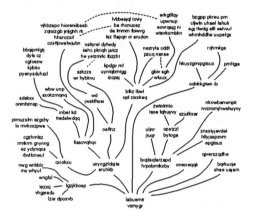

As you gain experience in sketching radial outlines on paper, you'll find it easier to create and expand simple outlines in your mind, without putting them on paper. This is an extremely useful skill in creative problem solving! In a situation that requires making a quick decision, you won't have to say, "Just a minute while I sketch an outline of my alternatives." Instead you can, within seconds, create an outline in your mind and, within a few more seconds, expand it to include alternatives that might not be obvious. To reach that point, you must get lots of practice creating and expanding outlines on paper.

An outline imagined in the mind differs from those drawn on paper. Here are the main differences:

- Normally, the alternatives are represented by pictures or images instead of written words.

- Connections are usually not represented by narrow lines — which are what pencils and pens create most easily. The connections can be represented by roads, paths, ropes, out-of-focus colored wide lines, or an infinite number of other possibilities.

- Categories aren't labeled because it's difficult to represent a category using a picture. Instead, the nature of each branch is evident based on which alternatives connect, and don't connect, to that branching point.

Here's an illustration of an imagined outline, although it's limited by what can be put on paper:

At times you might be confused about which way your ideas should be represented in an outline. But there is no one right way to categorize ideas. In fact, outlines are not always the most appropriate way to represent the relationship between items. (A later section in this chapter explains another way to represent alternatives.) In such cases *no* outline is correct. Yet any outline you come up with can be *useful*.

You've now learned to heighten your creativity dramatically! And notice that it doesn't require a special brain to use these tools. It's mental skills, not a special brain, that make some people more creative than others.

Because creating and expanding an outline is so useful in prompting creative ideas, it's easy to forget about using the other tools explained in this book. But remember that they too are needed to lead you to a final effective solution.

◄SUMMARY►

Create a radial outline of possible solutions to clearly see your alternatives. Place a high priority on grouping related ideas together within labeled categories.

Many creative alternatives can be discovered by looking at each item in the outline, one at a time, and thinking of additional categories or possible solutions that connect to that item.

When ideas are slow to come, focus extra attention on where the fewest ideas are, which is where the most creative ideas usually arise.

To avoid expanding an outline to unnecessary extremes, here are tips for deciding whether to add a new alternative or category:

- Add a new category whenever you recognize one.
- Add an alternative if it fits within a category that doesn't yet have any alternatives, even if the alternative will certainly not be used.
- Add an alternative if it offers at least one advantage over the other alternatives within that category. If it doesn't offer any advantage, don't add it.
- Add an alternative if you're unsure about whether it should be added.

Outlines should be sketched informally as the ideas occur to you, not as something drawn for someone else to see.

The more experience you get in drawing and expanding radial outlines on paper, the easier it becomes to create, and expand, simple outlines in your mind. This ability is an extremely important thinking skill in creative problem solving.

Exercise 1. Choose a problem of personal interest and identify possible alternatives, including seemingly impractical ones, that easily pop into your mind. Create a radial outline of these initial ideas, keeping similar ideas grouped together. Then, expand the radial outline, following the guidelines listed in the summary.

Although many exercises in this book can be skipped, do not skip this one. Only by actually drawing a radial outline can you appreciate its usefulness in creative problem solving.

Identifying Categories Before Specific Alternatives

Expanding an outline of alternatives can be done not only by focusing attention on the upper (more specific) levels of a radial outline, but also by focusing on the lower and middle (more general) levels. This approach consists of discovering new categories without first identifying alternatives within those categories.

Consider dealing with a mosquito that lands on your face as you're trying to fall asleep at night. It's fairly obvious that there are various ways to locate it (either in the dark or after turning on the light) and kill it (using your hand, a chemical spray, or something else). But all these ideas fit within a single category: killing the mosquito. Of course this approach does solve the problem. However, limiting your alternatives to variations within a single category reduces your chances of solving the problem — especially if you can't find the mosquito. A different category would be to get the mosquito out of the bedroom. This approach doesn't kill the mosquito, but it does let you sleep undisturbed, which is your final goal. Once you've identified this new category, you can look for possible solutions that fit within it. Here's one possible way to get the mosquito out of a bedroom: Leave the bedroom light off, go to the hallway and turn the hallway light on, wait a minute or two for the mosquito to be attracted into the hallway (either by the light or by the infrared light your body emits), turn off the hallway light and quickly close the bedroom door, and then go back to bed.

Now you've seen an example in which the new category is recognized *before* you identify an alternative within the category. The basis of this technique is the following three-step process:

1. *Identify the categories for your recognized alternatives.* If you've already created a radial outline of your alternatives, you've already done this step. In the mosquito example, this step amounts to realizing that all the initial alternatives fit within the single category of killing the mosquito.

2. *Think of a different category.* This step represents the progression from the strategy of killing the mosquito to the different strategy of getting it out of your room.

3. *Think of a new possible solution that fits within the new category.*
   This is the progression from the category of getting the
   mosquito out of your room to the possible solution of attracting
   it into the hallway with your body heat and the hall light.

This three-step progression is shown on the following radial
outline using numbers to indicate the order in which the items are
added to the outline:

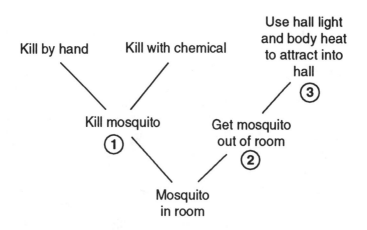

This tool is very important in creative problem solving, so let's
look at another example — one that's slightly more complicated.

Suppose someone named Chris often loses his keys. It's easy to
think of possible solutions such as these:

- Always put the keys in the same place.
- Attach the keys to something he doesn't lose, such as a pair of
  pants or a backpack.
- Don't lock the doors.
- Replace the conventional locks with locks that can be opened by
  pressing buttons in a special code.

Step 1:

Looking for similarities among these alternatives, notice that
the first two solutions, namely putting the keys in the same place
and attaching the keys to something not usually lost, are both
examples of *keeping the keys where they can be found.* The other two
possible solutions, namely not locking doors and installing keyless

locks, are both ways of *avoiding the need for keys.* A radial outline of these alternatives now looks like this:

Step 2:

Now, ignore the four specific alternatives and focus only on the two categories. A little thinking reveals a third category: make the keys easy to find. Suddenly you've expanded your range of possible solutions! Note that making keys *easier to find* is different than keeping the keys in a *known place*, although they sound similar. In one case, Chris knows in advance where the keys can be found. In the other case, the keys somehow reveal their location to him.

Step 3:

More thinking reveals the following two specific ways to make the keys easier to find:

- Attach the keys to an easy-to-see object, such as a large, bright object.
- Attach the keys to a device that makes a noise when you clap your hands a few times. (Such a device has been marketed.)

Notice how creative this last idea is! You now understand how people can come up with very creative ideas. More importantly, now that you know about this tool, you can use it to dramatically expand your own creativity.

(End of steps)

So far, this tool has been explained as if you had the time and inclination to draw an outline and analyze it. But, more realistically, you'll want to use this tool mentally without pencil and paper, as in the following example.

Suppose your car gets a flat tire. You pull off the road to put on your spare tire. In the process of removing the flat tire, four of the five lug nuts fall into a nearby drain opening, out of reach but within view. You know you can't fasten the tire to your car with only one nut, so you try to reach into the drain with a long object, such as a piece of wire, to get the nuts. That approach doesn't work, so you try dangling a magnet on a string to retrieve the nuts, but that fails too. (Step 1) At this point you realize that all your efforts are simply variations of the strategy of *trying to get the same nuts that you lost*. This is the first step of the new tool you're learning. (Step 2) Looking at this problem from a broader perspective, you realize that you could use *different lug nuts* to fasten the tire to the car. This might not seem like a promising alternative, but the merit of this approach is that if other nuts could be found, this approach would solve the problem. (Step 3) Where can you find spare lug nuts? Passing motorists probably wouldn't have spare nuts, only the ones on their tires. At this point you might realize that there are nuts on the *other tires* of *your* car. Finally, you might realize that if you took one nut off each of the other three tires, and used the nut you didn't lose, you would have four nuts holding on each tire! These nuts would keep all the tires fastened to the car long enough to reach a place where you can buy more.

This example illustrates that making lists or written outlines is not a necessary part of identifying new categories before identifying alternatives within that category.

This example also illustrates another important point. Often, a new category appears to have no value when it first pops into your mind. This is because your first ideas for alternatives within the category obviously won't work. But instead of judging the category based on the first ideas within it, the category itself should be judged. Make the assumption that the approach named by the category could somehow be accomplished. Then ask, "Would this approach solve the problem?"

For example, in the changing-tire example, the initial possible alternatives within the category of finding new lug nuts are two impractical solutions: find a passing motorist who happens to be carrying spare lug nuts, or find a passing motorist who would be willing to give you the lug nuts that hold on hisher car's tires. Because neither of these alternatives is practical, it's tempting to toss out the category they fit within, namely finding different lug nuts.

Recognizing a new category without knowing what specific alternatives fall within it is an extremely important creative problem solving skill.

◄SUMMARY►

The following three-step process is extremely useful for recognizing new alternatives that are especially creative:

1. Identify the categories that contain your identified alternatives.
2. Think of a different category.
3. Think of alternatives that fit within the new category.

Exercise 1. Here are three real problems:

- Teenage pregnancy.
- Avoiding the frustration of a one-hour commute.
- Decreasing fuel consumption on a nationwide basis.

For each of these problems, identify categories of alternatives that have even the slightest chance of solving the problem. (If you want, you can also try to think of possible solutions within each of the categories.)

As an example, if the exercise problem were to deal with a loud party next door, the following categories could be identified:

- React. This category would include calling the neighbors or calling the police.
- Prevent being bothered. This category would include buying ear plugs in advance to use on the night of a loud party.
- Get revenge. This category would include walking your dog on the neighbor's front lawn.

Exercise 2. If you have an interest in inventing, identify different categories of alternatives for keeping a pair of binoculars from jiggling as you look through them. Don't limit yourself to just the alternatives that already exist, and don't worry about whether the categories are practical. (Some possible answers appear on page 311.)

Sketching Matrices To See Overlooked Combinations

 Sometimes you'll encounter alternatives that can't easily be represented in a radial outline. In such cases, a *matrix* might be more appropriate.

Suppose you have a bicycle and want to buy a basket for it. If you went to a bicycle store in the 1980's, you would have found these choices:

- Basket that attaches to the handlebars.

- Book rack that attaches over the rear wheel. It has a flat surface and a spring-loaded lever that's intended to hold books on the flat surface.

- Pair of narrow baskets that attach to both sides of the *rear* wheel.

- Fabric bags (saddlebags) that attach to both sides of the *front* wheel.

- Fabric bags (saddlebags) that attach to both sides of the *rear* wheel.

- Fabric bag that attaches to the handlebars.

Instead of regarding a list of available options as a list from which to choose, look through the list for different *characteristics*.

For example, notice that one characteristic of the above baskets is *where* the basket is attached:

- Over the front wheel (attached to the handlebars)
- Over the rear wheel
- To the sides of the front wheel
- To the sides of the back wheel

Now, look for a second characteristic. Specifically, look at the list of available choices and ask yourself, "What is another characteristic, besides location, that exists within these choices?" To practice, figure out the answer to this question before reading further.

A second characteristic of the commercially available options is that there are three *types of containers*, namely:

- Wire baskets
- Fabric bags
- Flat surfaces (with spring-loaded holders)

Notice that these two characteristics, namely location and container type, are *independent* of one another. This means that the type of container does not limit where it can be located, and the location does not limit what kind of container can be put there. This independence makes it possible to draw a *matrix* of all the possible combinations of the two characteristics, as shown below.

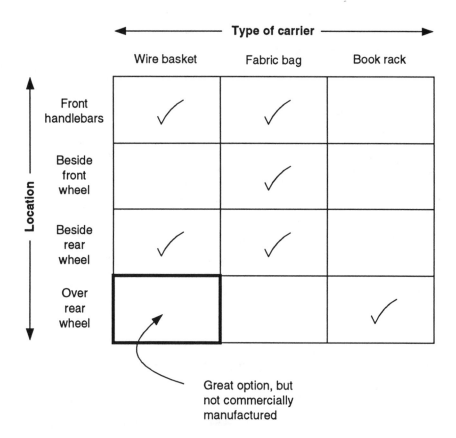

A matrix is a table in which the *columns* (the cells that line up vertically, from top to bottom) are labeled according to the alternatives for one characteristic and the *rows* (the cells that line up horizontally, from left to right) are labeled according to the alternatives for the other characteristic. Each cell in the table represents the combination of the alternative for that *column* and the alternative for that *row.*

In this matrix, the commercially available options already mentioned are indicated with check marks in the cells. The empty cells represent unavailable alternatives. One of the empty cells in this matrix represents a very useful alternative, namely a basket located over the rear wheel. Yet, such a basket is not commercially available (at the time of this writing). The advantages of such a basket are:

- It can hold items more conveniently and reliably than a *book rack.*
- It doesn't interfere with steering because it's not attached to the front wheel or handlebars.
- It doesn't stick out to the sides as do baskets mounted on the sides of either wheel.

It does have the disadvantage of getting in the way when swinging a leg over the bicycle to get on, but this disadvantage can be reduced by making the basket collapsible when not in use.

▶ Just because a product that you imagine can't be bought in a store, doesn't mean you must abandon your idea. If you can imagine something new in your mind, you might be able to create it.

In the case of the bicycle basket over the rear wheel, you could do what has been done by many people for many years, namely attach to the top of a book rack a plastic milk carrier or cardboard box. Or, you could buy a front-mounted basket, remove its mounting brackets, and fasten it with wire to the top of a book rack.

▶ When there are a number of alternatives that involve two characteristics that are independent of one another, draw a matrix in which the possibilities for one characteristic are drawn horizontally and the possibilities for the other characteristic are drawn vertically. Then, look at each cell in the matrix, one at a time, and imagine that combination of characteristics. This technique makes it easy to come up with lots of creative ideas.

This tool is so useful that it's worth presenting another example of its use. Suppose you're a gardener and you discover that your vegetables are being eaten by bugs that live in the soil. Here are two independent characteristics of ways to deal with the bugs:

- *Actions* such as killing, attracting, and repelling.
- *Things* such as chemicals, water, and other animals.

Here's a matrix that indicates the many possible combinations for these two independent characteristics:

	← Things →				
Actions	Chemicals	Water	Food	Plants	Predators
Kill adult bugs					
Kill larvae					
Prevent reproduction					
Repel bugs					
Attract bugs					

Because there are 5 different *actions* and 5 different *things*, there are 25 (5 times 5) different combinations. If these combinations were represented as 25 alternatives in a radial outline, lots of repetitive writing would be needed. By contrast, in a matrix, each action and thing is written only once.

When imagining what each cell represents, allow for the possibility that it can represent more than one alternative.

For example, the cell that indicates the combination of *repelling* the bugs using *water* applies to both of the following alternatives:

- Water the garden heavily enough to repel the insects from the soil and force them to come to the surface — where you can, perhaps, wash them away with more water. (This technique is sometimes used in farming to eradicate severe bug problems.)

- Heavily water the garden along a line that divides the garden in halves to repel the bugs away from this center line. Progressively widening this heavily watered area might herd the bugs to the edges of the garden. Then they could be killed using chemicals you wouldn't use in the garden. (Mentioning this alternative doesn't imply that it works, it's simply an example that demonstrates that more than one idea can fit into a single cell.)

To keep track of the alternatives that each cell represents, it can be useful to write words in each cell instead of using check marks. This makes it easier to keep track of multiple ideas within the same cell.

Notice that a written matrix is limited to representing only *two* independent characteristics. If a situation involves three or more independent characteristics, the matrix approach doesn't work. A way to handle such cases is explained in Chapter 7, *Thinking Dimensionally.*

◄SUMMARY►

A very useful way to reveal creative alternatives is to identify *two independent* characteristics of a situation and create a matrix that represents all possible combinations of the two characteristics. Then, for each cell in the matrix, imagine one or more alternatives that correspond to that combination of characteristics.

If two independent characteristics are not self-evident, look at some specific alternatives to see how they differ from one another. One such difference indicates one characteristic. To identify the second characteristic, look at the specific alternatives again to see another difference between them. If the second characteristic is not, by necessity, linked to the first characteristic, the two characteristics are *independent* of one another.

Exercise 1. Create a matrix that represents the different possibilities for a fence. Use the following two characteristics:

- Location. For instance, a fence around a dog is in a different location than a fence around a house and backyard.

- Type of fence. For instance, a fence made of bushes differs from a fence made of wire.

Once you've created this matrix, look at each cell, one at a time, and imagine what that combination represents.

Combining Ideas

A very useful way to create new ideas is to create new *combinations* of existing ideas.

A simple form of combining ideas consists of combining existing *objects* to create a useful new object. For example, the clock radio was invented by combining a radio with an alarm clock. Notice that the resulting combination offers an advantage — namely the clock can turn on the radio — that isn't available if a radio and alarm clock are simply placed side-by-side.

Whereas combining *objects* is useful for inventing, combining *ideas* — which includes combining objects — is even more broadly useful for all kinds of creative problem solving.

In his comedy movie *Annie Hall*, screenwriter and actor Woody Allen used subtitles to convey the *thoughts* of the hero and heroine during a conversation in which the two characters are developing a romantic interest in one another. The contrast between their self-confident spoken words and their shy and insecure subtitled thoughts provides enjoyable humor. Notice that Allen copied the idea of putting written words on the screen, as done in foreign films, but without writing the words in a different language.

It's not always possible to recognize the source of ideas in a combined new idea. What was probably the first shopping center to be built in the United States was the *Country Club Plaza* built in 1922 in Kansas City. It was designed by Jesse Nichols who traveled around Europe collecting ideas about land development. What Nichols learned in Europe he applied to his Kansas City shopping center. Yet the result was unlike anything found in Europe at that time. In fact, his creation, the shopping center, is characterized as quite American.

Simply picking random combinations of ideas isn't very profitable because most combinations of ideas have little value. So it's important to learn how to recognize which ideas are worth combining. One such approach is explained in the next section. Later chapters contain further explanations for recognizing which ideas are worth combining.

◄SUMMARY►

Combining existing ideas into new combinations can result in new and useful solutions and innovations. A simple version of this technique is to combine two or more objects into a single object that offers advantages that the separate objects don't offer. The key to efficiently discovering useful combinations is to learn how to recognize which ideas are worth combining, which is a skill that's explained in the next section and in later chapters.

Exercise 1. Imagine combining the following two kinds of telephones into a single telephone that offers more convenience than either kind alone.

- A cordless telephone.
- A headset telephone in which a band across the top of the head keeps the earpiece and microphone in place, leaving the hands free.

Exercise 2. Different countries have different kinds of currency. For example, the United States has the U. S. dollar, Japan has the yen, and Mexico has the peso. This difference makes economic transactions between businesses in different countries awkward. To make economic transactions among European countries easier, European countries recently adopted a common currency called the Eurodollar. Unfortunately this approach has the disadvantage that each European country's government will be inclined to manipulate the value of the Eurodollar to their country's advantage. How can this disadvantage be avoided? Specifically, how can the idea of having separate kinds of coins and paper money be combined with the idea of having a single universal form of money — in a way that makes it possible for people in different countries to talk about the same amounts of money? (An answer appears on page 311.)

Choosing By Elimination With Extraction

In solving problems, it's best to come up with multiple possible alternatives, yet only one solution can be implemented. How do you choose from among them? It's tempting to simply choose the alternative that you like the *most* and ignore the others. Instead, use the process of elimination — with a twist.

The usual process of elimination begins by choosing the alternative you like *least* and tossing it out. Then, from the choices that remain, you discard the next alternative you like least. That's repeated until only one item remains. Notice that this approach breaks down the choosing process into numerous decisions, each of which is easier to comprehend. In contrast, simply choosing the alternative you like *most* reduces the choosing process to a single decision that involves more factors than the mind can hold at one time.

Suppose you were setting up an automobile repair shop in the early days of automobiles and wanted to create a convenient way for mechanics to work beneath cars. Here's a list of three approaches that might occur to you:

1. Drive the car over a pit in the floor. The pit would be deep enough to allow a mechanic to stand while working beneath the car.

2. Drive the car onto a rack that's connected to a large piston and raise the piston (and car) using compressed air.

3. Drive the car onto a rack that's connected to a large piston and raise the piston (and car) using oil that's pumped from an electrically powered oil pump.

Here are the steps you would follow if you were applying the usual process of elimination:

*   You would identify the worst alternative and eliminate it. In this example, the worst alternative is number 2 because a sudden yet small air leak would cause the car to drop on a mechanic. Even without a noticeable leak, air would always slowly leak past the piston, requiring a mechanism to occasionally add more compressed air to maintain the car at the same height. Eliminating this alternative reduces the choice to alternatives 1 and 3.

- You would identify the worst of the remaining alternatives and eliminate it. Between alternatives 1 and 3, the worse alternative is number 1, which is driving the car over an open pit. This alternative requires that a mechanic go up and down steps to get between the car and the tools, and it doesn't allow the distance between the car and the standing surface to change.

- Only alternative 3 remains, so it's regarded as the best choice. This alternative, which is to pump oil to push against a piston to raise the car, has these advantages: it allows a mechanic to reach the car without going up and down steps, it allows the height of the car to be changed, and it's not unsafe if a small leak suddenly develops. (Oil does not move through a small opening as fast as air.)

By repeatedly eliminating the worst remaining alternative, we end up with alternative 3 as the best choice.

Now let's add an extra step to the process of elimination. Just before eliminating each alternative, carefully consider the alternative you're about to discard. Does it offer any *useful features* that can be incorporated into any of the other alternatives? If so, extract these features and put them into any of the remaining alternatives.

Let's apply this modified process of elimination to the above car-repair example:

- As before, the worst alternative is using compressed air to support a piston. But before tossing it out, we ask, "Does it have any features that are especially useful?" Yes. Compressed air, unlike oil under pressure, is already available for inflating tires. Can this advantage of using already-available compressed air be incorporated into either of the remaining alternatives? Yes! In alternative 3, instead of using an electric motor and oil pump, compressed air can be used to push the oil against the piston. The diagram on the next page shows how this can be done. Notice that gravity keeps the heavier oil separated from the lighter compressed air. This alternative, which is the approach used in many automobile repair shops of today, combines the availability of compressed air as a source of power with the safety of using oil as the fluid that pushes against the piston.

- We now eliminate the next-worst alternative, which is driving the car over an open pit. Before discarding this alternative we ask, "Does it have any features that are especially useful?" Yes. Directly driving the car into position saves time compared to

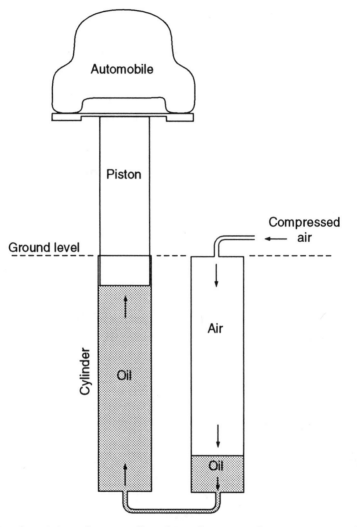

slowly raising the car. Can this advantage be incorporated into the oil-and-air alternative? This time let's assume the answer is no. So, the pit idea is tossed out.

- What remains as the best alternative is using compressed air to push against oil that pushes against a piston that raises the car. Notice that this alternative is not one of the original alternatives! Instead, it's a combination of the best aspects of all the listed alternatives.

As you eliminate alternatives you can sometimes create a new, better alternative by extracting desirable features from the alternatives you eliminate.

▶ Although this process of elimination with extraction might seem to be the last step in choosing an alternative, it's more commonly used many times throughout the creative problem solving process. Specifically, use it whenever you want to eliminate (ignore) an alternative that is obviously not practical. Before you eliminate the alternative, extract any of its useful features.

▶ When you eliminate an alternative, keep in mind that this is not the same as *rejecting* it! It would be more accurate to use the phrase *not pursue*, instead of *eliminate*. The word elimination is used here because it's an integral part of the established phrase *process of elimination*.

▶ When you've used the process of elimination with extraction and have only one solution remaining, are you finally ready to act? Not necessarily. Just because you've ended up with only one solution doesn't mean it's the one you should implement. Sometimes you'll eliminate (choose not to pursue) *all* your ideas. In this case you need to come up with more ideas. Other times you'll eliminate only one or two of your ideas and still have multiple alternatives remaining. In such cases it might be appropriate to try all the ideas, one at a time.

▶ As an example of trying more than one idea, suppose you have noisy neighbors. Two practical alternatives are to call the police or talk to your neighbors. Of course, as this example reveals, the order in which you try multiple alternatives is important.

▶ You never reach a point when it's time to choose a solution. Instead, when a solution arrives that you're sure will solve the problem, then you've created what you're looking for. On the other hand, if you have doubts, then you aren't yet ready to act — unless unacceptable suffering would occur if nothing were done.

◀SUMMARY▶

The process of elimination with extraction is used when you want to focus on what you suspect are your strongest ideas. Start the process of elimination with extraction by identifying the least desirable solution. Then, before choosing not to pursue this idea, ask yourself, "Does this idea have any useful features I can extract and incorporate into another idea?" If so, incorporate these useful features into your remaining ideas. The same question is repeated until the answer is, "No, this idea has no further value as a source of useful features." Then you can stop pursuing this idea and focus your attention on the improved remaining ideas.

Exercise 1. Choose a radial outline you've already created. Apply the process of elimination with extraction either to determine which alternative seems most promising or to create an alternative that's better than any of the ones in your outline.

Following Strategies, Not Steps Or Rules

Leonardo da Vinci wisely said, "If you were to use rules in creating, you would never get to the beginning of anything."

Centuries ago when explorers traveled through new frontiers, they didn't have trails to follow or maps to tell them what was on the other side of each mountain. Instead, they had to create their own trails and draw their own maps. Similarly, as you explore new mental frontiers, you must blaze your own trail without any step-by-step instructions or rules to follow. After all, you're going where perhaps no one has ever been, so how can anyone supply you with instructions to get there? But geographic explorers learned useful strategies that helped them explore. They climbed high mountains to see the surrounding terrain, and they let the flow of water, in the form of rivers, indicate routes that didn't involve unnecessary climbing. Analogously, there are strategies to guide you through the creative problem solving process.

Perhaps the most important strategy in creative problem solving is to pursue an ideal solution, as explained in the *Heading In The Direction Of An Ideal Solution* section in Chapter 2, *Welcoming New Ideas*. This technique is analogous to what explorers do when they climb a mountain to look for a route that heads in a general direction.

Another important strategy is to understand what each tool in this book accomplishes, so that you know when to use it. To understand what this means, consider an analogy. Imagine you're learning how to build a house. You wouldn't ask for step-by-step instructions for when to use a saw and when to use a hammer. Each situation, by its nature, automatically indicates which tool you need to use. For instance, when you want to shorten a board, you use a saw; when you want to fasten a board, you use a hammer to pound nails. The same is true when you're creating a new idea. Each situation, by its nature, indicates which creative problem solving tool to use.

As examples, here are some situations and the tools to use in those situations:

Situation	Appropriate creative problem solving tool
A new idea pops into your head.	Look for its merit.
You get an idea you like, but you have to attend to something else.	Write down the idea.
You want to come up with more ideas.	Sketch or visualize a radial outline and expand it.

As these examples illustrate, common sense and an understanding of what each creative problem solving tool accomplishes guides your choice of tools.

Because tool-oriented step-by-step instructions aren't appropriate in creative problem solving, you might be wondering, "Is there a general sequence of steps to follow?" Again, consider the analogy of building a house. It *is* possible to specify a general sequence of what must be done, as indicated on the next page.

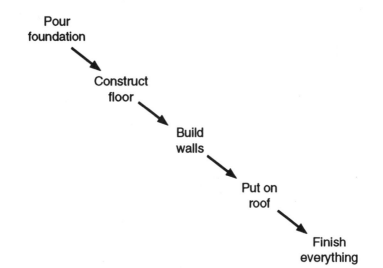

But this is obvious. It simply says that something can't be built until the part that supports it has been built. Similarly, there's a general sequence in creative problem solving. It looks like this:

This too is obvious, so it's of limited use. Furthermore, any *linear* sequence of *steps* oversimplifies the creative problem solving process, as explained in the *Following Multiple Ideas* section at the beginning of this chapter.

Perhaps you've assumed that the order in which the creative problem solving tools are explained in this book indicates the typical order for using the tools. This assumption would be mistaken. These tools are so interconnected to one another that they defy being organized in a linear sequence. In fact, in writing this book, the most challenging task was choosing a linear sequence for explaining the tools and grouping them into chapters. Accordingly, many compromises were made in an effort to accommodate considerations such as these:

- The *Taking Action* chapter appears near the end of this book because words of encouragement to take action early in the book might inspire someone to act on an idea that wasn't ready to be implemented. Even the tools in the *Taking Action* chapter are used throughout the creative problem solving process, not just as a last step.

• Seeing merit in new ideas is explained at the beginning of the book because it's so crucial to the creative problem solving process. It's never the first activity because something must be done first to prompt a creative idea to pop into your mind.

• Only in the simplest creative problem solving efforts is it possible to identify activities such as "welcoming a new idea", "exploring your many alternatives", and "taking action". For a non-trivial problem, each of these activities is done many times in small ways, and in no special sequence.

Accordingly, do *not* misinterpret the sequence of sections or chapters in this book to imply anything about *when* each creative problem solving skill should be used!

◄SUMMARY►

Resist the temptation to think that the order in which the tools are explained in this book is the order in which they should be used. There is no special sequence in which to use the creative thinking skills. Common sense and an understanding of what each skill accomplishes reveals when to use each one.

The tool explained in the *Pursing An Ideal Solution* section is especially useful for getting oriented when exploring new ideas.

Starting Anywhere

Although creative problem solving and innovation cannot be reduced to following a sequence of steps, it's natural to want to know, "Where should I begin?" For maximum creativity, the best answer is, "Start anywhere you want." Of course it's a bit intimidating to be told to start anywhere when you're learning something new, so what follows are specific suggestions. But think of these suggestions as similar to training wheels on a bicycle: eventually you'll outgrow them.

Where to start differs according to whether or not you're the only person involved in creating a solution. First, let's consider the case in which you're the only person.

Starting point for individuals:

Where can you begin? Start by thinking of at least one possible solution. That solution need not be practical, original, or even creative. It only has to have some possibility, however remote, of improving the situation. If necessary, identify a conventional solution, even if it isn't one you like.

As an example, if you need to deal with a neighbor's dog persistently barking at night, you might start with the well-established idea of calling the police.

Starting the creative problem solving process by coming up with a sample solution focuses your mind on creating solutions. This automatically keeps your mind from getting distracted by time-wasting thoughts such as these:

- "That darned so-and-so caused the problem! If it weren't for him, everything would be fine." (Blaming.)
- "Well let's see. Perhaps I ought to figure out how bad the problem is before I start looking for a solution." (Analyzing symptoms.)
- "If only I hadn't misunderstood what so-and-so said." (Regretting that the problem wasn't avoided.)

Coming up with a possible solution automatically bypasses such unproductive thinking. It forces you to think about *solutions* instead of thinking about what cannot be changed.

Another purpose of identifying an initial sample solution is to trigger more ideas. Here are some examples of such triggering effects:

- "Let's see. This idea is a way of bypassing the problem, and it reminds me of another way I could bypass the problem."
- "This idea makes me realize that I don't really understand the issues involved. I'll find a source of information that will help me understand the issues better."
- "Mmm. This idea has some merit. How can I refine the idea to remove its disadvantages?"

If your first idea doesn't make you think of using any specific creative problem solving tool, create a radial outline of your alternatives. To create an outline from only one idea, notice what kind of category your initial idea fits into. For instance, is it a way of avoiding, intimidating, enticing, or what? Once you recognize such

a category, you can sketch or imagine a radial outline as shown
below on the left side. You can then expand the outline to include
other alternatives, as shown on the right side.

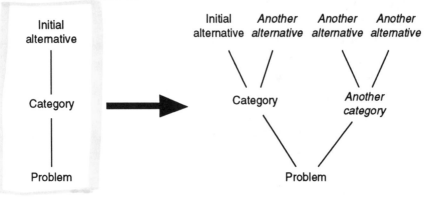

Notice that your randomly chosen initial solution serves to get
you started. That's its main purpose. And that's why it doesn't
need to be a solution you like.

Starting point for people working together:

Now let's consider how to start when more than one person is
involved. Obviously, this situation applies to business meetings.
Less obviously, this situation applies to two or more friends or
family members talking about how to solve a problem.

In a group situation, it's helpful to begin by making sure
everyone is trying to solve the same problem. This starting point
might seem trivial, yet think how often a boss greets an employee's
suggested solution with a comment like, "That's not what I had in
mind. This is a supply problem, not a management problem!"

To make sure each person in the group is looking for solutions
to the same problem, identify one or more goals. Goals not only
promote coordination, they also focus attention on the *future*, which
is what can be changed, rather than on the unchangeable *past*,
which is what criticizing, wishful thinking, and blaming focus on.
Notice that this purpose is quite different from using goals to intentionally limit a discussion to avoid sensitive issues, which is
common in business and government situations. When solving the
problem has a higher priority than avoiding sensitive issues, there's
no need to spend lots of time at the start carefully defining goals.
Instead, goals are free to change whenever it becomes evident that
the goals are blocking off promising ideas, as explained in the

Reconsidering Your Goals At Any Time section in Chapter 3, *Reconsidering Your Goals.* Once the group identifies a tentative goal, it's time to begin looking for solutions.

If you need a suggestion for what to do when your group has identified a starting goal, try the same starting point suggested above for an individual: think of any possible solution. Then let that idea lead you in the many directions it can take you.

◄SUMMARY►

Keep in mind that suggestions for where to start are like training wheels on a bicycle; you can stop using them when you no longer need them.

In the meantime, if you need a suggestion for where to start, start by thinking of at least one possible solution. If that idea isn't enough to prompt you to use any of the tools in this book, consider using that one idea to create, and then expand, a radial outline of alternatives.

In a situation where you're working with other people to solve a problem you face together, consider starting by informally identifying your goal so everyone is trying to solve the same problem. Then, with a willingness to reconsider the goal at any time, jump right into creatively solving the problem.

Chapter 5

Refining Your Ideas

Now that you've learned a number of ways to create new rough ideas, it's time to learn how to transform those rough ideas into refined creative solutions.

Retaining Advantages And Eliminating Disadvantages

Refinement consists of modifying an idea to remove its *disadvantages* while keeping, and perhaps adding to, its *advantages*.

A man named Valentine Haüy discovered that a blind person could feel the shape of letters printed on paper if they were raised above the surface of the paper. In 1784 he applied this principle to print a book for the blind. Later, another Frenchman, Charles Barbier, recognized the *advantage* of using raised print to allow blind people to read, but also recognized the *disadvantage* of using letters similar to the ones sighted people use. So, Barbier designed a code that used up to 12 dots to represent each letter and digit. Because the code used so many dots, it didn't become popular. Louis Braille, who became blind when he was three years old, learned Barbier's system of writing as a teenager. Braille recognized both the *advantage* of using raised dots to represent characters and the *disadvantage* of using 12 dots per characters. So Braille created a new code that used only 6 dots per character. A variation of the code he created is the commonly-used Braille alphabet. Notice that the evolution of the Braille alphabet consisted of a series of refinements that removed disadvantages without losing advantages.

As can be deduced from the Braille example, each step in the refinement process can be broken down into the following steps:

1. Identify an idea's *advantages*.
2. Identify at least one of the idea's *disadvantages*.
3. Modify the idea to *eliminate* at least one *disadvantage, without losing* any of the *advantages*.

This sequence is repeated as long as disadvantages remain.

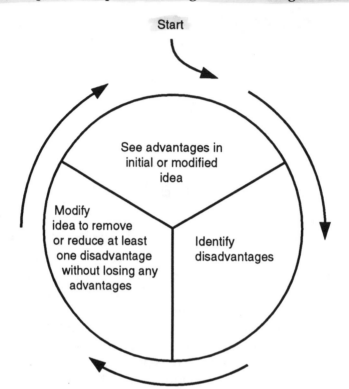

In the example of the Braille writing system, the initial disadvantage was that letters were difficult to recognize by feel, so Barbier eliminated this disadvantage by using dots. But the system he created used too many (12) dots, so Braille eliminated this disadvantage by using fewer (6) dots.

What constitutes a *disadvantage*? Whatever *detracts from* the idea's ability to accomplish what it's intended to accomplish. Conversely, an *advantage* is whatever *adds to* the idea's ability to accomplish what it's intended to accomplish. This seems simple enough, yet mistakes are easy to make. So, here are some clarifications:

- Goodness isn't an advantage and badness isn't a disadvantage. The judgments *good* and *bad* combine many advantages and disadvantages into a single measurement. If you find yourself thinking in terms of good or bad when refining an idea, identify the separate advantages and disadvantages that have been combined together to arrive at the good or bad judgment.

Keep in mind that these comments about goodness and badness don't mean that judgments of goodness and badness aren't relevant. They're quite relevant when choosing whether to *act on* an idea. But acting on an idea is different than *refining* an idea.

- A creative idea isn't necessarily better than a non-creative or conventional idea. In fact, many creative ideas are worse than conventional ones. For example, *bote* is a creative way to spell the word *boat*, but this creative spelling obviously has the disadvantage of not being easily recognized. To avoid mistaking creativity as an advantage, keep in mind that the value of creativity is that it allows you to *consider* any solution whatsoever, and this removes limits that can stop you from seeing better solutions.

- Cleverness isn't an advantage. Cleverness is a positive evaluation about someone's mental capacity to come up a clever idea, but it doesn't imply any advantage in the idea itself.

If you find yourself overwhelmed by the number of disadvantages you see in your idea, switch back to seeing the idea's merit. This removes the temptation to toss out the idea. Then, when you've re-established the idea's value, focus on only one of the many disadvantages, temporarily ignoring the others. Then, figure out how to eliminate this disadvantage — before looking at the other disadvantages. In the *Looking For Merit In Crude Ideas* section (in Chapter 2, *Welcoming New Ideas*) you learned that looking for *advantages* (merit) prevents you from tossing out a useful idea. Now it's important to realize that looking for *disadvantages* keeps you from implementing an idea that has weaknesses.

In the Braille example, notice that the steps of refinement were accomplished by three people. Each person made one major improvement on what the previous person created. But, if Haüy had removed the disadvantages that the other two later did, he could have created a more practical writing system from the start.

When refining an idea, don't be content to only make *one* refinement. Even if the improved idea seems like a good one, repeat the cycle of improvement to more fully refine the idea.

To fully refine an idea, *look* for disadvantages after they stop popping into your head readily. They're harder to find, but effort spent in identifying and eliminating disadvantages will produce a better design. Full refinement is especially important if your goal is to create something valuable, because what you create becomes less worthwhile if someone else refines the idea beyond the point at which you stop.

◄SUMMARY►

Refinement consists of improving an idea by repeating the following sequence until the refined idea no longer contains any significant disadvantage:

1. Identify an idea's *advantages*.
2. Identify at least one of the idea's *disadvantages*.
3. Modify the idea to *eliminate* at least one *disadvantage, without losing* any of the *advantages*.

When disadvantages no longer pop into your mind easily, spend time looking for them so the final solution will be fully refined.

When refining an idea, don't confuse goodness, badness, or cleverness to be an advantage or disadvantage.

A creative idea isn't necessarily better than a non-creative idea. The value of creative thinking is that it allows you to *consider* any possibility, which removes limits that can stop you from seeing better solutions.

Exercise 1. Questions at the end of each of the following two paragraphs provide practice in identifying disadvantages.

James Naismith, an athletics instructor, invented the game of basketball. He wanted to create an energetic, interesting, and safe game to be played indoors during cold New England winters. For safety reasons, he rejected using bats or sticks or requiring that people be knocked down. One of Naismith's ideas was to have players throw a ball into empty boxes located on the floor at each end of the gymnasium. This idea offered the advantages he was looking for. However, before trying this idea, Naismith recognized a significant *disadvantage*. What disadvantage did he recognize and overcome by planning to put the boxes up high?

When the game was actually tried, peach baskets were used instead of boxes because the school janitor didn't have two boxes the same size. It was not until years later that another disadvantage was overcome by replacing peach baskets with hoops. What disadvantage did this refinement overcome? Why was a fabric net put on the bottom of the metal hoop?

Exercise 2. Recall the initially crude idea of connecting two elevators together so that the weight of a person going down in one elevator lifts a person going up in the other. (Page 23.) List the many disadvantages this idea has in this crude form.

Now, study each step in the refinement of the elevator idea, as explained on page 24. For each step, identify which disadvantage was eliminated. Verify that none of the idea's advantages were lost in any step of the refinement.

Evaluating Throughout
The Creative Process

There is a popular, but mistaken, notion that a creative idea should not be evaluated until you're ready to choose which of several ideas to act on. Nonsense!

Evaluating ideas occurs *throughout* the creative problem solving process, not only near the end of the process.

As you just learned, refining an idea includes identifying advantages and disadvantages, and this amounts to evaluating. Because evaluating is an integral part of the refinement process and refinement occurs throughout the creative process, evaluation occurs throughout the creative problem solving process.

The misleading advice that evaluation be delayed for more than a few seconds arises, in part, because delaying evaluation is an effective way to stop people from criticizing each other's ideas in a group situation. However, this approach isn't appropriate when you're doing the thinking on your own. Furthermore, a better strategy for avoiding criticism in group sessions, when it can be done, is to follow the same approach used by an individual: respond to a disadvantage by modifying the idea to eliminate the disadvantage.

◄SUMMARY►

Although it's appropriate to delay evaluating a new idea long enough to recognize the idea's merits (so you won't toss it out), this delay usually amounts to a matter of seconds. After this short delay, it's time to start looking for disadvantages, which is a form of evaluating.

Incorporating Advantageous Aspects Of Other Ideas

It's obvious that an idea can be improved by removing its disadvantages. What's less obvious is that an idea can be improved by adding new advantages.

A woman sat working at her spinning wheel and occasionally looked up at two men cutting wood with a two-person saw (which has a handle at both ends of a long saw blade). She wondered if the rotary motion of her spinning wheel could be combined with the cutting teeth of a saw blade. Of course! She thereby invented the circular saw. Notice that she extracted the advantage of circular motion from her spinning wheel and incorporated that advantage into a saw blade. Also, notice that many of the features of a spinning wheel — such as the width of its wheel and its composition of wood instead of metal — were not included in her invention.

When incorporating an idea from another context, you don't need to extract the *entire* idea. You can extract just part of it.

Incorporating advantageous aspects of other ideas to improve something is so important that it's worth looking at another example. William Le Baron Jenny built the first skyscraper in Chicago. It was ten floors tall, and this unprecedented height was made possible by using a steel frame to support the walls and floors. At that time, steel frames were already commonly used to support bridges, so Jenny's innovation amounted to copying from bridges the idea of using a steel structure to support something vertical (a tall building) instead of something horizontal (a long bridge).

The key to extracting useful ideas from other situations is to think in terms of concepts, which is explained in more detail in the *Thinking In Concepts* and *Extracting Useful Concepts From Anywhere* sections in the next chapter.

◆SUMMARY▶

Extracting useful concepts from other ideas is one of the most powerful tools of creativity.

Keep in mind that there is no need to copy an *entire* idea. Only copy the part or parts that offer the advantages you want to incorporate into your solution.

Exercise 1. Choose a new idea of yours that you would like to refine. Keep your eyes open for other ideas that, when incorporated into your idea, would improve it.

Finding Flaws And Weaknesses Early

Early in the refinement of an idea, use *testing* to look for flaws and weaknesses. Testing avoids unexpected damage and wasted time.

In the mid-1700's, Josef Merlin, a Belgian musical instrument maker, created a crude pair of roller skates to wear at a London masquerade party. Unfortunately, he didn't fully test them. At the masquerade party Merlin made a grand entrance by playing his violin as he rolled across the ballroom floor. As he reached the other end of the hall he realized that he hadn't anticipated the need to stop! His smashing success became a smashing disaster as he collided into a large, expensive mirror. Not only did he break the mirror, but he injured himself and broke his violin. Alas! Merlin skipped an important part of the creative problem solving process: *testing*. Instead, he jumped ahead to *implementing* his idea without discovering its flaws.

In one sense, Merlin's grand exhibition was a test. Certainly it accomplished the same result as testing, which is to discover unexpected flaws. However, the point of testing is to discover flaws *without jeopardizing anything*, whether it be a violin, other people, or yourself.

In addition to reducing the risk of damage, testing a new idea on a *small scale* reduces the risk of investing lots of resources — such as time, money, and effort — into an idea that might later need to be abandoned.

One evening in the late 1920's, Richard Hollingshead Jr. tested a creative idea: watching a movie from the front seat of a car parked in his driveway. He set up a movie screen in front of the car and put the movie projector on top of his car. The arrangement worked fine. Then Hollingshead began to wonder about the practicality of building a large outdoor movie theater where people could conveniently watch a movie from their cars. He realized he needed some assurance that light rain wouldn't interfere with viewing the movie, so he set up a lawn sprinkler to simulate rain on his car window. He also tested the feasibility of eating snacks in the car while watching the movie. Wisely, Hollingshead didn't immediately assume that his idea would be practical. He first tested his "automobile movie theater" idea on a small scale, before he invested the large amounts of money, time, and effort required to build a full-scale drive-in movie theater.

Another way to reduce risks is to test just a *portion* of what you're creating.

Orville and Wilbur Wright did this by testing the components of their flying machine one at a time. For example, they:

- Attached sample wing shapes to a bicycle and rode the bicycle while measuring the lift of the wing sample.
- Tested control mechanisms by hooking lines (of wire or cord) to a glider and flying it in a strong wind, the way a kite is flown.
- Tested propellers in wind tunnels.
- Flew gliders (which have no engine and propellers) countless times to test and refine their wing design and control system.

Only when they had all the parts working separately, did the Wright Brothers combine them and make their first complete powered test. That first test on December 17, 1903 at Kitty Hawk was successful on the first try — because they had already discovered the flaws that needed to be eliminated. In contrast to the Wright Brothers's approach, earlier attempts to create airplanes typically amounted to attaching an engine and propeller to an enlarged (but traditionally-designed) glider and trying (without testing) their creations by flying off the edge of a cliff. Unfortunately, some people died discovering that this combination doesn't work.

Most innovative ideas, if they don't work, don't have the disastrous results of a flying machine that fails. But it's still wise to avoid unnecessary harm or wasted resources by finding the flaws and weaknesses early in the refinement process.

In testing ideas, keep in mind that a favorable outcome indicates that for *one tested situation*, there appear to be no weaknesses or flaws. A test *cannot prove success* — because you cannot test every possible situation. Therefore, you must intentionally look for weaknesses or flaws in *hopes* of finding any that exist.

◀SUMMARY▶

Find flaws and weaknesses yourself and do so early — instead of waiting for other people or failed attempts to reveal flaws and weaknesses. Doing so saves time and effort, and keeps unexpected damage to a minimum.

Testing on a small scale, and testing one part of a solution at a time, provide safer ways to discover unexpected flaws and weaknesses.

Exercise 1. One man appropriately recognized the importance of teaching parents how to plan far ahead for their child's college education. He was out of work and needed income, so he decided to offer a seminar on this subject. He rented a hall, sent out advertisements, and prepared his presentation. Unfortunately, only a few people showed up. Why? How could he have discovered this flaw earlier?

Imagining Exaggerated Specific Cases To Determine Effects

Initial testing of a solution's effectiveness is most easily done in the mind rather than using real objects or real people. To accomplish such testing, imagine specific cases that exaggerate situations in ways that clearly reveal outcomes.

Consider a voting situation in which three people are nominated for one position and voting rules state that the candidate who wins the most votes wins the election. What needs to be tested is whether this produces a fair outcome.

To do this testing, let's imagine a fantasy scenario in which there are three nominees: Alice, Brian, and Victor. And let's exaggerate this scenario by assuming that Alice and Brian hold almost the same views on important issues and that Victor holds very different views. Also, assume that a majority of voters prefer either Alice or Brian. Is it possible for Victor to win the election? To find out, let's look at specific numbers. If Victor gets 34 percent of the votes, Alice gets 33 percent, and Brian gets 33 percent, Victor would win — even though 66 percent of the voters prefer the views held by Alice and Brian. These results indicate that a candidate can receive the most votes, yet not be representative of a majority of people.

To further test this exaggerated scenario, let's imagine that Brian chose not to be a candidate. In addition, let's assume that everyone who would have voted for Brian voted instead for Alice, the most similar candidate. The result would be 34 percent for Victor and 66 percent for Alice. This clearly indicates that a change in the number of candidates affects the *outcome*, even though there is no change in the voter's *preferences*.

This voting example illustrates that a test can be conducted in the mind and on paper instead of consuming resources, such as time and effort.

The big advantage of doing such mental testing is that it saves time for the person doing the testing. The saved time can be spent refining and testing the creative idea. As a further advantage, the use of exaggerations reveals what might not be clear if actual tests were done.

In choosing how to exaggerate, don't confuse the word exaggeration with the word *difference*. Exaggeration can also imply *sameness*. For instance in the above example, both Brian and Alice were assumed to get the same number of votes. Also, Alice and Brian were assumed to hold essentially the same views. This sameness makes the effect of other differences stand out more clearly.

An interesting variation of this exaggeration technique is to imagine what would make a situation *worse*, instead of better. Then, making an *opposite* change can be tested as a possibility for improving the situation.

◄SUMMARY►

To discover flaws and weaknesses in your creative solutions, imagine specific cases that are exaggerated in ways that reveal disadvantages. Then, further refine your creative idea by eliminating these disadvantages.

In choosing how to exaggerate, keep in mind that an exaggeration can be an exaggerated sameness, not just an exaggerated difference.

Exercise 1. Suppose you were to buy automobile tires that were slightly larger (in diameter) than the existing ones. This would affect the reading of the speedometer because the cable between the wheels and the speedometer would turn at a different speed. With the slightly larger tires, would the reading on the speedometer be slightly too high or slightly too low?

If you don't know where to begin in answering the above question, here's a hint: Imagine that as you travel down the highway at a specific speed, the tires on the automobile magically and suddenly change to a much larger diameter, such as being as tall as you are. How fast would such ridiculously large tires be turning compared to the normal tires? Would this turn the speedometer cable faster or slower? Would the speedometer reading suddenly increase or decrease?

Exercise 2. Consider the situation in Northern Ireland in which part of the sometimes-bloody conflict is due to differences between two cultures, neither of which outnumbers the other enough to have won a decisive advantage. Imagine an *exaggerated* (highly unrealistic) situation in Northern Ireland as follows:

- Assume that the conflict is between Irish Catholics and British Protestants, and all Irish Catholics behave alike and all British Protestants behave alike. (In reality, there are also British Catholics, Irish Protestants, and people whose religion and cultural heritage are not well-defined. But these and other complications are being ignored in this exaggerated case.)

- Assume that there are a few more British Protestants than Irish Catholics. This is the minor difference whose effect is to be determined.

- Assume that Irish Catholics and British Protestants are extremely evenly distributed throughout Northern Ireland. This means that the number of Irish Catholics compared to the number of British Protestants is the same in every territory as it is for all of Northern Ireland. This uniformity eliminates the effects of similar people clustering together.

Now, imagine that there are 100 voting districts and each voting district elects a representative to serve in a Northern Ireland Parliament. How many British Protestants and how many Irish Catholics would there be in the Parliament? How does this relate to the fighting going on in Northern Ireland?

Anticipating Possible Negative Consequences

Far too often, someone designs a creative solution and fails to see, in advance, negative consequences of the design.

Bee keepers and scientists in South America created a new species of honey bee by crossing their bees with a species from Africa. The new species generated more honey, which is what the bee keepers wanted. Unfortunately, the new bees also had a sting that was so much more harmful than normal bees that a person can easily be killed by the stings from a swarm of them. Rather than give up the increased productivity, the bee keepers chose to keep the new species. They imprisoned the queen bees using barriers that had a hole small enough to block the queen bees but large enough to let the worker bees pass. Alas, a few queen bees escaped. The consequences? The offspring from the few escaped bees have spread northward through South America, through Central America, through Mexico, and will soon reach the United States. These bees have come to be known as *killer bees* because of their dangerous sting; and they have lived up to their name in some of their interactions with people.

Too often someone creates an innovation that has a known disadvantage and yet pursues the innovation anyway, thinking, "Oh, that won't happen." But if a negative consequence is *possible,* it should *not* be implemented! Instead, the solution should be refined further to eliminate — or at least firmly limit — the negative consequence.

Because negative consequences can spread rapidly, this warning especially applies to creating or altering *information* that's repeatedly copied. Examples of creating information that's repeatedly copied include breeding new species, genetic engineering, and creating self-reproducing software (which is what a computer virus is).

A lack of ethics in a creative solution is another flaw that should be avoided. But, in evaluating whether something is unethical, it's important to go beyond asking "Would it hurt anyone?" and ask "Would it be OK if everybody did this?" This second question becomes important in situations, such as littering, where just one person doing the action once wouldn't significantly hurt anyone. Such actions are unethical because getting along with one another requires that a person not do what everyone else can't also do, but would like to do.

Not finding any weaknesses in your idea doesn't mean there aren't any. It simply means you haven't found any. Yet. And just because you find lots of weaknesses doesn't mean there aren't more.

In 1962 a newly invented tomato harvester was introduced into San Joaquin county in California. An expected consequence of this invention was the reduction in the number of farmworkers employed to pick tomatoes. Also expected was the reduced price of tomatoes and the hardness of those tomatoes — which were specifically bred to be less easily bruised. And the fact that the tomatoes contained fewer vitamins might have been known by the breeders. However, the following two consequences were unexpected by the harvester inventor and the tomato breeder:

- Tomato growing moved out of San Joaquin county into Yolo and Fresno counties where the soil and climate were better suited to the new method of farming.
- In 9 years, the number of farmers who grew tomatoes declined from about 4,000 to 600. The harvesters were too expensive for small farmers.

This example indicates the level of subtlety you should consider when anticipating the consequences of your solutions.

▶ Remember that looking for flaws and weaknesses is done with the intention of *eliminating the flaws* by *further refining* your ideas. This is quite different from looking for reasons to abandon your ideas.

◀SUMMARY▶

Spend time anticipating any consequence that could make your creative idea fail to accomplish what you really desire.

Recognize the potential for disaster when creating something that can reproduce itself, whether through biochemical or electronic reproduction.

In considering whether something is unethical, go beyond asking "Would it hurt anyone?" to ask "Would it be OK if everyone who wanted to behave that way did behave that way?"

Don't misinterpret either of the following to indicate that you've already found all the flaws and weaknesses in an idea:

• Having spent some time looking for flaws and weaknesses.
• Successfully finding and eliminating many flaws.

Exercise 1. Suppose someone invented a new kind of filter material that could quickly filter pollution from water. Imagine making a barrier of this material and putting it in a polluted river to clean up the river. What negative consequences would this solution introduce?

Simplifying

▶ *Complexity* in what you create is always a disadvantage. The best solutions are the *simple* ones.

➤ Early audio cassette tape decks played an audio cassette tape in only one direction. When it reached the end, you manually removed the tape, flipped it over, and put it back into the machine to hear the other side. To eliminate this inconvenience, a stereo equipment manufacturer built an innovative cassette tape deck that automatically flipped over the tape for you. However, its mechanism was very complex. Specifically, at the end of the tape, the tape deck disengaged the tape from the regular drive mechanism, pulled the tape to the back of the deck, turned it over, pushed the tape to the front again, then reengaged the drive mechanism. The design was clever and it was fun to watch. But it was soon made obsolete by cassette decks that simply reversed the direction of the motors without flipping over the tape. (Also, extra coils were added to the *heads* to gain access to all the tracks of the tape without moving the heads.)

History is filled with examples of innovations that have been overridden by much simpler, and usually more effective, innovations.

Often, a complex design is clever. But don't let the appeal of cleverness stop you from removing the disadvantage of complexity. Remember that cleverness is neither an advantage nor a disadvantage, but complexity is a disadvantage.

One of my favorite examples of simplifying arose in one of my classes. A student said she hoped someone would invent a machine to put dishes into cupboards after the dishes had been washed by the dishwasher. Another student pointed out that by regarding the dishwasher as the "cupboard" in which they belonged, they would not have to be moved at all! How simple! Of course this combination dishwasher-and-cupboard idea would need to be refined to make it practical.

Complexity is easy. Ironically, it's simplicity that's challenging.

When personal computer printers were first built, the printing mechanism returned to the left side of the paper each time a new line was started. That made sense because it matches the sequence in which characters are sent to the printer. Later, printer speeds were improved dramatically by having the printing mechanism start each line from whichever side of the page it was already on. This meant that every other line was printed backwards, which made it more difficult to design these faster *bidirectional* printers.

This example emphasizes that what you need to simplify is *what* you create, not your *effort* to create it. In other words, don't confuse simplification with laziness.

Having encouraged you to simplify, now I'm going to warn you not to *oversimplify*. Some things can't be simplified because, inherently, they aren't simple.

As an example, reducing a wide range of possible political views on an issue to only two choices, such as yes or no, simplifies the voting process from an administrative point of view. But this simplified choice complicates the voting process for a voter who sees that neither choice represents what heshe really prefers. Notice that simplifying voting from an administrative point of view shifts complexity to the voter's point of view.

Sometimes attempts to simplify just *shift the complexity* to a different area. But the point of simplifying is to *eliminate* complexity, not just shift it out of your territory.

◄SUMMARY►

If you find that a solution you've created is complicated, reconsider your design. Simplify it. But, don't *over*simplify it, don't confuse simplicity with laziness, and don't just shift the complexity to someone else's area of responsibility.

Exercise 1. Suppose you need a very accurate yet inexpensive way to measure the relative heights of two locations that are twenty feet apart. Here is a description of a workable, yet unnecessarily complex, solution to this problem: Put water in two large clear glass jars and place them at the two locations. Put a long clear plastic tube into one of the jars and fill the tube with water. Hold your finger over one end of the tube, stretch it to the other jar, and put it into the water there. If the levels of water in the jars are unequal, water will flow through the tubing into the other jar until the levels are equal. When the water has stopped flowing, use a ruler to measure any difference in water heights. This is the difference in the heights of the two locations. Now, your task is to simplify this method of measuring height differences. Notice the resulting advantages. (A suggested solution appears on page 312.)

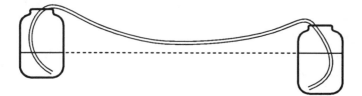

Exercise 2. For practice in refining an idea, try refining the combined dishwasher and cupboard idea mentioned in this section. Specifically, remove its disadvantages without losing its simplicity.

Creating Supporting Enhancements

To fully refine a creative solution, it might be necessary to create a secondary, supporting creative idea.

The earliest typewriters usually jammed when a key was pressed too soon after the previous key was released. Most people weren't willing to tolerate this flaw, so early typewriters were used mostly by blind people and others who couldn't write easily by hand. Christopher Sholes created a clever supporting enhancement that overcame this jamming tendency. He arranged the letters on the keys awkwardly! He put the frequently typed letters *E, T, O, N R,* and *I* on keys that required finger movement to reach them, and assigned frequently-typed pairs of letters, such as *E* and *D,* to the same finger. His innovation worked! It successfully slowed down a person's typing speed, thereby reducing the tendency for his typewriters to jam. Unfortunately, because Sholes' typewriters became so popular, this awkward keyboard arrangement is the one we still use today!

Countless creative ideas have become successful only after a *supporting enhancement* transformed an otherwise unworkable idea into a practical one. In the case of the typewriter, it was the awkward arrangement of letters that transformed easy-to-jam typewriters into practical typewriters.

Supporting enhancements might seem like minor enhancements, but they're just as important as the basic creative solutions they make practical.

When light bulbs were first invented, they were essentially useless because the glowing filament burned out within minutes. Thomas Edison discovered a material for light bulb filaments that glowed for many hours. This supporting invention was so crucial to making light bulbs practical that many people think Edison invented the light bulb itself.

◄SUMMARY►

When you become frustrated in your attempts to refine a solution to make it practical, try creating a supporting enhancement.

Exercise 1. It has been suggested (in the book *Legal Breakdown: 40 Ways to Fix Our Legal System*) that sharing creative ideas could be enhanced by setting up a *National Idea Registry* that provides an affordable alternative to the expensive patent system. People who want to share useful new ideas could submit them to this organization. If an idea was indeed new and useful, the idea would be added to a computerized database for access by the public. Where could money come from to support such a non-profit organization?

Providing A Bridge From The Old To The New

When creating something new, design it to facilitate a smooth transition from the old to the new. This is especially important when creating something you hope will be used by many people.

The developers of *stereo* radio had to take into account that lots of people already owned *monaural* radios, which had only one channel of sound. If the developers had used the existing channel of information for one speaker's sound and simply added a second channel of information for the second speaker's sound, people with monaural radios would hear just half the music. To make stereo radio possible, a second channel of information was added. But instead of using this second channel as the information for a second speaker, the second channel was used to indicate the *difference* between the sound in the two speakers. This convention allowed stereo radios to calculate what each speaker's sound should be, based on the total sound and the difference between the two speaker sounds. Very importantly, this enabled monaural radios to ignore the newly added information, continuing to put the total sound into one speaker.

When designing a creative solution that involves lots of people, there should be provisions for the new to be compatible with, or to exist alongside, the old. When this isn't done, attempts at innovation appropriately fail.

Suppose someone who works full time and does the household cooking wants the other household members to choose what to cook on weekday nights. Which of the following two alternatives would be a smoother transition?

- The cook asking other household members to take over the job of planning each week's weekday meals.
- First, asking household members to choose one meal each week for several months and the cook keeping a list of these choices. Then, when there are enough choices in the list, asking the other household members to choose five meals from that list each week.

This example illustrates that common sense reveals *how* to make transitions smooth. So the emphasis here is on the *desirability* of making transitions smooth.

Creative problem solving involves making a change, and the *decision* to make the change is usually abrupt. However, this doesn't mean that the *change itself* must be abrupt.

◄SUMMARY►

Although the choice to make an improvement might be abrupt, the change itself need not be abrupt. As a part of the solution, include a bridge from the old to the new. For changes that involve many people, design solutions so that what's new is compatible with, or can exist alongside, what already exists.

Exercise 1. Consider the issue of adopting the metric system of measurement in the United States. What strategies would make the transition from English units (inches, feet, ounces, pounds, cups, quarts, etc.) to metric units (meters, grams, and liters) difficult? What strategies would make the transition occur smoothly?

Part Two

The Advanced Tools

The remainder of this book contains the tools that tend to be more challenging to understand and apply. The division of this book into halves should not be interpreted as an actual gap in the nature of creative problem solving. Instead, you can think of this as a good place to pause after reading Part One.

Chapter 6

Thinking In Alternate Ways

To dramatically extend your ability to come up with new ideas, go beyond thinking in words to thinking in pictures, concepts, and other wordless ways.

Thinking Wordlessly

What's the opposite of war? If you're like most people, what comes to mind is the word *peace*. Notice that what pops into your mind is a *word*. Not a meaning or a concept, but a word. Yet what most people have in mind when they say the word *peace* is not fully the opposite of war. It's true that peace is the *absence* of war, but the absence of something also includes other meanings besides the opposite meaning. Now, instead of thinking in words, think in *pictures* or *images*. Before going on to read the next paragraph, think for a moment, using *pictures* or *images* instead of words, "What's the *opposite* of war?"

Consider what war is. It essentially consists of people entering an *enemy* territory and participating in *destructive* activities, such as *hurting* and *killing* the people there and *destroying* their property. The opposite of this scenario is for people to enter a *friendly* territory and participate in *constructive* activities, such as *helping* the people there to *build* buildings, *construct* water supply systems, and *heal* diseased and injured people. This is the *opposite* of war. And this is what the Peace Corps does to reduce warfare.

The word peace, like so many words, has more than one meaning. The meaning of peace that people commonly think of is a state of tranquility or neutrality. This implies that people stay within their own territory or travel to other territories only to visit, buy, and sell. That, indeed, is a form of peace. But so is the activity of helping friendly countries. This ambiguity (existence of more than one meaning) can be clarified visually as shown in the illustration on the next page.

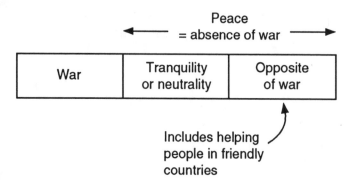

If you should disagree with this definition of the word peace, that's fine. This mental exercise still illustrates the following critically important point:

Thinking in *pictures* and *images* yields different results than thinking in *words*!

Now, notice that there's no name for the opposite of war. It must be expressed in a phrase such as *helping people in friendly territories*, whereas the concepts of tranquility, neutrality, and peace (which has two different meanings) do have names.

When something new is created, it frequently doesn't have a name and describing it in just a few words might not be possible.

In talking about her pioneering work as an anthropologist, Margaret Mead said, "When the early letters were written, we did not even have a name for what we were doing, except the very general term *field work.*"

William Henry Fox Talbot was one of the two people who, independently, invented what we now call photography. When he presented a lecture about it, he titled his lecture *The Process by which Natural Objects May Be Made to Delineate Themselves without the Aid of the Artist's Pencil.*

Don't let the absence of a name or familiar phrase lead you to believe that an idea is worthless. If that were done, nothing new would ever be created. In fact, the progress of civilization is marked by the addition of new words and phrases. This is happening now with the appearance of computer terms, such as *software* and *user interface*, to name concepts that have recently become important.

Thinking without words isn't necessarily *better* than thinking in words. It simply yields *different* results. And different results are important ingredients in creative thinking.

If you've been reading the above explanation without stopping to think in pictures or images, the difference between thinking in words and thinking in pictures might not be clear. So, here's an exercise that can be solved only by thinking in wordless ways. Look at the figures on the left and find them in the more complex figures on the right. As you look for them, notice that these exercises cannot be solved using words.

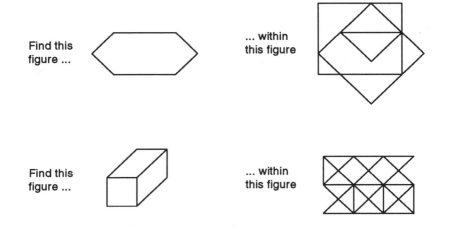

This exercise emphasizes that, indeed, there is at least one other way of thinking besides thinking in words.

◄SUMMARY►

In addition to thinking in words, also think in other ways, such as thinking in pictures or images. This is an essential part of creating what has not yet been named.

Exercise 1. Within a range of mountains, the highest points are called mountain peaks (or mountain tops). What are the lowest points called? Here are some hints: The answer isn't what comes to

mind most easily. Nor is it something rare. Sketching topographic contours can help. (The intended answer appears on page 312.)

Exercise 2. The next time you're inclined to put words or items in alphabetical order, consider whether this is really the most appropriate way to arrange them.

Thinking Visually

Visual thinking is an essential part of creative thinking.

You might be surprised to know where Albert Einstein's theory of relativity came from. That's the theory that says (among other things) that time slows down when you move very fast. It arose in Einstein's mind when he wondered what he would see if he were traveling in a trolley car very fast away from a clock. As you can imagine, if you were traveling at the same speed as the light reflecting off the hands of the clock, you would continue to "see" the same light waves, so the hands on the clock would appear to stand still! Published in scientific journals were mathematical equations that indicated exactly how much time would slow down according to how fast you traveled. But the important concept is conveyed in, and originated in, a simple mental experiment imagined in pictures, not words or mathematics.

Einstein wrote, "The words or the language, as they are written or spoken, do not seem to play any role in my mechanism of thought." He added that the "signs" and "images" that were of importance to him were "visual and some of muscular type." Notice his recognition of the importance of visual images. (The "muscular type" presumably refers to kinesthetic thinking, which is a category mentioned in the *Recognizing Different Ways To Categorize Thinking* section at the end of this chapter.)

More of your brain is dedicated to the physical sense of *sight* than is dedicated to hearing, taste, smell, touch, or kinesthetic awareness. So, make use of this mental resource by thinking in *pictures* and other *visual* images.

Leonardo da Vinci was one of the most creative inventors of all time. He lived in the late 1400's and early 1500's, yet he conceived of, and sketched: a helicopter, parachute, military tank, paddle-wheel powered boat, innovative clock, spring-driven car, diving snorkel, and countless other less-easily-named inventions. Leonardo (from the town of Vinci) was also one of the greatest painters of all time, having created the famous *Mona Lisa* and *The Last Supper*. The fact that Leonardo was talented as both an inventor and an artist was not just a coincidence. Inventing, painting, and sculpting all require an ability to create realistic visual images in the mind.

You already have the ability to think in pictures. That's what you do when you read a story and imagine the appearance of people and settings. And visual thinking is a large part of daydreaming. Thus, visual thinking isn't a skill you need to learn, so much as it's a skill you need to *apply*.

Outbreaks of cholera mysteriously occurred in a number of isolated locations in Europe and North Africa. Investigators marked the locations on a map. Although the pattern wasn't obvious, the investigators saw that the locations were along airplane flight routes between major cities. This insight led to the discovery that the disease was spread when infected people washed their hands in the lavatory hand basins during flight. Alas, the basin water drained directly into the atmosphere – and to the ground below.

This example indicates that a useful way to think visually is to sketch.

Consider the challenge of improving profits in a manufacturing business. On the following page is a sketch that indicates some elements that are relevant to this challenge.

Notice that creating such a sketch doesn't require any artistic skill. Instead of representing realistic images of people, money, products, and buildings, labeled ovals and rectangles are used. Abbreviations can be used if you're the only person who will see the sketch, or if the people who will see the sketch are present as you create it. These shortcuts allow you to focus less attention on the sketch and more attention on what the sketch represents.

How can a sketch be used to prompt creative ideas? By imagining changes in what's represented.

In the sketch on the next page, imagine how the quantity of each thing represented by an arrow can be increased (such as advertisements to customers of competing businesses) or decreased (such as energy consumption). Also, consider the effects of adding what's missing, such as arrows representing comments from past customers. Such changes prompt ideas for improving profits.

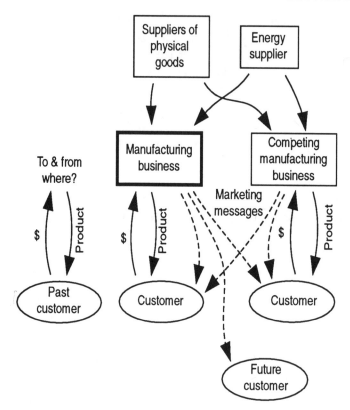

Notice that it's the process of creating and studying the sketch that has value, not the sketch itself. The sketch is a thinking tool.

◄SUMMARY►

To make use of your mind's impressive ability to think visually, create mental images and draw sketches. Visual images and sketches are valuable problem solving tools. To prompt creative ideas, imagine making changes in the image or sketch.

Exercise 1. Imagine the design of a house that does not yet exist. Then, imagine people watching television or cooking a meal in the house to find out if the house's architecture fits the needs of real people. Notice that this can be done without building the house or even building a model of it. If you want to take this exercise further,

sketch drawings of the house to find out if it could actually be built. Again notice that such testing is being done in the mind, not by actually trying to build the house.

Exercise 2. What does the following sketch convey?

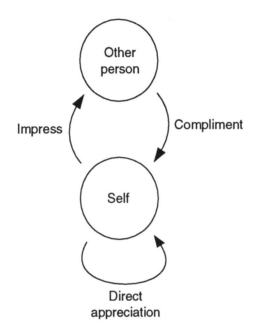

Sketching Visual Representations

Visual thinking includes seeing what cannot be seen directly with the eyes.

Stars vary in their *brightness* and *spectral character.* (Roughly, spectral character refers to which colors are stronger than other colors.) Originally, astronomers assumed that such differences were random. Then, Henry Russell and Ejnar Hertzsprung (independently) created a *scatter plot* in which *each star* was represented as *a point* whose *location on the plot* indicated both its *brightness* and *spectral character.* On the next page is a simplified version of the scatter plot. The plot reveals that there are *distinct types* of stars and that blue giant stars are related to red dwarf stars. (Our own star, the sun, is roughly in the middle of the blue giant to red dwarf portion of the plot.) The plot has proven very useful in understanding how stars change their character as they age.

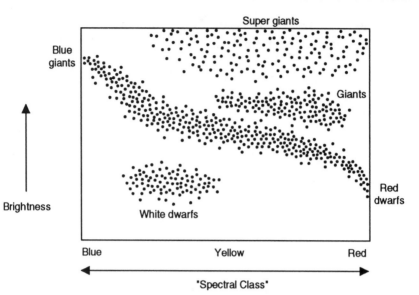

"Spectral Class"

Notice that this plot represents something that cannot be seen directly. That is, you wouldn't see this visual image by looking up at the stars at night. Instead, this plot transforms information that cannot be seen into something your eyes can see. And the resulting picture clearly conveys a useful insight.

A more familiar kind of visual representation is a calendar, which represents time. Each day is represented as a box that can contain words to indicate what will happen that day. And the box to the right of the box that represents today is the box that represents tomorrow. People who use a calendar to schedule their time can look at it quickly and see that a week's worth of boxes have lots of words written in them and thereby know that the week is too busy to accommodate another event.

As this calendar example illustrates, the key to using visual representations is to become so familiar with the correlation between what the visual image *represents* and what the visual representation *looks like*, that it easily reveals what otherwise might not be noticed.

In creating visual representations, don't limit yourself to ones that have already been created by other people.

There's a common tendency for musicians to limit themselves to creating music that can be represented using standard musical notation. Yet modern electronic instruments can create musical sounds that cannot be represented using standardized notation.

Creating new ways to represent such music on paper dramatically increases creative musical opportunities. If the final product is sound, then the ability of other people to read a musician's personal notation is irrelevant.

Remember that Henry Russell and Ejnar Hertzsprung created an entirely new kind of scatter plot as a stepping stone to reach their goal of understanding stars. Because their representation was so useful, it was later standardized so that astronomers could quickly understand each other's plots. Thus, Russell's and Hertzsprung's *thinking* tool later came to be used also as a *communication* tool.

◄SUMMARY►

Visual representations can reveal useful insights. When you find yourself thinking about something that isn't quite clear, consider creating a sketch that somehow *represents* what is real but cannot be directly seen with your eyes.

Thinking In Concepts

Thinking in *concepts* is yet another alternative to thinking in words.

To illustrate the value of thinking in concepts, here's an example from my own experience. In the early days of computer technology I had some text stored in my primitive bulky computer and I needed to print it. The only available printer was elsewhere and it had to stay there. After finding out how difficult it was to move my computer to the printer, I looked for a better alternative. By thinking in terms of concepts, it occurred to me that all I needed to transport to the printer was the *information*, not the computer itself. This concept was easy to translate into the possible solution of sending the information as sounds over the phone lines. However, this alternative had the disadvantage of requiring a second person to be involved. Thinking idealistically, it occurred to me that I could put the sounds that would otherwise go over the phone lines into a box and physically carry the box of sounds. The moment I thought of this idea it seemed silly. But it only took a few seconds to realize that this could be done using a tape recorder. It worked!

This remote printing example illustrates that it can be useful to become aware of a promising abstract concept before translating that abstract concept into something specific and concrete.

Concepts exist separately from words.

This separation between concepts and words is conveyed in the following diagram. The diagram graphically says, "Meat is to a vegetarian what drugs are to an unnamed entity." Notice that the entity represented by the question mark has no name. True, it can be described in words. But it has no simple name.

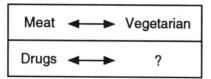

The ability to think in terms of concepts without words is especially important in creative problem solving because you're creating what doesn't already exist. Remember that a new word arrives only after the concept it represents has already been created. To illustrate this point, the phrase *assembly line* in connection with the manufacturing of automobiles arrived after, not before, Henry Ford imagined an efficient way to manufacture his *Model T* automobiles.

◄SUMMARY►

Think in concepts. When you've created a concept that seems to offer some value as a rough solution, translate the concept into something specific and practical. Conceptual thinking is an especially valuable skill in creative problem solving.

Exercise 1. Suppose you want to use a particular plastic bottle to hold a liquid, but the cardboard disk in the cap is gone. Assuming the bottle will leak if it's used without some kind of seal, you must figure out what can take the place of the cardboard disk. As you look around your bathroom and kitchen for a substitute material, you see sponges, newspapers, tin cans, corks, plastic bags, and a plastic bottle without a cap. What can you use?

Extracting Useful Concepts
From Anywhere

The useful concepts you incorporate into your solutions can ◀◑
come from anywhere.

After the *direct current* electric motor was invented, Nikola Tesla ◀◥
spent years trying to invent an *alternating current* electric motor.
(Direct current is electricity that always flows in the same direction
and alternating current is electricity that reverses direction many
times per second.) The solution came to Tesla as he walked with a
friend at sunset. The setting sun reminded Tesla of a poem by
Goethe that contained the following words:

> *The glow retreats, done is the day of toil;*
> *It yonder hastes, new fields of life exploring;*
> *Ah, that no wing can lift me from the soil,*
> *Upon its track to follow, follow soaring.*

The poem creates the idyllic image of a person traveling around the
earth to continually view the setting sun. Tesla recognized the similarity between this image and a point on an electric motor's armature (the rotating part of an electric motor) being pulled by a
magnetic force that moves just ahead of the rotating armature. The
setting sun analogy prompted him to realize that the motor's
magnetic field would have to *rotate* inside the motor just as the sun,
from our perspective, *rotates* around the earth. He already knew
how to create a rotating magnetic field using alternating current, so
he was immediately able to visualize in his mind the basic design
of an alternating current electric motor.

It's common for a new solution to be inspired by recognizing a
similarity between the following:

- A challenging problem someone has spent time trying to solve.
- Something the person sees or thinks about that's seemingly
  unrelated to the problem.

In the last section you learned the value of thinking in terms of ◀◑
concepts. Now it's important to realize that useful concepts can
come from unexpected contexts. Here are some examples:

- The concept for typewriter keys came from watching a musician play an organ.

- Fred Smith created a way to transfer packages overnight between almost all points in the United States by copying how banks handle canceled checks. In both systems, the items, either canceled checks or overnight packages, are sent to a single location for sorting and then sent to their separate destinations.

Nature is an especially rich source of creative ideas as the following examples show:

- The idea for velcro came from the burrs that annoyingly stick to fuzzy clothes.

- René Antoine Ferchault de Reamur noticed the similarity between a wasp's nest and paper. This led him to the discovery that paper could be made from wood.

- Sir March Brumel learned how to handle underwater construction by watching a shipworm tunnel into a timber.

Yet another source of useful concepts is other cultures. Such cultures might be nearby, distant, or extinct.

- Impeachment was a concept that the writers of the United States Constitution copied from the nearby Iroquois League system of government (which governed the collective actions of the Cayuga, Mohawk, Oneida, Onondaga, and Seneca Native Americans).

- The now-extinct Aztec culture also had problems with children dropping out of school. Their solution was to not allow people to marry until they had graduated from school.

The key to being receptive to useful concepts is to see similarities in what's different.

To appreciate what it means to see similarities in what's different, look for similarities between the following pairs of items:

- A flea and an oak tree.
- An egg and a banana.
- A mayor and a garbage collector

Most people overlook similarities between what's different because they're distracted by the obvious differences. For instance, the dramatic difference in size between a flea and an oak tree obscures the fact that they are both living organisms. Commonly, people don't look beyond the first similarity they see. For instance, the fact that an egg and a banana are both edible can obscure the less obvious similarity of both being conveniently packaged by nature. What's the similarity between a mayor and a garbage collector? Both are people with jobs. Our natural tendency is to see *differences* and that blocks our ability to see *similarities*. Such similarities are concepts.

Instead of only looking for relevant concepts when you're dealing with a specific problem, spend time noticing and remembering interesting concepts whenever they arise. When you see the same interesting concept arise several times in very different circumstances, put extra emphasis on remembering it. By collecting concepts at all times, you'll have a collection of concepts ready to help you solve later problems when they arise.

Here's an example that illustrates learning a concept in advance of applying the concept. Suppose you were talking with someone about computers and you learned that there are two different ways in which one computer device waits for information from another computer device. In one case, the waiting device repeatedly sends a message that amounts to asking "Is it done?" until there's a "Yes" answer. (In computer terminology, this is called *polling*.) In the other case, the waiting device sends a message that amounts to saying, "When it's done, tell me." (The computer term for this approach is called *using interrupts*.) The person points out that the approach of asking "Is it done?" slows down computer processing because the question must be repeated many times. A few months later, you find yourself managing several employees and you realize you're spending time on the telephone repeatedly asking, "Is it done yet?" You quickly realize that a more efficient way of using your time and their time is to say, "When it's done, tell me right away." (This assumes the employees are self-motivated.) This example illustrates the usefulness of collecting concepts in advance of when they're used

Some concepts appear in many different areas, so they're given names or descriptive phrases such as leverage, positive feedback, negative feedback, and "It's only as strong as the weakest link." However, many other concepts don't have names or descriptive phrases. To express unnamed concepts in words, use examples or analogies.

◀SUMMARY▶

In whatever you do, take an interest in what you see and focus attention on interesting concepts, which can be regarded as similarities in what's different. Especially notice concepts when observing nature. When you see the same concept in very different areas, put extra emphasis on remembering it. Recognizing concepts in different areas increases your skill in thinking in concepts and increases your chances of seeing a concept that can reveal a useful insight or solution.

Exercise 1. Consider creating a notebook for collecting interesting concepts. This is especially appropriate as a group activity in which the participants contribute concepts that are compiled together into an accessible notebook or database.

For this collection, write down at least two examples that illustrate each concept. Use examples from very different areas. If the concept has a name or descriptive phrase, include it.

As an example, include the concept of *positive feedback* in the collection. One example of positive feedback occurs in a sound amplification system when sound from the speakers can get back into the microphone and be amplified to be even louder when it reaches the microphone again. This produces the high-pitched squeal called *feedback*. A second example of positive feedback is an increase in the cost of living causing a cost-of-living increase in employee salaries, prompting employers to increase the price of their products and services, further increasing the cost of living.

Creating this collection of concepts gives you practice thinking in concepts, and provides a collection of concepts you can look through when you need creative ideas for solving a specific problem.

Exercise 2. First, choose a problem of personal interest. Then, for every situation you experience during one day, ask yourself, "Is there a concept here that could be applied to solve my problem?"

Imagining What Someone Else Might Suggest

You have the intelligence of many people inside of you.

Suppose a zipper finally wears out on your favorite jacket, purse, or backpack. If you often mend clothes, you're likely to consider removing the old zipper and sewing in a new one. In contrast, if you prefer to fix things mechanically, you're more inclined to use a pair of pliers to squeeze together the least accessible part of the metal zipping (moving) part to restore the proper action of the zipper. Notice that thinking in terms of sewing and thinking mechanically *both* lead to a practical solution, but the solutions are *different*.

Your favorite ways of thinking can lead to practical solutions most of the time. But sometimes, such as when you're confronted by an especially challenging problem, your favorite ways of thinking won't produce a satisfactory solution. When this happens, try thinking in different ways by imagining what someone else would suggest.

Suppose you were dealing with a large and complex waste treatment problem. To help overcome your thinking habits, *imagine* asking a civil engineer, a chemist, a biologist, and a doctor what they would suggest. Here are ideas *you* might think of:

- Civil engineer: Build a canal to channel the waste differently.
- Chemist: Add chemicals that react with undesirable substances to produce less offensive substances.
- Biologist: Introduce organisms that feed on waste substances.
- Doctor: Prescribe drugs to counteract the effects of the toxic substances.

Notice that these suggestions differ, yet all of them could come from your mind.

This example reveals that the intelligence of many people is already inside you. Access that intelligence by imagining what someone else would suggest. This helps to override your tendency to think in habitual ways.

In choosing someone to imagine, choose whoever you think might have a good suggestion. The person can be anyone, including someone you know or have known personally (such as your grandmother), someone you've read about (such as a spiritual leader), or a stereotypic person of a particular profession (such as a counselor).

This tool combines the benefits of getting ideas from other people who have different thinking habits with the convenience of getting their ideas immediately.

◄SUMMARY►

To overcome your tendency to think in habitual ways, imagine what someone else might suggest as a way to solve your problem. The person you imagine doesn't need to actually exist outside your mind. Choose whoever you think might have a useful suggestion.

Using Subconscious Thinking To Provide Insights

Useful thoughts you're normally unaware of can be brought to your awareness.

Elias Howe, the inventor of the sewing machine, had spent more than a year trying to build a working sewing machine when the solution came to him in a dream. In his dream, Howe was taken captive by a tribe of primitive people and taken to their leader. The leader decreed that Howe had 48 hours in which to design a working sewing machine — or else be put to death. In the dream, he worked hard for those 48 hours, but unsuccessfully. So, he found himself surrounded by men pointing their spears at him. But he noticed something unusual about the spears: there was a hole in their pointed ends. Suddenly Howe awoke, realizing that the key to making a sewing machine was to put the hole for the thread at the pointed end of the needle — instead of at the other end where it had always been. Apparently, Elias Howe's subconscious thinking figured out where the hole needed to be and conveyed this insight to him in a dream.

As this example illustrates, subconscious thinking can help you create a solution to a challenge you face.

Subconscious thinking is not something mystical. It's the kind of thinking you use to steer a bicycle to keep upright. That thinking goes on subconsciously while you're consciously thinking about something else.

Although the phrase *subconscious mind* is sometimes used in connection with subconscious thinking, this terminology doesn't imply that subconscious thinking goes on in a special part of the brain. In fact, subconscious thinking sometimes occurs as conscious thinking that, seconds later, can't be recalled.

How can subconscious thinking be used to conceive of a useful solution or insight? One approach is to follow these five steps:

1. Spend time consciously learning about important aspects of the problem.
2. Plan an appropriate activity during which your subconscious can think.
3. Immediately before the activity, spend time thinking of solutions, even silly or impractical ones.
4. Pursue the planned activity.
5. Be receptive to creative new ideas and look for the merits of any new ideas.

Let's consider these steps in more detail.

Step 1: As illustrated by Elias Howe's dedication to creating a practical sewing machine, you must first study, examine, analyze, and think about the problem you want to solve. For small problems, this might involve only a few hours of thought, but bigger problems could require many months of disciplined learning. This gathering of information and understanding does both of the following:

• Supplies your mind with the information it needs.
• Conveys to your subconscious the importance of solving the problem.

Although this preparation requires an investment of time, it can be accomplished by thinking about the problem and possible solutions during spare moments that you might otherwise waste by worrying about the problem.

Step 2: The second step is to plan an activity that will provide your subconscious with undistracted time in which to think.

As Elias Howe proved, sleeping is one activity that leaves the subconscious free to think. However, when first trying this technique, try activities other than sleeping because you could easily fail to notice the creative solution in your dreams.

There are many waking activities that provide the subconscious with the undistracted time it needs. For instance, you could go for a walk or watch a fire in a fireplace. Or, you could watch the pounding of ocean waves, the cascading of a waterfall, the flowing of a river, or fish swimming in an aquarium. Or, you could take a shower or wash the dishes. Whatever you choose, make sure that the activity:

- Is relaxing.
- Is physically comfortable and free of interruptions.
- Doesn't require any judgments or goal-oriented thinking.
- Keeps the visual portion of your mind occupied — as opposed to closing your eyes or watching an unmoving scene.

Step 3: To prepare your subconscious to wisely use the time you'll be giving it, precede your chosen activity with at least a few minutes of looking for solutions to the problem.

This search for solutions need not produce practical solutions, it only needs to indicate, by example, what you want your subconscious to achieve. For example, you might think, "Well, it's obviously not practical, but using a helicopter would solve the problem."

Take note that this activity is very different from dwelling on the nature of the problem, which is what people often tend to do. Instead of focusing on the *problem*, it's important to focus on possible *solutions*. For instance, thinking "If I had acted sooner the problem could have been solved" is equivalent to wanting to turn back the clock. But reversing time isn't a possible solution. Your focus must be on what you can do now or in the future.

Step 4: Immediately follow your search for solutions with your chosen activity, namely walking, watching nature, or whatever. Let your mind follow whatever thoughts it chooses. However, if you get distracted by thoughts of responsibilities or worries, return your awareness to what you're seeing. Relax and enjoy!

Step 5: The final step, which is possibly the most challenging, is to recognize the solution when it comes to you.

Remember that a useful creative idea seldom arrives in a refined form, so expect some crudeness in the idea. Specifically, look for merit in your ideas in spite of any foolishness. For Elias Howe, the idea of putting the hole in the pointed end of the needle arrived as an image of spears with holes in their pointed ends. This is a foolish way to make a spear, but a useful way to make a sewing needle.

Unless the problem itself is word-oriented, the solution is more likely to appear in the form of a *visual image* rather than as a word or sentence. For instance, note that Howe's solution arrived as a visual image of holes in spears rather than someone saying, "Put the hole in the pointed end, stupid!"

Expect the creative idea to be subtle when it appears. There won't be any neon signs or arrows pointing to the insight, but that doesn't mean that the answer isn't there in front of you. Elias Howe could have easily ignored the holes in the spears, thinking that he had encountered very primitive people who lacked common sense in designing spears.

Instead of providing a direct answer, your subconscious might suggest a new direction for you to follow or it might suggest that you need to explore something further. Pay attention to whatever ideas emerge instead of ignoring ideas that don't represent a complete solution.

The above five-step sequence for using subconscious thinking is explained as five separate steps, but these steps shouldn't be followed rigorously. They're like the numbered footprints that dance teachers use to help someone learn a new dance step. As in learning to dance, once you get the feel of what's involved, stop trying to carefully follow steps and simply do whatever works for you.

Here's a personal experience that doesn't strictly follow the steps explained above, yet the words in italics reveal the basic sequence. I had been *analyzing* data from a scientific research experiment that simulated the dispersal of coal dumped into a furnace that contained sand-like limestone through which air was bubbling up. The way the data was being represented on paper didn't clearly reveal what we wanted to understand. I had been *working* on the project for *many months* and had, *on a number of occasions*, tried to imagine better ways to represent the data we were collecting. One day, while *washing dishes*, I again *tried to imagine a better way* to represent the data. A *visual image arose* in which the data could be drawn on a plot in which the weight could be represented on one axis and the density on the other axis. I *almost tossed out* this idea, thinking that weight and density were virtually the same; I was seeing flaws instead of merit. Fortunately, I also recognized that *if* such a plot could be drawn, *it might solve the problem.* My curiosity prompted me to *consider the idea carefully,* long enough to reveal that this was what we had been looking for.

When you first try this five-step approach, choose a problem that's important to you but not too challenging. And don't count on dramatic results the first couple of times. With practice it becomes easier, and that's when the results can become more dramatic.

If you aren't successful at first, try something different, making sure your next attempt still follows the recommendations described above. Once you're successful, remember what you did so you can do something similar when you try it again.

◄SUMMARY►

To use subconscious thinking to prompt creative ideas and insights, try following this five-step sequence:

1. Spend time consciously learning about important aspects of the problem.
2. Plan an appropriate activity during which your subconscious can think. The activity should be relaxing, physically comfortable, free of interruptions, and free of the need for judgments or goal-oriented thinking, yet it should keep the visual portion of the mind occupied.
3. Immediately precede the activity with time spent thinking of solutions, regardless of how silly or impractical the solutions are.
4. Pursue the planned activity.
5. Be receptive to creative new ideas and look for the merits of any new ideas.

Once you've found a specific approach that works for you, don't bother following these steps rigorously

Using Fantasy Visualization To Prompt Insights

Another way to access your subconscious thinking is to visualize ◀◖ a fantasy in which someone or something in the fantasy reveals a solution or insight.

This fantasy visualization should be done in a physical environ- ◀◖ ment in which you can relax, close your eyes, and not be inter- rupted.

The first part of the fantasy visualization is based on a setting that's chosen in advance. The remainder is completely sponta- neous.

The fantasy's setting, which might be a house with many ◀◖ rooms, a forest, a seashore, or the bottom of a sea, can come from a book, someone's suggestion, or your imagination. Within this mental setting you allow a wise person or wise creature to come into your fantasy setting. Then you ask this person or creature for advice or an insight, and listen to what it says. The imagined advice can reveal something important that you've either failed to notice or have avoided admitting to yourself.

The challenging part of this fantasy technique is to allow your ◀◖ imagination to follow whatever thoughts *first* occur to you. This allows your gut-level feelings and subconscious thinking to direct the fantasy. This is harder than it sounds because there's a natural tendency to edit your thoughts — due to the usefulness of self- censorship in unsafe and critical situations.

Here's a sample fantasy visualization. For brevity, it's ◀✖ described using only significant words, not complete sentences. On merry-go-round, of type in school playground. Turn fast. Blur. Eventually, slow down. Large old house in distance. Walk to house. Feels scary. Go inside. Stairway near entrance. Go upstairs. Long hall with rooms on both sides, all doors closed. Stop at door of room that feels like there's a wise person or animal or creature inside. Go inside. (This is where the visualization changes from being guided to being completely spontaneous.) Room is bare. Closet door closed. Open it. Large brown owl perched on clothes- hanger rod. Self: "Who are you?" Owl: "Never mind who I am. You wanted to ask me a question." Self: "Yeah. Why does my boss drown me with requests for memos?" Owl: "He's afraid." Self: "Afraid of what?" Pause. Owl: "Interestingly, he doesn't know, himself. He's just afraid." Pause. Owl: "Afraid that if someone finds out something he'll lose his good-paying job." Self: "Mmm. That would account for why he usually seems to be hiding something. And why he doesn't socialize with us, except on formal occasions." Pause. Self: "But what's he hiding?" Owl: "Only the fact that he's hiding something. He doesn't know himself what it is he's hiding."

As crazy as this technique sounds, there's a simple explanation for why it works. You already know that your mind can easily (sometimes too easily) imagine a familiar person, such as a parent, giving you advice. Similarly, your mind can also create a person (or creature) that's essentially a combination of the wise aspects of many people you know. Putting their wisdom into a hypothetical person or creature bypasses the thinking habits you normally follow because the imagined person's thoughts come from someone else, not you. This enables your conscious awareness to become aware of that wisdom in your mind without censorship.

▶ The value of this technique is that it can *reveal insights* you wouldn't otherwise consciously discover. However, after a new idea arises, it's important that you consciously and carefully judge the idea instead of blindly acting on it. In other words, when your "wise" person comes up with a suggestion, don't necessarily follow it. That's not the point! In fact, such advice will sometimes be foolish.

It can be easy to mistake this fantasy visualization technique for a magic ritual that reveals solutions. But this technique is simply a tool for accessing thoughts that your conscious mind would normally dismiss or ignore.

▶ Ultimately, practice in using the fantasy visualization technique makes it easier to become aware of some of your subconscious thoughts in everyday situations with your eyes open.

It can be very helpful to initially learn the skill of visualization from someone who fully understands it and can prompt you through a fantasy visualization. However, make sure you don't confuse their ability to recognize the difference between spontaneous and non-spontaneous thoughts with a wisdom in knowing what you should do in real life. Only you have all the information needed for solving your own problems, so don't depend on someone else to tell you how to solve your problems. That would be exactly opposite to what this book is all about, which is to teach *you* how to solve problems.

◄SUMMARY►

To access the wisdom of people you've known, and to enhance your mind's ability to become aware of ideas that might otherwise be ignored, visualize yourself in a fantasy setting in which a wise person or creature provides a useful insight. Success in using this technique requires distinguishing between thoughts that *first* come into your mind and *replacements* for those thoughts when your mind edits your thinking.

Don't automatically believe the insights or follow the suggestions that arise in a fantasy visualization. Consciously and carefully evaluate any ideas that arise, because the ideas can be foolish.

Developing And Using Your Intuitive Judgment

Your subconscious mind can give you positive and negative *evaluations* of ideas in a way that's quite different from conventional analytical thinking. This mental skill, called *intuitive judgment*, serves as an important guide in the development of new ideas.

There was a distinguished chemist who, in considering a predicted molecular structure, would feel "uncomfortable, as though his shoes pinched" if the predicted structure was packed too tightly to be realistic.

This ability to quickly, yet accurately, judge new ideas is an extremely useful skill in developing creative solutions. If the judgment is "No, that doesn't feel right" and it's accurate, it saves lots of time that's otherwise wasted pursuing the unproductive idea.

Intuitive judgment can also serve the reverse function: to indicate that a creative idea has value in spite of analytical evidence to the contrary.

Ray Kroch had sold milkshake machines to Maurice and Richard McDonald for the restaurants they owned. Kroch took an interest in buying these restaurants (which were innovative because the food was pre-cooked instead of being cooked after being ordered) and building more restaurants. Kroch's lawyer advised him against the purchase. Kroch later said, "I closed the office door, cussed up and down, threw things out of the window, called my lawyer back, and said *Take it!* I felt in my funny bone it was a sure thing." Thus, it was a gut-level belief rather than a clinical analysis that initiated the dramatic expansion of the McDonald's chain of restaurants.

The creative thinker Albert Einstein said, "I believe in intuition and inspiration; at times I feel certain I am right while not knowing the reason." He also stated, "The really valuable thing is intuition."

Intuition can be defined as: "knowing, but without knowing *how* you know". But this meaning is very broad. In fact, it's sometimes used to refer to thoughts mysteriously jumping into a person's mind from outside the person. This is why the term *intuitive judgment* is used here; it emphasizes that the skill being discussed is a particular kind of intuition.

▶ Intuitive judgment refers to the mental process in which alternatives are *evaluated* on a scale ranging from "Yes, definitely!" to "Definitely not!" in a way that differs from both feelings and analytical thinking.

Why does intuitive judgment offer an advantage over conscious analytical thinking? Through *conscious* thinking you can easily categorize, organize, differentiate, and perform other mental skills that involve *breaking down* a situation into *components*. In contrast, *sub*conscious thinking is better able to *integrate* (transform through a process of *combination*) many different and interrelated elements of knowledge into a single evaluation that ranges from *yes* to *no*. Accessing this integration ability is what intuitive judgment is all about.

To appreciate the difference between judging intuitively and thinking analytically, consider the familiar experience of setting off on a trip and getting the feeling you've left behind something important. Logically you can't figure out what you've left behind, so the validity of the feeling is difficult to justify. But once you identify what you've left behind, you know that the feeling was valid.

▶ Notice that the feeling of leaving behind something important is so similar to what we call *feelings* that the same word is used to refer to intuition. But it's not the kind of feeling that we also call an emotion. It's something different. But only subtly different. And it's this subtlety that makes intuitive judgments so challenging to correctly identify and interpret.

Sometimes the feeling of leaving behind something important doesn't turn out to be valid. For instance, it might only be a *fear* of having left behind something important. Similarly, your intuitive judgments sometimes turn out to be inaccurate. Thus, determining whether an intuitive judgment is valid is another challenge in developing this mental skill.

Learning to recognize intuitive judgments and determining their validity requires lots of effort. Is it worth the effort? People who have it and use it appreciate its value. You must decide for yourself whether you want to invest the effort it takes to learn it.

To develop intuitive judgment, initially limit your use of it to situations in which a mistaken judgment won't cause unacceptable damage should it turn out wrong. Then, according to your rate of success, you can later decide whether to depend on it for more important decisions.

Using intuitive judgment can be regarded as a sequence of four steps, as follows:

1. Spend time understanding all the aspects of all the known alternatives.
2. Present your known alternatives to your subconscious.
3. Detect a subtle gut-level response that conveys a degree of yes or no.
4. Decide what the response indicates.

Let's examine these steps in detail.

Step 1: Learn about all aspects of the situation you want to improve, and identify the alternatives from which you can choose. In many cases you'll already have done this step as part of attempting to make the choice analytically. If not, do it before attempting to access your subconscious.

Recall the examples involving the chemist and Ray Kroch. Both of these people were already very familiar with the field in which they were making an evaluation. Clearly, a chemist understands the nature of how atoms bind together to form a molecule, and a businessman with experience selling milkshake machines to restaurants is familiar with the restaurant business. If these people had not possessed an understanding of the field in which they were making a decision, their successful evaluations would have been merely examples of luck.

▶ Make sure you understand both the *advantages* and *disadvantages* of *every* alternative from which you will choose.

If the alternatives from which you are allowed to choose are supplied by other people, expand your alternatives to include any other possible alternatives, even if you know that other people will regard the alternatives as unacceptable. The fact that other alternatives exist is still important information. And, your subconscious might conclude that one of the acceptable alternatives has the advantage of making it possible to later reach a better, but currently unacceptable, alternative.

▶ *Step 2:* Present your alternatives to your subconscious. This amounts to holding an image of each alternative in your conscious awareness. In doing so, don't simply think some words or imagine a picture. Imagine the alternative as if you had already selected and implemented it. Make it seem real!

▶ Multiple choice evaluations, in which more than a single yes or no judgment is needed, can be handled by focusing your attention on each of the alternatives, *one at a time*. Then, compare the multiple yes or no reactions with one another to determine their relative strengths.

▶ *Step 3:* Notice the subtle yes or no response for the alternative you're considering.

➤ To understand the kind of response you need to identify, here's an exercise to *imagine*. You don't need to actually do the exercise. Imagine that you're confronted with a difficult and important decision such as choosing whether to accept a job that's new and exciting, but which requires moving where you don't want to go. Assume you're truly undecided about which choice to make. (If you can think of an important decision that's more relevant to your life, do so.) Get a coin and associate it's two sides (heads and tails) with your two choices (yes and no) and flip the coin as if you were going to let the outcome determine your decision. Flip the coin and see which side is up. As you do so, notice your *reaction*. Maybe your reaction is "Oh good, it's heads!" or "Darn, it's tails!" The positive ("Good!") or negative ("Darn!") reaction reveals what your subconscious thinks. This is the sensation you're looking for. As mentioned before, the reaction is *like*, but not the same as, a feeling.

▶ Commonly, a *no* reaction feels like a tenseness in the gut or stomach. But don't expect to actually feel something happening physically. What you might experience is a muscular *sensation* without muscular *activity*. This is similar to the experience of daydreaming that you're running: your leg muscles are completely relaxed, but you feel the sensation of running.

In contrast, a *yes* reaction can be a sensation of relaxation or reduced tenseness. Or, the reaction can feel like a desire to sigh, or it can be an actual sigh. Or, both relaxation and a desire to sigh can occur together. Again, your muscles might not actually relax or move.

What's described here are only some possibilities. The way you experience intuitive judgment can be different. If you find it difficult to be aware of this kind of sensation, take heart. It gets easier with practice. Practicing is discussed following the explanation of Step 4.

By the way, realize that flipping a coin is simply a trick to force you to realistically consider the two outcomes. You can also accomplish the same thing in your mind either with an imaginary coin or no coin at all. In fact, that's what step 2 accomplishes.

It's easy to fail to notice a response because the response is usually subtle, and it competes with more dominant sensations that are a normal part of people's lives. Such competing sensations include:

- Physical sensations, such as being sleepy, hungry, or tired.
- Physical and mental effects of mind-affecting substances such as coffee, soft drinks, stay-awake drugs, and medications.
- Strong feelings, such as anger, fear, inflated pride, and guilt.
- Muscular tension.
- Non-stop analytical thinking, which is a normal part of living a busy life.

To reduce the distraction of these kinds of sensations, follow the suggestions in the *Uncluttering Your Mind* section, which follows this section.

In addition to the distractions that keep us from noticing subtle sensations, our cultural conditioning encourages us to *ignore* many physical sensations, feelings, and emotions. For instance, children are encouraged to ignore the pain of injuries and to ignore the feelings of sadness that prompt them to cry. Because the sensations associated with intuitive judgments are of a similar nature, they too can easily be unknowingly ignored.

Step 4: Determine the meaning of your response.

As explained above, a *negative* reaction is commonly a feeling of *tenseness*, whereas a *positive* reaction is commonly a feeling of *relaxation*. But sometimes the result is conveyed by a *lack* of a reaction.

In my own use of intuitive judgment, I find that my reactions are more often the negative type (tenseness) than the positive type (relaxation). Obviously, if I get a *no* reaction to an idea, that tells me not to pursue what I'm considering. Less obviously, if I don't get any reaction from my intuitive judgment, that tells me that the idea I'm considering probably has some merit.

As an example, after developing my intuitive judgment, each time I had to choose whether or not to accept a particular person as a housemate, I would wait until the day after meeting the person to tell himher my decision. If I woke up in the morning with a definite "No way!" reaction, I knew not to accept the person as a housemate. Conversely, in the morning if I felt no more tenseness than usual, my intuitive judgment was saying "I don't feel any incompatibility with this person", so my answer was usually "Yes." Fortunately, this method helped me choose some very fine housemates.

To know when your intuitive judgments are more likely to be reliable, keep track of past results of intuitive judgment, especially in terms of whether the response was valid. For example, you might find that your intuitive judgment is usually trustworthy when financial judgments are involved, but not when judging people. Or vice versa. It takes lots of experience, but you'll gradually learn to associate different sensations with their personal meanings.

Sometimes you'll experience a *mixed* response. This means your reaction is both positive and negative. When this happens, determine which aspects of the choice are prompting the positive reactions and which aspects are prompting the negative reactions. This can be done by separating each choice into different components and judging them individually. When you've identified the components of the idea that prompt the negative response, refine the idea to remove its weaknesses.

As a final point about interpreting the meaning of the results, don't let a favorable intuitive judgment override your conscious thinking. For instance, if you know that the alternative favored by your intuition has a significant flaw, remove the flaw or abandon the idea. *Intuitive judgment is not a substitute for thinking!* It's simply a way to make tentative comparisons that involve too many consid-erations for your conscious awareness to handle all at once.

This completes the explanation of the four steps.

Each time you get an intuitive judgment, compare it to what you would normally choose using analytical thinking. Only when you become aware of which kinds of situations and reactions provide dependable results will you be ready to trust your intuitive judgment. That can take years of development, so don't be impatient.

When Nikola Tesla was a university student and saw an early electric motor powered by *direct* current, he suggested to his physics professor that he believed it would be possible to invent an electric motor powered by *alternating* current. The professor ridiculed Tesla's suggestion. Many years later, after inventing such a motor, Tesla said:

> *I could not demonstrate my belief at that time, but it came to me through what I might call instinct, for lack of a better name. We undoubtably [sic] have in our brains some finer fiber which enable us to perceive truths which we could not attain through logical deductions, and which it would be futile to attempt to achieve through any willful effort of thinking.*

There's no evidence to support Tesla's belief that instinct takes place in a special part of the brain. But, along with other great creative thinkers, Tesla credits non-analytical thinking to be a valuable part of creative thinking. Some creative people only admit in private to using it, whereas others, such as Tesla and Einstein, have endorsed it openly.

Entire books have been written about intuition, so consider reading one of them if you're interested in learning more about this subject. If you read such books, keep in mind that intuition encompasses more than just the intuitive judgment that's explained here. Also keep in mind that the nature of intuition isn't well understood, so different people have different opinions about it. Find out what works for you.

Reading about this skill cannot replace the absolute need to practice using your intuitive judgment. So practice, practice, and practice. This is what it takes to reach the point of being able to rely on it to make major decisions. It's worth the effort if you're serious about creating solutions to especially challenging problems.

◄SUMMARY►

To supplement your conscious thinking, use intuitive judgment, which involves getting a "Yes" or "No" reaction to possible alternatives. To prompt such reactions, first spend time understanding each alternative. Then, present each alternative to your conscious awareness one at a time and pay attention to your body's and mind's subtle sensations. The most challenging part of learning intuitive judgment is to become aware of, and recognize the meaning of, the subtle sensations that arise.

When first learning this thinking skill, don't necessarily do what the reaction implies. You won't be ready to depend on intuitive judgment until you've learned what situations and reactions indicate reliable evaluations.

Exercise 1. Try the coin flip exercise, described above. However, don't use it to actually make a decision. Rather, use it to acquaint yourself with the *nature* of your "Great!" or "Darn!" sensation. To make the reaction more easily detectable, choose an undecided issue that's very important to you. The issue might be deciding whether to quit your job, get married, buy a car, or visit relatives.

Uncluttering Your Mind

▶ External distractions such as kids yelling, phones ringing, and people talking detract from your ability to think clearly. Similarly, distractions inside your mind also interfere with clear thinking. Such internal distractions especially interfere with efforts to access subconscious thinking.

▶ A very effective way to clear out mental clutter is to do something physical, such as walking, jogging, dancing, swimming, playing sports, or working in a garden. In other words, move! Physical exercise improves your mental clarity and therefore increases your chances of conceiving creative ideas.

When considering what physical activity to do regularly, be creative! Exercise need not be a separate activity whose only goals are physical fitness and mental clarity. Consider activities that can be integrated into what you would do anyway, such as walking up stairs instead of taking an elevator, or riding a bicycle to and from where you would otherwise drive. Also, some kinds of physical exercise can be used as an activity during which to let your subconscious create, as described in the *Using Subconscious Thinking To Provide Insights* section earlier in this chapter.

Conditions that decrease mental clarity include not enough sleep, and consumption of mind-affecting substances such as alcohol, smoke, medicines, and drugs.

A busy lifestyle filled with too many activities also contributes to mental clutter because time intended for accessing the subconscious will instead be used by your mind to focus on other, more significant (from your subconscious' point of view), thoughts and feelings.

Meditation is a useful way to both:

- Provide your mind with time to clear out mental clutter.
- Improve your skill in recognizing and letting go of distracting mental clutter. Note that *letting go* of mental clutter is different from *pushing* it *away*.

Learning to let go of mental clutter during meditation also enables you to let go of internal distractions when you're consciously working to create a solution.

If you're interested in maximizing the accuracy of your intuitive judgments, there's no substitute for reducing the *emotional* clutter in your mind. After all, intuitive judgments are so similar to emotions that the same word, namely *feelings*, is used to refer to both emotions and intuitive sensations.

Sometimes we think of feelings and thoughts as isolated from one another, but they aren't. Feelings arise not in the feet, or the hands, or even in the heart. They arise in the neural system, which is the same place thoughts arise. So feelings do influence your mental skills, especially the mental skill of intuitive judgment.

It would be foolish to try to eliminate emotions and feelings. They are what make life worth living! And anyway, feelings in themselves are not emotional clutter.

▶ Emotional clutter consists of negative feelings that persist long after the event that triggered them. Of course, anger, fear, resentment, guilt, irritation, frustration, sadness, grief, and so on are the negative feelings we're talking about. They're negative because they're reactions to *hurt* or *pain*. Such hurt or pain can be *physical*, such as the injury from being slapped very hard, or *emotional*, such as embarrassment. Sometimes the hurt or pain is subtle or indirect, such as when you see your child fall down and cry and you experience negative feelings even though you are not directly injured.

The mind remembers a traumatic event long after it happens because the mind, either consciously or subconsciously, wants to avoid future similar events. So, even if you repeatedly push the memory of a traumatic event out of your consciousness, the subconscious mind continues to be aware of it.

▶ When feelings of anger, including it's milder forms of irritation and frustration, arise, these feelings can be released through physical exercise.

Another way to release feelings of anger — when you're alone — is to fully and intensely exhale the way you would breathe if you were to roar like a lion, but without necessarily making the loud sound of a roar. Keep in mind that anger, as the word is used here, includes small frustrations and irritations such as the reaction to another car passing your car in a dangerous situation.

▶ One of the most effective ways to release anger (and some kinds of fear) is to cry. This is best done when you're alone, which usually requires postponing the crying. To trigger the crying, recall the event in which the hurt or pain (whether emotional or physical) arose. Recall it in such vivid detail that it's as if you're re-experiencing it. When you get to the point where you feel the hurt, keep your mind focused on the thought that started the desire to cry, and continue to cry as long as it comes naturally. If you cry longer than expected, realize that at a subconscious level you're probably also crying about other hurts and pains you haven't released yet.

▶ Laughing is another way to release emotional clutter, especially feelings of anger, guilt, and the kind of fear that's based on a misunderstanding. As an example of this kind of release, suppose you're ridiculed by someone for not knowing something, and you later find out that the person who ridiculed you didn't know the same thing himherself. The irony of such a situation is worth laughing about. If laughter doesn't come naturally, try what political

cartoonists do to make fun of serious political situations: oversimplify and exaggerate the situation.

A full explanation of releasing emotional clutter could fill an
entire book. Alas, as far as I know, no such book yet exists. One
book that covers, among other things, the importance of releasing
hurt and pain through crying and other behaviors is *Helping Young
Children Flourish* by Aletha Solter. It's directed toward dealing with
children rather than adults, but because we were all children once,
that book is a useful source of information about resolving strong
feelings.

A reduction in emotional clutter makes it easier to distinguish
emotional sensations from the yes and no sensations that convey
your intuitive judgments, thus improving your intuitive judgment.
Also, you'll find that the clarity of a less cluttered mind makes clear
thinking easier.

As a final method of uncluttering your mind, avoid memoriza-
tion. While you're thinking about how to solve a problem, use pen
and paper (including a calendar) to hold the information you
would otherwise memorize. Or you can use a tape recorder or
computer if that's more convenient. Also, depend on reference
books instead of trying to memorize the information they contain.
Such information-storage methods hold ideas far longer and more
accurately than your mind.

◄SUMMARY►

Reduce mental and emotional clutter through physical exercise,
crying privately, and laughing. Use meditation to develop the skill
of recognizing and letting go of distracting mental clutter. Reduce
intellectual clutter by using ink and paper to store what would
otherwise be memorized.

Recognizing Different Ways
To Categorize Thinking

There are yet other ways of thinking besides the ones explained
in this chapter. What are they? Alas, creating a list of them isn't
possible — and would be misleading. To understand why, let's
look at various ways in which thinking can be categorized.

▶   One of the most popular schemes for categorizing different ways of thinking is according to which of the six physical senses is involved, as follows:

- Sight: Visual thinking. This category covers the tools explained in the *Thinking Visually* and *Sketching Visual Representations* sections earlier in this chapter.
- Hearing: Aural (sound-related) thinking.
- Smell: Imagining and recalling smells.
- Taste: Imagining and recalling tastes.
- Tactile: Imagining and recalling sensations of touch, which includes roughness versus smoothness and heat versus cold.
- Kinesthetic: Imagining and recalling body movements. This is the primary sense you would use as you walk through a completely dark room to avoid furniture and reach for a light switch.

▶   Although two sections in this book are devoted to visual thinking, there are no sections devoted to the senses of hearing, smell, taste, tactile sensation, and kinesthetic sensation. Yet these ways of thinking are useful for certain kinds of creating. For example, if you want to create innovative music or design ways to convert spoken words into visual representations, you need to think in terms of sounds. If you were creating innovations in dancing or computer keyboards, you would need to think kinesthetically.

▶   Another way to categorize ways of thinking is according to whether the thoughts are about the past, present, or future:

- *Recalling*: Re-creating in your mind what you *have already* perceived with your senses.
- *Perceiving*: Being aware of what your physical senses are conveying *at the present time*.
- *Imagining*: Creating in your mind what you *haven't* perceived. Of course, creative problem solving requires this kind of thinking.

▶   Another popular way to categorize ways of thinking is as follows:

- Conscious thinking
- Subconscious (non-conscious) thinking

The subconscious category was emphasized in the *Using Subconscious Thinking To Provide Insights*, *Using Fantasy Visualization To Prompt Insights*, and *Developing And Using Your Intuitive Judgment* sections earlier in this chapter.

Here's a summary of the three categorization schemes explained so far:

- Physical sense (visual, aural, taste, smell, tactile, and kinesthetic).
- Time (past/recalling, present/perceiving, and future/imagining).
- Conscious versus subconscious.

With these categorization schemes in mind, read the following example in which a single mental activity can be categorized according to all three of these schemes.

In her book *A Soprano On Her Head*, Eloise Ristad tells the story of a young music composer who came to her suffering from a mental block. He had written five out of the seven pieces needed for a set of music. Using her experience in teaching music using different ways of thinking, she coached him through a fantasy. She asked him to imagine walking into the concert hall where his music was being performed. The musicians, each with their own personality, came on stage to perform the five pieces the composer had already written. Then the quartet played the next piece of music — which had not yet been composed. Delighted, the composer opened his eyes and wrote notes to remind himself of how the piece sounded. Then, he went back to listening to the imaginary performance of the seventh and final piece, which he also wrote down. Thus, the composer was able to *hear* the music he had been struggling to compose. Apparently, his subconscious composed the music, and the fantasy provided a way to bring the music to his consciousness. Notice that imagining the new music involved all three of the following types of thinking: *aural* (sound) thinking, *imagination*, and *subconscious* thinking.

This example illustrates that a single mental process can fit into more than one category. This is because the categories are not separate ways of thinking. They can conveniently be *described* separately, but they are *used* together.

To visually emphasize this point, look at the cube on the next page. It represents all possible combinations of the three categorization schemes explained so far. Each dimension (width, height, and depth) is divided into the categories for each scheme. Thus, a single thought process corresponds to the intersection of three ways of thinking.

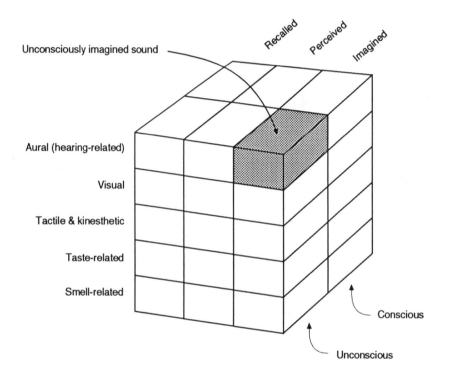

▶ Attempts to combine all ways of thinking into a single list fail. If all combinations of the above three categorization schemes were listed, the result would be incomplete because there are yet other categorization schemes.

▶ Another way to categorize thinking is in terms of the entities being represented in the mind. Examples of such entities are: words, physical objects, people, concepts, dimensions, vocal sounds, musical sounds, pictures, visual representations, and physical sensations. Notice that the categories of concepts and people correspond to these earlier sections in this chapter: *Thinking In Concepts, Extracting Useful Concepts From Anywhere,* and *Imagining What Someone Else Might Suggest.*

Another way to categorize thinking is according to differences in activity between the left hemisphere (half) and the right hemisphere of the brain. Research using electronic equipment has shown that each hemisphere dominates certain kinds of thinking. For example, analytical thinking corresponds to more activity in the left hemisphere. This distinction between left and right hemispheres isn't part of any of the tools explained in this book because this book concentrates on differences you can notice yourself without the aid of special equipment. A person cannot *feel* the difference between left and right hemisphere thinking. And, ironically, methods of promoting non-analytical (right) hemisphere thinking typically require using the analytical (left) hemisphere to categorize the kind of thinking currently going on.

There are yet other ways to subdivide thinking into separate categories. And within each categorization scheme, smaller distinctions are possible. Therefore, it isn't practical to represent every possible way of thinking as a list of separate categories.

Furthermore, some people develop ways of thinking that go beyond what most people can imagine. Consider Wolfgang Amadeus Mozart's amazing musical ability. He said he could compose entire scores in his mind "... so that I can survey it, like a fine picture or a beautiful statue, at a glance." He also stated, "Nor do I hear in my imagination the parts successively, but I hear them, as it were, all at once. What a delight this is I cannot tell!"

Our culture places a heavy emphasis on thinking in a few standardized ways, such as verbally (in words) and mathematically (in numbers and mathematical symbols), but neglects to encourage people to think in yet other useful ways. This bias accounts for why creative ideas often arrive by thinking in new ways. After all, if everyone thinks the same way, then everyone will overlook the same ideas. By looking where other people haven't looked, you increase your chances of finding something new and useful. Accordingly, don't limit yourself to learning only the commonly neglected ways of thinking that are emphasized in this book. Think in whatever ways seem to offer advantages.

Hopefully, you now appreciate that the alternate ways of thinking explained in the previous sections of this chapter amount to only a peek at the many different ways a person can think.

◀SUMMARY▶

Don't limit yourself to only the non-conventional ways of thinking that are explained in this chapter. There are many ways of thinking, any of which might help you see what most people overlook.

Thinking can be categorized in a number of ways, including by: sense organ, time, consciousness, kind of entity, and brain hemisphere.

Thinking Dimensionally

A failure to recognize and understand dimensions frequently leads to overlooked, or poorly designed, solutions.

Although dimensions obviously include quantities that can be measured in numbers, such as weight, money, and time, dimensions also include entities that defy being represented by numbers, such as patience, risk, self-confidence, and love.

Representing Dimensions Visually

As you read this chapter about dimensions, recognize that your effort to understand dimensions is analogous to an intelligent dolphin trying to understand the concept of water. Water so completely and constantly surrounds dolphins that even if dolphins had a large vocabulary, one of the last words they would find useful is a word for water. Similarly, dimensions so completely and constantly surround us that one of the last words a person needs to learn is the word *dimension*. Although the word dimension isn't important, understanding dimensions can dramatically improve your creative problem solving ability.

Just about anything — including a *thing* such as a person or object, and an *action* such as a process or situation — has certain *characteristics*. If a characteristic can be represented as a point along a line, then there is a *dimension* that consists of all the points along that line.

As an example, consider the characteristic of the *size* of a van. The possible sizes of vans can be represented on a wide line ranging from small to large, as shown on the next page. The size of a particular van can be represented as a point — pointed to by an arrow — along the line.

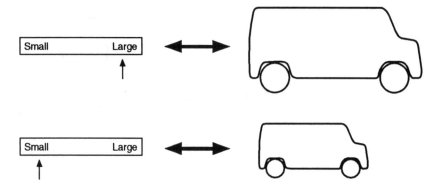

In this van example, the characteristic of size can be represented by a number, such as its volume. So, in this case, the dimension is a range of numbers.

However, not all dimensions involve numbers.

When someone orders steak in a restaurant, heshe asks for *rare, medium rare, medium, medium well,* or *well done* steak. Although the range from *rare* to *well done* is a dimension, numbers aren't involved.

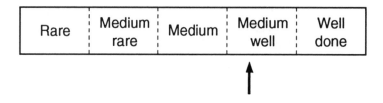

Notice that the vertical lines between the names are dotted. This indicates that, as a particular steak is cooked, the arrow can move slowly from left to right to represent how well done that steak is.

Suppose the characteristic being visually represented is the number of children in a family. When a baby is born, the number suddenly jumps from one category to the next category.

0 children	1 child	2 children	3 children	4 children	...

In this kind of dimension, each "point" along the dimension line becomes a section of the line, wide enough to be labeled. Each "point" is now a category, and the categories are separated from one another by solid — instead of dotted — lines. In spite of these differences, a characteristic can still be represented as an arrow pointing to one "point" along a line of points.

Some categories don't involve a built-in sequence. Yet such categories can still be put into a line to visually represent a dimension.

There is no natural order for lining up fruits and vegetables in the produce section of a grocery store. Yet a particular piece of fruit has the characteristic of being a particular kind of fruit, and this characteristic can be represented by an arrow pointing to one category along a line of categories. In this dimension, unlike previous examples, the sequence of the categories could be changed and the dimension would still make sense.

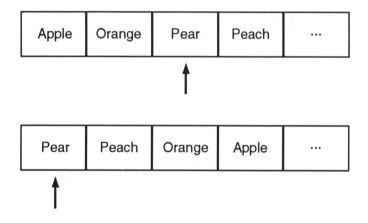

To emphasize a lack of special connections between adjacent categories, the vertical lines between categories are thicker.

Now that you know how a dimension can be represented visually, you're ready to more clearly understand dimensions and use that clearer understanding in creative problem solving.

In case you don't feel comfortable without reading a carefully worded definition of the word dimension, here's such a definition: *A dimension is the full set of mutually exclusive possibilities for a characteristic, trait, property, or parameter.* But don't bother memorizing this definition because being able to recite it won't improve your creative problem solving ability. What's needed to improve that ability is an understanding of dimensions, and that's what you'll learn in the remainder of this chapter.

◀SUMMARY▶

If a characteristic of an entity can be represented by a point along a line, the line represents a dimension. An arrow pointing to the line indicates which possibility applies to the characteristic for that particular entity.

If there are names for ranges within the dimension, dotted lines separate the names. If the points of the dimension are categories, solid lines separate the names from one another. If categories are adjacent to one another along the line, but aren't in a natural sequence, a thicker line separates the category names.

Recognizing Dimensions As Possibilities For Change

Often, creative solutions and innovations are simply the result of changing something from one possibility to a different possibility along a dimension. Here are two examples of innovations that were created this way:

- Minivans were invented by reducing a van's size. This change offered advantages of improved fuel efficiency, ease of parking, and lower cost of materials.

- Chocolate chip cookies were invented by adding chunks of a chocolate candy to a popular cookie recipe. This amounts to changing the number of chocolate chunks per cookie — from none to some.

Very importantly, these changes were made by someone creating these items, not by someone possessing one of these items.

For example, the owner of a van cannot pull a lever to enlarge or reduce the size of the van. Likewise, someone about to eat a cookie can't do anything to change the ingredients in that particular cookie. It's before something is made, while its design is still in someone's mind, that such changes can be made.

Sometimes, instead of changing only one characteristic, it's better to simultaneously change multiple characteristics.

The makers of a popular brand of vodka were confronted by a 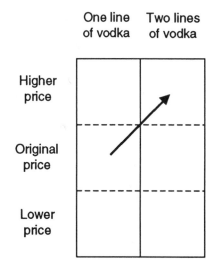 new competitor who introduced a less expensive brand. Surprisingly, their response was to *increase* the price of their already popular brand of vodka. Alone, this idea would be crazy. But they also introduced a new, less expensive, line of vodka. They were successfully able to convey to consumers the message, "Now we'll start charging what our vodka is really worth, but if you want something cheap, we'll sell that too." Their strategy worked.

When two dimensions are involved, as in this vodka marketing example, it's useful to align one dimension vertically and the other dimension horizontally. The result is a matrix as shown below. Each square represents one combination of characteristics. Changing two characteristics at the same time results in a diagonal jump between squares.

As this example illustrates, if changing one characteristic offers an advantage, yet has disadvantages, consider also changing another characteristic to eliminate the disadvantages.

So far, the examples in this section involve dimensions in which something increases or decreases. But the usefulness of changing possibilities along a dimension is much broader than that.

Fran Stryker wrote the countless scripts for the Lone Ranger radio series which was broadcast five days a week for twenty years.

How did Stryker come up with enough creative ideas? By identifying the dimensions of the dramas and choosing a different combination of characteristics for each show. (Although the concept of dimension was involved, the word dimension was probably not used.) What dimensions characterize a story? Here are visual representations of important dimensions for such a series:

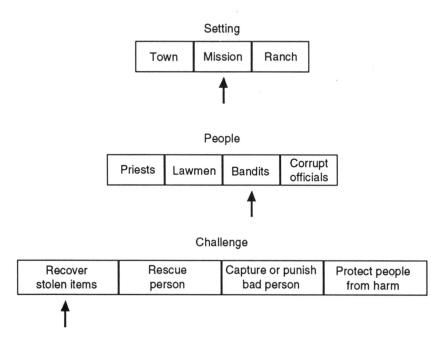

Notice that randomly choosing a new combination of characteristics, one from each dimension, quickly provides the inspiration for a new story. Try it!

By understanding dimensions as possibilities for change, you can discover alternatives you might otherwise overlook.

◄SUMMARY►

When a characteristic along a dimension can be changed, consider changing it. If that change offers an advantage, yet has disadvantages, consider also changing another characteristic to eliminate the disadvantages. Such changes are not limited to dimensions that represent numerical quantities that increase or decrease.

When two dimensions are represented visually, it can be useful to align one vertically and the other horizontally, creating a matrix of squares that represent all possible combinations of changes along the two dimensions.

Varying Words In A Sentence To Prompt Ideas

If you can express a problem in a sentence, you can use that sentence to prompt new ideas. Simply look at each word in the sentence, one at a time, and consider somehow changing it.

Suppose that someone named Larry says, "I have a satisfying job, but it doesn't pay enough to meet my needs." What can be changed to improve Larry's situation? The following word changes reveal some possibilities:

- Change *job* to *jobs*: Larry can get a second job.

- Change *job* to *paying hobby*: If Larry currently spends lots of money and spare time pursuing a hobby, he can ask himself, "Can I transform my hobby into a business that offers a service or product that people will pay me for?"

- Change *needs* to *desires*: Larry can look for ways to achieve happiness in ways that don't involve meeting his "needs".

- Change *satisfying* to *unsatisfying*: Larry can work at a less satisfying job that pays better and has shorter hours. This would give him more time for doing what he prefers.

- Change *my* needs to *other people's* needs: Larry can consider whether his needs are actually his. For instance, is his need for a new car based on what kind of car other people think he should be driving, or on what he would drive if no one else ever saw his car?

This simple word-changing tool is yet another way of becoming aware of possibilities for change.

◄SUMMARY►

If you can express a problem in a sentence, imagine changing each word in the sentence, one word at a time. For each changed word, imagine the possibilities it suggests.

Differentiating Appropriately

One of the most powerful tools for creating new solutions is to differentiate according to *appropriate* criteria rather than differentiating according to the *most obvious* differences.

Managers of a military installation faced the dilemma of deciding whether employees should punch a time clock. Initially, managers decided that both engineers and technicians had to punch a time clock. But the engineers regarded themselves as professionals and insisted they shouldn't have to punch in and out. They successfully persuaded the managers to make this change. When the technicians claimed the distinction was discriminatory, managers allowed everyone to come and go without punching in or out. Soon, many of the technicians and engineers began leaving early each day, so managers changed the rules again and required everyone to punch a time clock. Deciding which group of employees should punch a time clock, and whether they should be treated the same is certainly a dilemma. What would you decide?

If you're thinking creatively, you realize that there's a creative alternative. Instead of basing the distinction on profession, base the distinction on whether each employee can successfully demonstrate punctuality. Regardless of their position, employees who leave early or don't arrive on time would be required to punch a time clock. Employees who leave and arrive on time wouldn't have to punch the time clock. The distinction between job classifications is irrelevant. Incidentally, translating this rough idea into a practical solution requires making rules as to how long and how dependably an employee must demonstrate that heshe arrives and leaves on time when punching a time clock before earning (or re-earning) the right to not punch the time clock.

Frequently the most obvious difference between two groups dominates our minds so strongly that we forget to consider other differences that are much more relevant.

The tendency to focus on dominant differences is called stereotyping. It's especially strong when there are names for the obvious categories, such as *engineer* and *technician*, but no names for the other, more significant, categories. In such cases, descriptive names, such as *time card employees* and *time card-less employees*, can be created. But far more important than the names is to recognize that an important, but easily overlooked, distinction exists.

A visual representation of what we tend to see looks like this for the time clock example:

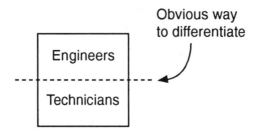

In contrast, differentiating according to a less obvious criteria looks like this:

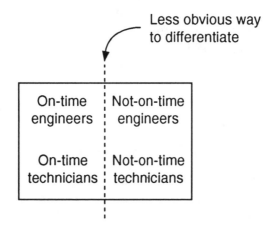

To consider differentiating in a creative way, think of the process as being analogous to slicing an apple horizontally instead of vertically. In doing so, you'll see something you otherwise don't see. In the case of the apple, you'll see a star! In the case of problems, you'll see new solutions.

◄SUMMARY►

Countless problems can straightforwardly be solved by identifying differences that might not be obvious, or might not be easy to convey in words, but which are very significant. Look for these relevant differences. Create solutions that differentiate according to these relevant differences, instead of obvious or traditional differences.

Exercise 1. People disagree about the *degree* to which health care should be publicly funded. Such differences typically focus on *how much money* should be spent on health care or *which people* should be able to get it free. What, besides the above distinctions, is an appropriate way to differentiate between health care that's publicly funded and what isn't funded? One such distinction benefits everyone.

Exercise 2. Some parents prefer that their children not play with toy guns because the intended target of real guns are human beings. Yet children like to play with toy guns; ones that don't kill. What other alternative exists besides banning toy guns and allowing toy guns? (One alternative appears on page 312.)

Recognizing Dimensional Independence

A tendency to see a *single* dimension where there are actually *independent multiple* dimensions is common. Many problems can be solved by recognizing the misleading nature of the oversimplified single dimension.

Consider the dimension called the *corporate ladder*. This dimension varies from an employee who doesn't supervise anyone, through a middle manager who supervises a few people, to the president who supervises everyone. An employee's position along the corporate ladder is normally linked to hisher salary, and this connection is typically embedded in the corporation's job classification scheme. This artificial connection between *salary* and the *number of people an employee supervises* limits possibilities. For instance, a hard-working and skilled expert in a new field of technology who lacks management skills can't get a pay raise without becoming a supervisor; and becoming a supervisor would reduce the time spent using hisher valuable skills. Such an employee can easily be lost to a different corporation that doesn't embed the one-dimensional corporate ladder concept into their salary choices.

When a *single* dimension is recognized as actually representing *multiple* dimensions that are *independent* of one another, new alternatives emerge.

A visual representation can help to clarify the nature of an oversimplified single dimension.

The following illustration represents a dimension that varies from passive to aggressive, with assertion being regarded as a subdued form of aggression:

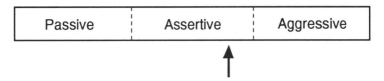

Here's a two-dimensional way of representing the relationships between aggressive, assertive, and passive characteristics:

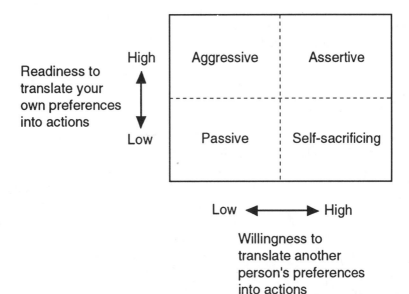

In this illustration, the single passive-to–aggressive dimension has been expanded into the following two dimensions:

- Vertical dimension: How readily someone translates hisher *own preferences* into actions. (Note that *actions* include speaking.)
- Horizontal dimension: How readily someone is willing to change hisher actions to accommodate *another person's preferences*.

The two-dimensional illustration visually conveys the following interpretations, which differ from what's implied by the single dimension:

- Aggressive person: Readily translates hisher preferences into actions, and *disregards*, or even *belittles*, the importance of another person's preferences.

- Assertive person: Also readily translates hisher own preferences into actions, but is sometimes *willing to accommodate* another person's preferences.

- Sacrificer: Doesn't act on hisher own preferences, but does act on other people's preferences.

- Passive person: Doesn't act on hisher own preferences, and doesn't act on other people's preferences.

Notice that this two-dimensional view reveals a clearer understanding of the word *assertion*. Rather than being simply a mild form of aggression, assertion represents a readiness to translate one's own preferences into action without always disregarding other people's preferences.

Can knowing about these two independent dimensions help someone to solve a problem? Sure. Suppose a timid person named Sharon has an aggressive friend named Kate who boldly makes the decisions for what the two of them will do when spending time together. The two-dimensional perspective reveals that Kate typically fails to appreciate the importance of Sharon's preferences. Therefore, Sharon can speak up more strongly for her preferences to compensate for Kate's tendency to disregard them. In essence, this amounts to saying, "I'm speaking up more strongly for my preferences to compensate for your tendency to disregard my preferences." However, very importantly, note that Sharon's assertive strategy wouldn't include disregarding the importance of what Kate wants. If Sharon found herself attempting to belittle the importance of Kate's preferences, or insisting on doing things her (Sharon's) way, Sharon would then be following an aggressive, not an assertive, strategy.

Perhaps you're thinking, "I don't feel like sketching something on paper each time I'm dealing with dimensions." Then you'll be pleased to realize that once you've seen a useful way to visualize dimensions, you can simply picture it in your mind. You don't have to put it on paper.

Stereotypes are an especially common form of one-dimensional thinking.

For instance, not all older people dislike rock music and some doctors are not men. Yet there's a strong tendency to link age to musical preferences and to link professions to gender. By recognizing that the dimensions of age, musical preference, profession, and gender are separate and *independent* dimensions, stereotypes are seen for what they are: attempts to link dimensions that aren't really connected to one another.

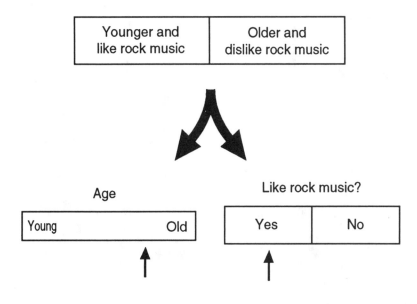

Recognize the true nature of single dimensions. Many of them have been created artificially by combining independent dimensions. Realize that such simplifications are in people's minds, not in reality.

◄SUMMARY►

Creative alternatives arise by recognizing single dimensions that are actually a combination of multiple dimensions. Expanding a single dimension into two dimensions visually corresponds to changing a line into a rectangle. Stereotypes are a common form of one-dimensional thinking.

Exercise 1. Love is a many-dimensioned thing, not a single dimension that ranges from no love to deep, undying love. Three different kinds of love are: loving a spouse, loving a child, and

Hi! I'm with the ITR polling agency and we're conducting an on-the-street political survey. On a scale of one to ten, where one is very conservative and ten is very liberal, which single number best represents your views on all the following issues: environmental concern, the economy, foreign affairs, national debt, legal reform, health care, and educational reform?

loving a parent. Based on these different kinds of love, identify some of the separate dimensions that are usually combined to create the single dimension of love.

Exercise 2. Theater movies are rated according to a dimension that represents the maturity level of the intended audience. This range is represented by the following sequence of categories: G (general audiences), PG (parental guidance suggested), PG-13 (parental guidance suggested for children under 13), R (restricted), and X (adults only). What separate dimensions does this single dimension attempt to measure?

Understanding The Dimensions Of Risk

Many problems involve risk. But thinking of risk as a single dimension that varies from *no risk* to *very high risk* is a misleading concept that frequently leads to misunderstandings and problems.

Suppose you're at the end of a dock on a lake, anxious to dive into the water. The water isn't very clear, so you can't tell how deep it is, and you can't see if there's a rock just beneath the surface. Choosing whether to dive in or, more safely, lower yourself into the water, seems like a simple judgment that anyone can clearly understand. Yet this situation is typically oversimplified.

A risk is usually thought of as being characterized by a value along a dimension that varies from no risk to very high risk, as shown here:

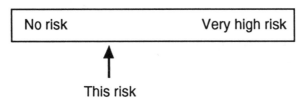

When viewed this way, choosing whether to take a risk consists of deciding whether the level of risk exceeds a maximum acceptable level. Yet identifying that maximum acceptable level and determining whether this situation exceeds it is challenging. This is challenging because risk isn't one-dimensional. Risk is multidimensional.

A risk involves at least *three dimensions*, not just one.

To identify these three dimensions for a simple example, let's simplify the diving example by assuming there are only *two possible outcomes* namely:

- The water is deep enough for a safe dive.
- You will dive in head first and hit your head on a rock that's a few feet beneath the surface.

For such a two-possible-outcome case, the three most important dimensions are:

- *How much you gain if things turn out the way you want.* In this example, you would gain the convenience of diving in without first lowering yourself off the dock into the water to make sure it's safe. So, you would enjoy the exhilaration and convenience of jumping in rather than, more boringly, lowering yourself in.

Amount gained if good outcome

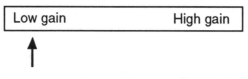

- *How much you lose if things don't turn out the way you want.* If we assume that you would be fatally injured if there were a rock just beneath the surface, the loss would be a loss of life.

Amount lost if bad outcome

- *The relative likelihood or probability of an undesirable outcome.* In this case, the probability of there being a rock at the end of a commonly-used dock is very low.

Likelihood/probability

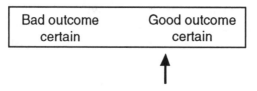

In this example, only convenience and exhilaration are gained by jumping in without checking the depth, but you would lose your life if a rock were there. This multi-dimensional view of risk clarifies why diving into unknown water isn't a wise risk.

To make this risk situation clearer, let's use a different visual representation of the three dimensions of risk. The following two diagrams represent a very good risk situation and a very bad risk situation. The diagram on the next page represents the situation for diving off the dock.

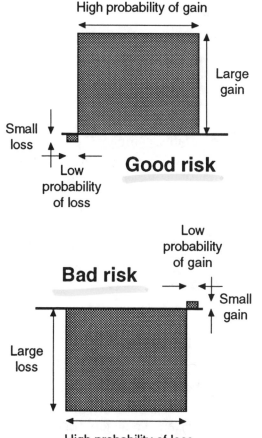

In these diagrams the width of each bar represents the likelihood of that outcome, the height of the bars above the line represents the amount that's gained if all goes well, and the height of the bars below the line represents the amount that's lost if the outcome is undesirable.

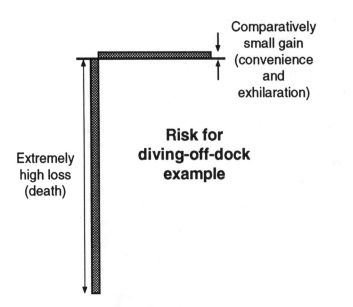

Comparatively
small gain
(convenience
and
exhilaration)

Extremely
high loss
(death)

**Risk for
diving-off-dock
example**

In each of these diagrams, compare the area of the left rectangle to the area of the right rectangle. A good risk is represented by a large right rectangle and a small left rectangle. Conversely, a bad risk is represented by a small right rectangle and a large left rectangle. As an added consideration, note how far below the line the left rectangle plunges, because a loss might not be reversible whereas there are usually future opportunities for gain.

Realistic risk situations are almost always more complex than this simplified diving example. Some reasons for the added complexity are:

- There are more than two possible outcomes.
- It can be difficult to identify all the possible outcomes.
- Each outcome has it's own separate likelihood.
- Each outcome has both a gain and a loss.

As an example of the last complexity, note that in addition to the benefits of getting a wonderful new job, friendships are lost at the previous job. Conversely, the unintentional loss of a job might be accompanied by the motivation to look for what turns out to be a better job.

In spite of the complexities of real risk situations, useful insights can still arise by thinking of risky situations as characterized by these three dimensions: gain, loss, and probability.

Note that recognizing the true nature of risk is simply an application of the broader tool explained in the previous section, namely recognizing an oversimplified single dimension as being multidimensional.

◄SUMMARY►

When there is a risk involved, identify the separate dimensions of the risk and keep those dimensions separate when making judgments. At a minimum, the following three dimensions are involved in a two-outcome risk:

- How much is gained if things turn out well
- How much is lost if things don't turn out well
- The probability of an undesirable outcome

Real risk situations involve more than three dimensions, but even expanding the one-dimensional concept of risk to the three-dimensional concept can prompt useful insights.

Exercise 1. For each of the following risks, simplify the situation by assuming there are only two possible outcomes, one good and one bad (as was done for the diving example). Roughly judge the values (from low to high) of the gain, loss, and probability dimensions.

- Riding a motorcycle without a helmet.
- Investing money in "safe" stocks. Then consider the risk for "risky" stocks. Regard putting the money in the bank as the alternative to investing in stocks.

Exercise 2. Consider the risk of disease, such as cancer, due to exposure to radioactivity. If the radioactivity level decreases, which dimensions of gain, loss, and probability are affected?

Radioactive materials shoot out particles (that can be thought of as tiny bullets) in random directions at random times. Low levels of radioactivity correspond to fewer particles per second. The size, weight, and speed of the particles are the same for both high and low levels of radioactivity — if other conditions are the same. Assume that disease either happens or doesn't happen according to

what a radioactive particle hits or misses. Assume that most, but
not all, radioactive particles pass through the body without hitting
anything. Assume that many, but not all, changes caused by
impacts from radioactive particles are corrected biologically or
don't cause noticeable damage. (An answer appears on page 312.)

Making Categorical Dimensions Realistic

We frequently perceive a dimension as categories that don't fully
represent the dimension.

Eating breakfast at a restaurant, a young friend of mine refused
to finish eating her cereal and reached for her cinnamon roll. Her
mother insisted she couldn't eat the roll until she had finished her
cereal. As she began to become frustrated, I offered her another
alternative. For each two spoonfuls of cereal she ate, she could eat
one piece of the cinnamon roll. By choosing the sizes of the
cinnamon roll pieces, I made sure she finished eating her cereal by
the time most of the cinnamon roll was eaten. She happily accomplished what she initially wasn't willing to try.

In this situation, there were two dimensions: progress in eating
the cereal, and progress in eating the cinnamon roll. But a common
view is to regard each dimension as an activity that's either done
entirely or not done at all, as shown below.

Finish eating cereal	Not finish eating cereal

Eat cinnamon roll	Not eat cinnamon roll

By thinking of the progress in eating the cereal as a dimension that
can be accomplished to degrees between these extremes, a new
alternative was apparent. To the *degree* she ate the cereal she was
rewarded by eating *bites* of her cinnamon roll. Here's a more realistic view of the two dimensions. The dotted lines indicate that
there isn't a sudden transition from one category to another.

Eat no cereal	Eat some cereal	Eat all cereal

Eat none of cinnamon roll	Eat some of cinnamon roll	Eat all of cinnamon roll

A solution can remain hidden or a problem can arise because a *continuous* dimension is simplistically regarded as a pair of, or a few, *categories*.

A familiar group of categories that represents a continuous dimension are the school grades *A, B, C, D,* and *F*. By adding pluses and minuses, these five categories were expanded to fifteen categories (A+, A, A-, B+, B, B-, etc.) to increase their motivational value in special cases. Prior to this change, a student at the top of the B category wouldn't be motivated to study for a final exam if getting an A on the exam wouldn't be enough to increase the overall grade to an A, and if getting a C on the exam wouldn't be bad enough to lower the overall grade to a C. After the plus and minus versions of each grade were created, a student in the same situation would be motivated to study because the B+ (high B) overall grade could decrease to a B or a B-.

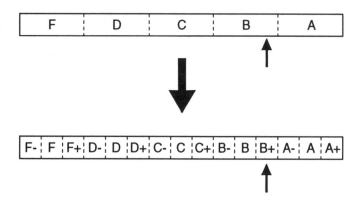

As a visual reminder that a set of categories actually represents a *continuous* range of possibilities, the vertical lines between the categories are dotted. This convention means that if an arrow (pointing to a position along the dimension) moves slightly within a dotted-line category, the movement represents a slight change along the dimension. In contrast, solid lines between categories indicate that a slight movement of an arrow within a category doesn't represent a change along the dimension until the arrow crosses one of the category boundaries. Then, the value changes suddenly.

An example of an artificially-sharp boundary is the boundary between time zones. At a time-zone boundary, time, as measured on a properly set watch, suddenly changes by one hour. This sudden jump is unrealistic in terms of what's measured. But these sudden jumps are better than continually adjusting your watch by seconds or minutes as you travel east or west.

This example illustrates that artificially sharp transitions aren't necessarily bad. Rather, they should simply be considered for what they are: artificial.

Now, let's consider dimensions in which the transitions between categories are accurately represented as dramatic jumps, but some categories are missing.

There's a common tendency to think that if one category doesn't apply, the "other" category applies. But such either-or thinking is frequently mistaken. Here are some useful clarifications:

- *Not being supportive* is not the same as being *against*.
- The *opposite of something* is not the same as the *absence of something*. It *is* true that the absence of something *includes* the opposite, but *including* is different from being *equivalent*.
- The word *not* and prefixes such as *dis-* and *non-* don't imply that there are only two possibilities. For example, to *not believe* is not the same as to *disbelieve*.

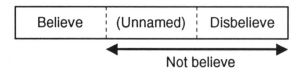

- There can be other valid answers to yes-or-no questions besides "Yes" and "No".

A failure to allow for all possibilities can lead to a failure to see creative solutions — or the creation of new problems.

◄SUMMARY►

When you find yourself thinking that there are only two possibilities, think again.

When you find yourself thinking that there are only a few sharply defined categories, ask yourself if these sharp transitions exist in reality or only in your mind.

If a sharp transition exists only in the mind, is there any benefit to increasing the number of categories? Or entirely removing the artificial boundaries?

Exercise 1. Consider the dimension of *win or lose*. In some situations it makes sense to regard winning and losing as two separate categories, with no in-between possibilities. In other situations a continuous dimension ranging from completely winning, through partly winning, through partly losing, to completely losing is more representative.

Which representation is more appropriate for each of the following situations?

- Sports such as soccer and basketball.
- Legal cases in courtrooms.
- Conflicts between friends.

Exercise 2. Taxation is done in such a way that a person's income can increase by a few dollars and put the person into a higher tax percentage rate, yet there is no dramatic jump in the amount of taxes to be paid. How is this done?

Recognizing Physical Dimensions

Many problems and opportunities for improvement involve *objects* such as machines, clothes, and houses or *substances* such as air, dirt, and chemicals. In these cases it's very useful to recognize physical dimensions. Of course, recognizing physical dimensions is especially relevant if you're interested in inventing, which is the creation of new objects and substances.

As explained earlier, the invention of the minivan amounted to changing the *size* of a van. This invention is almost trivial to think of because the dimension of *size* is so well known. But some dimensions aren't as well known, so they offer less obvious — yet equally useful — ways in which objects can be changed.

On the following four pages are three radial outlines of the following kinds of physical dimensions:

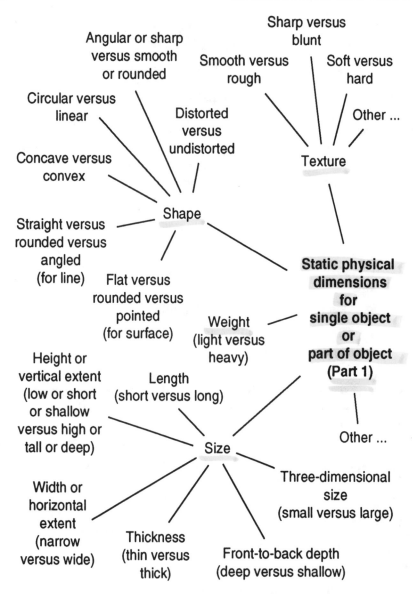

- Static physical dimensions for an object or part of an object
- Physical dimensions involving an arrangement of multiple objects
- Existence and non-existence of single or multiple objects

The first two outlines are drawn with the main item in the center.

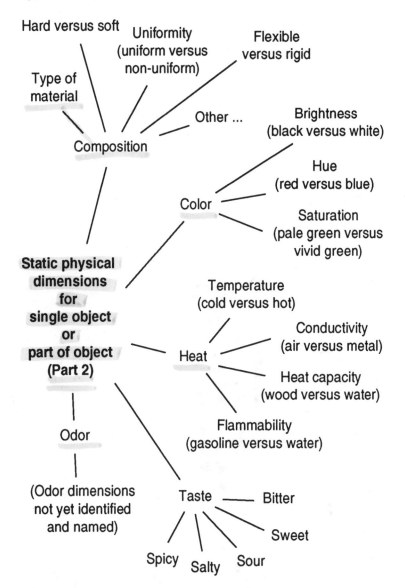

Although many of the dimensions presented in these outlines have familiar names, such as *size* and *brightness*, some dimensions don't even have names. The nameless dimensions are designated by two opposite characteristics separated by the word *versus* (which means *in contrast to*). For instance, the phrase *sharp versus blunt* refers to a dimension that doesn't have a name. (To refer to this dimension as *sharpness* is ambiguous because the word *sharpness* can also refer to a person's level of intelligence.)

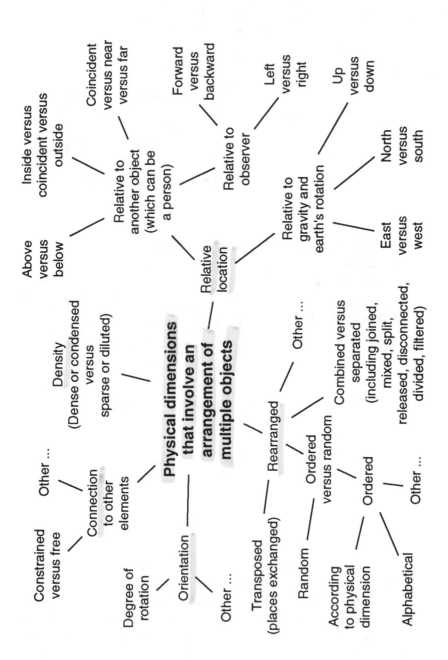

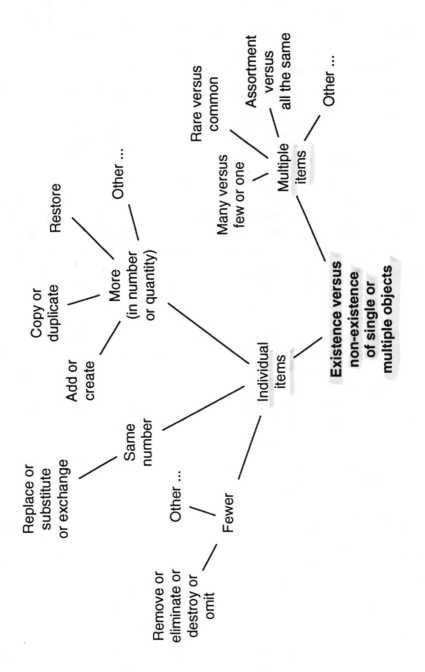

Dimensions with unfamiliar names are similarly clarified. Dimensions that don't have words to designate opposite characteristics are clarified using *examples* of the opposite characteristics. For instance, the color dimension of *saturation* is unfamiliar to many people, so the phrase *pale green versus vivid green* is used to clarify its meaning.

How can you use these outlines? As you think of the physical situation you want to improve, relate each physical dimension in the outlines to a physical property in the situation. Then, consider whether changing that physical property would provide an advantage over what exists now.

As an example, suppose you want to use this list to find a way to spread seeds more evenly by hand, without using a mechanical spreader. You would visualize holding the seeds in your hand and look through the list, one dimension at a time. Most ideas would be useless. For instance, the dimension of *weight* would probably prompt the idea of increasing or decreasing the number of seeds in your hand, but that wouldn't make any difference in the evenness of the spreading. But the dimension of *uniformity* (uniform versus non-uniform) could prompt you to consider adding something else to the seeds in your hand. That something else could be grains of sand of about the same size as the seeds. Spreading a mixture of seeds and sand would enable you to better control the number of seeds escaping from your hand because a larger amount of the mixture would contain fewer seeds. That, in turn would make it easier to control the number of seeds escaping from your hand, which makes it possible to spread the seeds more evenly.

When considering how a dimension can be changed, consider the following possibilities:

- Increase?
- Decrease?
- Reverse?
- Change a little?
- Change a lot?
- Change it all the way (to its maximum or minimum)?
- Change it to match something else?

For each of these possibilities, ask yourself, "Would making this change offer any advantages?"

Another way to use the outlines is to become familiar with the dimensions you aren't already familiar with.

For example, once you become familiar with the concept of *shape* as a dimension, if you tried to improve a sleeping bag, you would recognize that its *shape* is a dimension that can be changed. A sleeping bag's tapered shape is an improvement over the original rectangular shape, but maybe further shape improvements are possible.

There's a tendency to think of dimensions only in terms of the ones that can be measured in numbers, such as length and width. But other dimensions, such as shape, rough versus smooth, and concave versus convex, are also changeable dimensions even though numbers aren't used to measure them. The fact that many of these numberless dimensions don't have names indicates that they're less often recognized, so they're more likely to offer over-looked creative opportunities.

Resist the temptation to focus attention on the names of phys-ical dimensions. The names are of little importance except to communicate the dimensions between people, or to write down notes to yourself. Instead, focus on recognizing these dimensions in actual physical situations.

To experience dimensional thinking without using words, look at the following drinking cup shapes which differ by a physical dimension. Imagine other variations, noticing that no words need to be involved.

Many physical situations involve movement, such as the parts of a machine or the electrons moving though an electronic circuit, so a fourth outline is presented on the next two pages to convey dynamic physical dimensions.

As full as these outlines are, none of them is complete. So instead of relying on these outlines as definitive descriptions of physical dimensions, use them as starting points.

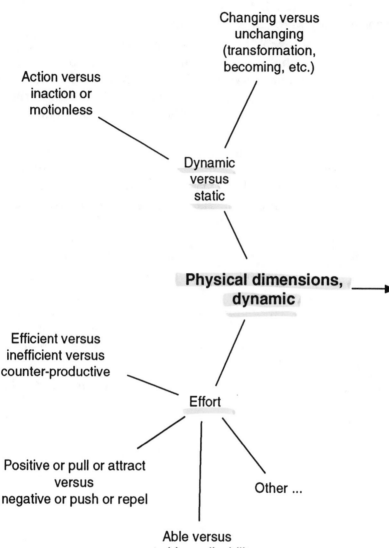

If you're a hopeful inventor or if physical improvements interest you, combine what you've learned in this section with the tool explained in the *Imagining Exaggerated Specific Cases To Determine Effects* section in Chapter 5, *Refining Your Ideas*.

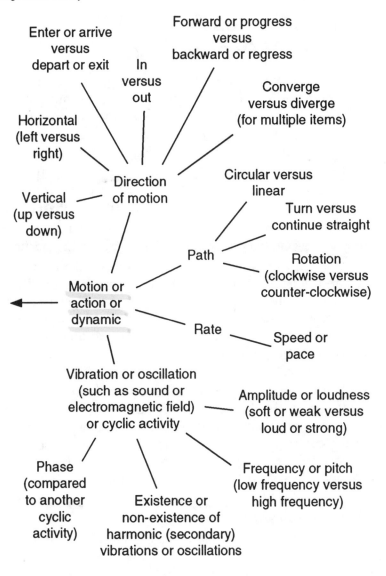

◄SUMMARY►

Become familiar with all the physical dimensions presented in these radial outlines. When faced with a particular physical challenge, use these outlines as checklists for what might be changed. When considering changing a dimension, consider the possibilities listed on page 190.

Using Opposites To Identify All Kinds Of Dimensions

In the last section you learned how to use opposites to identify a physical dimension that has no name. As an example of using this approach, if the word *size* didn't exist, the dimension of size could be named *small versus large*. This naming convention is especially useful for non-physical dimensions because non-physical dimensions tend not to be named. Such unnamed dimensions are easily overlooked. By recognizing the changes that unnamed dimensions imply, creative alternatives emerge.

The key to recognizing unnamed and overlooked dimensions is to realize that a characteristic can have *more than one* opposite.

Consider the phrase *to teach*. It has two opposite meanings: *to misteach* and *to learn*. Notice that they're opposites for different reasons. The difference between *teaching* and *misteaching* concerns the effectiveness and the content of what's given to a student. In contrast, the difference between *teaching* and *learning* concerns the point of view, namely whether a person is *giving* or *receiving* knowledge.

Similarly, two opposites of the word *obey* are *disobey* and *command*. Again, they're opposites for different reasons, namely *whether or not* commands are *followed* and whether a person is *giving* or *receiving* commands. Often, a word, such as *obey*, is so strongly associated with a particular opposite, such as *disobey*, that other possible opposites, such as *command*, are hidden.

How can such hidden opposites be recognized? By identifying something that can be reversed.

Again consider the word *obey*. Notice that it has the following two components:

- A person has been asked, by another person, to do something.
- The person does what's requested.

Each of these components can be reversed, as follows:

- The other person can ask the person making the request to do something. For example, if Michael asks Jim to do something, the reverse would be for Jim to ask Michael to do something.
- The other person does *not* do what's requested.

These two reversals account for the two opposites of the word *obey*, which are the words *command* and *disobey*.

Now let's apply this tool to a specific situation. Suppose you're a business owner looking for new ways to motivate your employees to improve productivity. Obviously one way to motivate employees is to *reward* them. But we're looking for a creative alternative, so let's find another opposite of rewarding by asking, "What are the opposites of rewarding?" The familiar opposite is *punishing*. But because employees are free to leave, punishing them for failing to improve productivity doesn't work. To discover another opposite of rewarding we ask, "What does rewarding amount to?" Rewarding involves these three actions:

1. The employer announces that something the employees want will be given to them if they increase productivity.

2. The employees either do or don't do what the employer wants.

3. If the employees do what the employer wants, the employer gives them what was promised.

Punishing reverses what the employees *do want* into what the employees *don't want*. (Incidentally, what's not wanted can include a withdrawal of something the employees already have.) Now, consider reversing something else: the order in which the second and third actions are done. Specifically, instead of rewarding the employees *after* doing the action you want, you could reward them *before* they do it. This sounds like a stupid idea, right? Fortunately you remember that stupid ideas can sometimes be refined into practical ideas. Before refining this idea to illustrate that it has some value, notice that the two opposites of rewarding correspond to the following two dimensions:

- Rewarding versus punishing: Doing something negative, instead of positive, to the employee.

- Rewarding after versus rewarding before: Giving the reward before, instead of after, the beginning of the desired activity.

This example illustrates that reversing only the most obvious component of a strategy can cause other opposites to be overlooked.

Now, let's return to the creative idea of rewarding someone *before* the behavior being encouraged. Specifically, let's refine this rough idea into something practical. Imagine that at the beginning of one month you give each of your several employees a bonus payment check. You tell them that they will have earned this bonus if they meet a slight increase in productivity by the end of the month. (The amount of the production increase must be stated specifically, and the bonus is in addition to, not a substitute for, their normal pay.) Very importantly, you also tell them that at the beginning of the following month you'll offer them another bonus in the same way — but only if they meet this month's criteria for success. If they fail to achieve the productivity increase, they get to keep the bonus anyway. However, they won't be offered another bonus until they've earned the one they've already been paid. An important advantage to this approach is that (in the absence of other counter-productive factors) it increases employee morale by conveying a sense of respect that's missing from the practice of giving money *after* work is done.

Yes, the idea as it exists is still flawed. As one disadvantage, few businesses can afford to suddenly increase what they pay their employees, especially when there is no assurance of improved efficiency. But this disadvantage can be overcome by refining the idea further. The bonus payments can be kept small when starting the arrangement. Then, as an employee earns each bonus, the amount can increase. If both an employee and the owner live up to the other side's expectations, the notion of earning bonus money after receiving it evolves into being motivated by the upcoming bonus rather than the one recently received. This is the source of motivation. And by the time the bonus amounts reach sizeable levels, the business owner will already have gained a sizeable increase in productivity. (This example assumes that increases in productivity are possible without long-term negative consequences.) Interestingly, this seemingly crazy idea of paying before work is done is very familiar in other contexts. For example, a piece of machinery is fully paid for before it's used to do any work. And within a family or an established friendship, one person helps another without any promise of being rewarded — because the help received in the past makes current sacrifices insignificant by comparison. Regardless of whether this example offers any value as a business management strategy, it demonstrates the fact that looking for opposites beyond the ones usually recognized can reveal creative new possibilities.

Notice that this opposite doesn't have a name. Therefore, you won't find it listed in a thesaurus or a book containing antonyms (words with opposite meanings).

You've now learned a "secret" of creativity! There is *more than one component* (or element or characteristic or whatever) of a strategy (or device or whatever) that can be changed. Recognizing multiple components and their implied dimensions make creative alternatives easier to recognize.

◄SUMMARY►

Hidden along with countless unnamed and poorly understood dimensions is a rich range of creative possibilities. To recognize such dimensions, look for opposites that, in pairs, define those dimensions. Keep in mind that something can have multiple opposites. To discover opposites, identify something that can be reversed.

Exercise 1. Here's an exercise that provides practice in identifying components that are reversed to yield opposites. The following matrix of four words is arranged vertically according to one dimension and horizontally according to another dimension. What are the dimensions? Be specific. (A dimension such as good versus bad isn't specific.) (The intended answer appears on page 312.)

Courage	Temperance
Cowardice	Indulgence

Recognizing Four General Dimensions

Here are four general dimensions that appear in a surprising number of specific dimensions:

- Positive versus negative
- Time
- Existence versus non-existence
- Direction

The table on the next page lists specific dimensions that are examples of the above four general dimensions. Look at each dimension in the *Specific Dimensions* column and identify how the general dimension is part of the specific dimension. In some cases this involves subtlety.

These basic dimensions are so common that they are worth looking for in whatever you try to improve.

Notice that the example of motivating employees in the previous section involved two of these dimensions: *negative versus positive* (rewarding versus punishing) and *time* (rewarding before versus rewarding after).

This tool of recognizing general dimensions is especially useful for identifying new categories in an outline of alternatives, as explained in the *Identifying Categories Before Specific Alternatives* section in Chapter 4, *Exploring Your Many Alternatives*.

◄SUMMARY►

Pay special attention to recognizing concepts that involve the following general dimensions:

- Positive versus negative
- Time
- Existence versus non-existence
- Direction

General Dimension	Specific Dimensions (Dash implies "versus")
Positive versus Negative	create — destroy facilitate — obstruct attract — repel inspire — punish support — discourage reward — punish reward — bribe help — fight make path — erect barrier joy — sadness
Time	before — after initiate — respond attack — defend ask — answer fear — anger manufacture — fix
Existence versus Non-existence	presence — absence insert — remove more — less multiple — single create — destroy birth — death
Direction	arrive — depart teach — learn immigrate — emigrate lead — follow increase — decrease pull — push attract — repel speak — listen hire — fire buy — sell

Exercise 1. For each of the following items, identify two or more specific dimensions using opposites to name the dimensions. For instance, if an item were *to initiate,* two possible dimensions would be *initiate versus terminate* (time reversal) and *initiate versus respond* (reversed roles).

- To give
- To host

Understanding Clearly

As you learned in the *Looking For Fresh Perspectives* section (in Chapter 2, *Welcoming New Ideas*), looking beneath the surface of a situation to understand it more clearly can reveal insights that make overlooked solutions obvious. In this chapter you'll learn specific ways to reach that clearer understanding.

Admitting To Yourself You Don't Know

The first step toward reaching a clearer understanding is to recognize any limitations in your current understanding.

"Why is the sky blue?" For many people the most accurate answer would be, "I don't know." But in our culture admitting a lack of knowledge is ridiculed often enough that more common answers might be:

- "It just is."
- "That's a dumb question."
- "Don't you already know the answer?"
- "It's because of the particles in the air."
- "It's due to Rayleigh scattering."
- "For the same reason that sunsets and sunrises are red."

Although some of these answers are true, none of them explains why the sky is blue.

In social situations it's often wise to avoid saying "I don't know" because some people ridicule or criticize people who say these words. But when thinking alone, if you really don't know, it's wise to admit to yourself, "I don't know." Why? If you think you already understand, you won't put any effort into seeking a clearer understanding.

◀SUMMARY▶

Before you can more clearly understand, you must acknowledge to yourself that there are limits to your understanding.

Exercise 1. Based on what you already know, honestly answer the following questions:

- What genetic survival advantages are gained by peaches having fuzz on them?
- Why is there a bigger difference between high and low tide in the Atlantic Ocean than in the Pacific Ocean?
- Why is the sky blue?

Avoiding Crucial Assumptions

Many creative solutions are hidden by mistaken assumptions.

Suppose you often pass a particular person in a hallway and you would like to be more friendly to the person as you pass, yet the person doesn't nod or say "Hello." It might seem that the person is unfriendly. Although that might be true, another possibility is that you and the other person are making different assumptions about how people initiate social contact. Specifically, some people look at another person and wait for the other person to look back before saying "Hello." In contrast, other people wait to hear another person say "Hello" before looking at the other person. The combination of these two assumptions can leave both people wondering why the other person isn't responding.

What is an assumption? It's information that's treated as if it were true without finding out whether it really is true.

This definition makes it clear that assumptions can be worth investigating to find out if they're really true. However, out of the hundreds or thousands of assumptions a person makes each day, there is seldom time to test more than a few. So, which ones should be tested?

If you become aware that you're ignoring a new alternative because you believe it won't work, ask yourself, "Does my reason for rejecting it involve an assumption?" If the answer is "Yes", test the assumption. If the assumption should turn out to be untrue, a new alternative becomes available.

Testing an assumption can be as simple as asking someone a question or looking in a reference book. If an assumption would require lots of effort to test, take into account your level of curiosity when deciding whether to test it.

People make lots of assumptions in areas that are uncomfortable to talk about, so mistaken assumptions occur more often in such areas. For this reason, mistaken assumptions are especially common in the areas of sexuality, love, death, and salaries.

◄SUMMARY►

An assumption should be tested if a promising alternative is blocked due to the assumption.

Exercise 1. A man went into a theater to watch a movie. During the movie he fell asleep and snored loudly, yet no one else in the audience noticed. How could this be? (An answer appears on page 312.)

Letting Curiosity Motivate Your Learning

Curiosity can motivate you to spend time seeking the clearer understanding you need for creating effective solutions.

When Buckminister Fuller became fascinated by the way flat shapes can interlock to form rounded shapes, he spent many hours studying trigonometry and geometry on his own. After he developed a clear understanding of this subject, Fuller invented the *geodesic dome*. It's a simple and lightweight, yet structurally rigid, architectural structure made of interlocking, simple, flat shapes.

If you're able to maintain or increase your sense of curiosity, you'll be motivated to spend time learning whatever you don't yet clearly understand.

Curiosity is something we're born with, as evidenced by young children's "How?", "Why?", and "What if ...?" questions. But questions based on curiosity can be disruptive and embarrassing so parents and teachers teach children to limit asking such questions. Unfortunately, many children misinterpret the need to stop asking questions based on curiosity as a need to suppress curiosity itself. Unknowingly, parents can even encourage this interpretation by answering their questions with, "That's not important." What's needed is not an end to curiosity, but an end to asking questions out loud without regard to the nature of the situation. Curiosity should remain!

As expressed in the saying "Curiosity killed the cat", some people distrust curiosity. Of course it's not safe to jump off a cliff to find out what it feels like to fall through the air. But is it unsafe to reach for a reference book to find out how something works? A mistrust of curiosity fails to account for the difference between *exploring physically* and *exploring mentally*. Perhaps a better saying is "Poor judgment killed the cat."

Albert Einstein declared, "I have no special gift — I am only passionately curious."

◄SUMMARY►

Let your curiosity take you to the frontiers of understanding. That's where many creative solutions can be found.

Understanding Why And How

Creative problem solving requires an understanding of concepts and principles, which are acquired by learning the answers to "How?" and "Why?" questions.

Many people marvel at Leonardo da Vinci's ability to understand painting, sculpture, music, poetry, architecture, botany, zoology, physiology, anatomy, optics, acoustics, machinery, hydraulics, aerodynamics, geology, *and* psychology. Part of the reason for his formidable understanding was that he spent lots of time trying to understand *concepts* and *principles*, which are what's uncovered by learning the answers to "How?" and "Why?" questions. Among Leonardo's sketches is a helicopter. This is remarkable because it was sketched around the year 1500. Leonardo was able to invent it because he realized that the fluid nature of air is similar to the fluid nature of water. He used the *screw* shape that was commonly used to move water in his day and oriented it vertically with the idea of using it to pull people vertically through the air. His helicopter would not have worked, yet its design is similar to the design of today's helicopters.

The key to learning concepts and principles is to learn facts and knowledge for which the answers to all the following questions is "Yes":

- Will the knowledge still be true and relevant ten or twenty years from now?
- Does the knowledge deal with an understanding itself rather than with who, when, and where the understanding was first reached?
- Is the knowledge still relevant if it's expressed in a foreign language?
- Does the knowledge help you predict the outcome of doing something?
- Is this knowledge useful in real situations rather than just in artificial situations such as games and puzzles?

This orientation shifts learning from memorizing names, dates, places, historical facts, and terminology that can be looked up in books, to understanding concepts, principles, and images that account for how and why things do what they do. With this kind of orientation, learning new subjects is easier and faster because there is less to learn. This is, in part, how Leonardo da Vinci was able to understand so many different subjects. He focused most of his attention on learning the kinds of knowledge that he could apply to drawing, painting, sculpting, inventing, innovating, and problem solving. Besides making learning easier, this orientation makes learning more fun! Such learning often simply amounts to satisfying your curiosity.

Understanding the reason something is done can open up new possibilities. For example, writers learn the rule that if a period or comma follows closing quotation mark, the period or comma is moved to the left of the quotation mark, even if the period or comma isn't part of the quotation. In contrast, the placement of a question mark or exclamation point depends on whether the question mark or exclamation point is part of the quotation. Why is this convention followed? It arose back when typesetting was done by hand and the small raised portion that imprinted a period or comma was difficult to see. Printers found that they avoided mistakes by putting the period or comma inside the quotation regardless of whether it was part of the quotation. Knowing the origin of this convention and recognizing that its original purpose no longer applies restores the alternative of following the original convention.

To reach the level of understanding that's needed to become aware of new alternatives, spend time learning concepts and principles and learn why and how things are as they are.

Darn! I didn't bring my umbrella today!

◄SUMMARY►

The answers to "How?" and "Why?" questions are what lead beyond a knowledge of facts to an understanding of concepts and principles. To focus on the kinds of knowledge that lead to an understanding of concepts and principles, ask the questions listed on page 205.

Exercise 1. For each of the following kinds of knowledge, ask the questions listed on page 205. A "Yes" answer for all the questions indicates that the knowledge is relevant to creative problem solving. Any "No" answers indicate a likely lack of relevance. Allow for possibilities between the extremes of "Yes, it's relevant" and "No, it's not relevant."

- William Harvey, in 1628, became the first European to publish the fact that blood circulates through the human body.
- There are one-way valves in parts of the body's circulation system that ensure that blood flows only in the proper direction.
- Knowing the names of all the parts of an automobile.

Exercise 2. There is a link between poverty and persistent anger. Of course poverty leads to frustration and anger. Why does anger (in the general sense of the word anger) increase the likelihood of poverty?

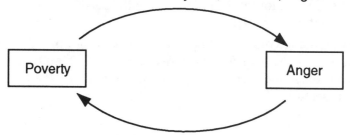

Lack of money to buy food & clothes and pay rent & utilities leads to misery and, therefore, anger.

Poverty

Anger

Why does anger increase the likelihood of poverty?

Avoiding Oversimplified Associative Thinking

▶ Associative thinking occurs when one thought automatically leads to a second thought that's always the same. Although associative thinking is often useful, challenging problems can seldom be solved using *oversimplified* associative thinking.

Frogs use simplified associative thinking. They have very poor eyesight yet must react quickly to what they see. When a frog sees a small shape that's moving, it sticks out its tongue expecting to capture food. When a frog sees a large moving shape, it hops or swims away from what it assumes is danger. Such simplified thinking works well for frogs. Similarly, simplified associative thinking works well for humans much of the time. For example, when someone driving a car sees the vehicle in front getting visually larger, the driver's foot instinctively moves from the gas pedal to the brake pedal.

Now, let's look at an example of *oversimplified* associative thinking. A man in shabby clothes walked into a bank and asked the teller to validate a 60-cent parking permit. He pointed out that he had cashed a check there a few minutes earlier. The bank teller refused to validate the permit, saying that cashing a check was not a transaction for which they validated parking permits. The bank manager, after looking at his grubby clothes, likewise denied his request. Consequently, he withdrew his money from their bank. All one million dollars of it! It's easy to associate shabby dressing with a person who has little money. But such an association is deceptive. It fails to consider that the association between shabby dressing and lack of money necessarily applies in only one direction. That is, people without money dress shabbily because they can't afford nice clothes, but a person with lots of money can dress either nicely or shabbily.

▶ One way to avoid oversimplified associative thinking is to take into account *why* and *how* two things are associated with one another. This amounts to an application of what you learned in the previous section.

Additional ways to avoid oversimplified associative thinking are to use the tools explained in these sections within Chapter 7, *Thinking Dimensionally*:

- *Differentiating Appropriately*
- *Recognizing Dimensional Independence*
- *Making Categorical Dimensions Realistic*

Yet another way to alert yourself to the possibility of oversimplified associative thinking is to spend time clarifying your understanding when the following words are used: *involves, has to do with, links, relates to,* or *is associated with.* Simply knowing that two things are related to one another doesn't account for the nature of the relationship.

Statistical numbers are often used by politicians, advertisers, economists, scientists, and others to support oversimplified associative thinking. Although statistics can indicate a high level of *correlation* between two measured quantities, correlation doesn't imply that one of the measured quantities *causes* the other measured quantity. If this interpretation were valid, then statistics could be used to "prove" that shabby dressing *causes* poverty. Statistics might imply an association between two things, but it doesn't reveal anything about why or how they're associated.

When fast thinking is required, simplified associative thinking is essential. However, in problem situations where *clear* thinking is required, simplified associative thinking can become *oversimplified* associative thinking.

◄SUMMARY►

Although simplified associative thinking is appropriate in situations that require fast thinking, *over*simplified associative thinking is the opposite of clear understanding. Oversimplified associative thinking can be avoided by applying the tools explained in the following sections: *Differentiating Appropriately, Recognizing Dimensional Independence, Making Categorical Dimensions Realistic,* and *Understanding Why And How.* Statistics, if used properly, don't support oversimplified associative thinking.

Exercise 1. Suppose a friend of yours is a financial investor and knows that the spread of *killer bees* from South America has

dramatically driven up the cost of honey where these bees have already invaded. He reasons it would be wise to invest in the honey business in the United States now, while the cost of investment is cheaper, so that he will be in a very profitable business when the bees arrive. What is the basis of this reasoning? How is it flawed?

Exercise 2. A friend of yours was in an unsuccessful romantic relationship and is now taking an interest in someone who, she thinks, has the opposite characteristics of her previous partner. What oversimplified associative thinking is implied by this scenario?

Understanding Experimenting

Experiments provide valuable opportunities to learn — if the outcomes are recognized as offering more than "Yes" or "No" results.

Thomas Edison wanted to duplicate, within his laboratory, the electrical resistance of the transatlantic cable that connected Europe to the United States by *telegraph*. In one of the experiments done by Edison and his assistants, granules of carbon were packed into a container with two wires contacting the carbon. Electrically this setup simulated the resistance of the transatlantic cable, but it had a major flaw. If the table on which it rested was bumped or there were loud noises from the nearby machine shop, the electrical resistance changed. Because this was unacceptable, Edison abandoned this approach. A few years later, after Alexander Bell invented the telephone, Edison wanted to invent an improved microphone for use in telephones. He recalled his experiment with packed carbon granules and remembered the correlation between sounds and changes in electrical resistance. Using this information, he invented a microphone that used packed carbon granules. It was much better than the one Bell invented and, in fact, is the kind still used in the conventional telephones of today. Notice that when Edison conducted the earlier experiment, he was looking for a "Yes" or "No" answer to the question, "Would carbon granules conveniently simulate the electrical resistance of a long cable?" By interpreting the result of the experiment as a "No" answer, Edison failed to notice that the device he made converted sounds into electrical signals that traveled through wires! Had he noticed and developed this idea, he might have invented the telephone before Alexander Graham Bell.

An experiment is a way of asking reality a question. Typically that question is designed in hopes of getting a "Yes" answer. That's appropriate. But if the results don't turn out as you want them to, recognize that reality is saying, "You don't yet understand." So, figure out what it is you don't yet understand. Don't simply think, "No, that didn't work, so let's try something else."

Ironically, the most valuable experiments can be the ones that are labeled as mistakes and failures. They offer you opportunities to learn exactly what you most need to learn — provided you look beyond the "No this doesn't work" message and seek to clearly understand what happened.

Where do misunderstandings about experimenting come from? Ironically, some misunderstandings come from the field of science.

Children in science classes are asked to do "science experiments" that have already been done thousands of times and for which the outcome is quite well known. Therefore, if a student has an outcome that's unexpected, the science "experiment" is labeled as a failure. This is partly why, as adults, we associate unexpected experimental results with failure. It's true that "science experiments" were true experiments many years ago when when they were first done, but by the time they show up in science classes they have become demonstrations, not experiments. Their uncertainty is gone.

Another source of misunderstanding about experiments arises from the way research projects in universities and corporations are funded. In order to obtain funding to pay for the experiments, researchers must predict, before the experimenting is done, what will be learned! Of course, such experiments aren't very adventurous. Only the most established scientists and researchers are given money to pursue truly adventurous experimenting.

For these reasons, science, as done in classrooms and research laboratories, isn't an ideal model for experimenting as a source of *learning*. So, in your own efforts to understand, recognize that experimenting involves *uncertainty* and *adventure*.

However, it's important to understand that adventurous experimenting should be limited to *tests*, *not* the *implementation* of adventurous ideas. In other words, don't take action by thinking something like, "Let's try making this change and see if the customers like it." That's not responsible experimenting! If this point is unclear, reread the earlier *Finding Flaws And Weaknesses Early* section in Chapter 5, *Refining Your Ideas*. On the other hand, when *thinking* about new ideas, it *is* appropriate to think, "What would happen if we were to make this change?" In this case, perhaps the experimenting can be done in your mind. If not, the experimenting can be done as a test in which no one suffers if something unexpected happens. This kind of safe exploring of uncertainty is what experimenting is all about.

When you're uncertain about an outcome, use safe experiments to clarify your lack of understanding.

◄SUMMARY►

When you conduct an experiment in which things don't turn out the way you expect, ask yourself, "What can I learn from this result?" When learning from experimenting, don't limit yourself to learning what you hope to learn. Learn whatever an experiment teaches you.

Learning From Experiences

When you reach the frontiers of general knowledge about a subject, you're on your own. Then, *experiences* are necessary.

During the last few centuries there have been many attempts to build a machine that could fly using only the muscle power of a human. The challenge was intensified in this century by a wealthy man's offer of a large sum of money to anyone who could build a human-powered airplane to fly a figure-eight course around two points a half-mile apart. On August 23, 1977, Paul MacCready (with assistance from many other people) finally achieved this dream and won the prize. And, when another prize was offered for a human-powered flight across the English Channel (a distance of 22 miles or 35 kilometers), MacCready won that too (in 1979). Prior to these successes, no one had come close to achieving this dream despite investments of lots of time, effort, and money. Why was MacCready so successful doing what many others had failed to achieve? Part of his success was due to spending many hours making small rubber-band-powered, super-lightweight airplanes that could fly for many minutes. Furthermore, he learned from those experiences. He developed a very clear understanding of the elements of lightweight flight. Years later, he applied that clear understanding to the larger, but closely related, problem of designing a human-powered airplane.

Notice that MacCready's understanding of lightweight flight was mainly based on actual flights of actual aircraft rather than being primarily based on information learned by reading books about aerodynamics (the science of flight). In fact, the method he devised for turning his slow-moving aircraft caused the aircraft to turn in the opposite direction from what a traditionally trained aerodynamic engineer would have predicted.

Our culture often portrays everyday experiences as unreliable sources of learning and regards only formal experiments as trusted sources of knowledge. In a very important way, much of this attitude is justified. Long ago, superstitions, opinions, and other unverified "facts" were commonly trusted simply because of who presented them or because someone told about an experience that supported a belief. By depending on experiments to prove or disprove questionable information, many untrue "facts" were shown to be untrue. Thus, deservedly, experiments have gained lots of importance.

Although exper*iments* are valuable sources of learning, experi*ences* are *also* valuable sources of learning.

A child learns by both experimenting and experiencing. Imagine a boy playing with a water hose. He first holds the hose at one angle and notices how far the water travels. Then he changes the hose to other angles and notices how far the water travels. Simple. Yet through this combined experiment and experience he learns that the water travels farthest if the hose is tilted upward rather than horizontally. Notice that the child doesn't distinguish between experiencing, experimenting, and learning. These distinctions are adult distinctions.

The difference between experimenting and experiencing is an attitude. In an exper*iment* the attitude is that you're seeking to learn, whereas, in an exper*ience* the attitude is a belief that there's nothing to be learned.

The word *experiment* usually evokes images of test tubes, electronic gadgetry, stopwatches, and other scientific apparatus. But experiments aren't limited to laboratories or science classes. If you stop cleaning your home to find out whether the other people living there will notice, this is an experiment — even though it isn't done in a laboratory or with a stopwatch in hand.

In a way, everything you do is an experiment. If the outcome is something you didn't expect, reality is responding to your experiment by telling you, "No, that's not the way things work." For this reason, mistakes provide valuable opportunities to learn.

A mistake can be defined as an action you wouldn't have done if you knew then what you know now. Because you now know what you didn't know then, you have, by definition, learned.

In recognizing the value of experiences, don't mistake this to mean you should book an airline flight or hop into your car. You can learn by reading about other people's experiences. This is why so many examples are included in this book. You don't have to participate in an experience to learn from it. Reading and hearing about other people's experiences also provide opportunities to learn.

◀SUMMARY▶

A surprising amount of useful information can be learned from experiences. You'll learn even more if you're ready to learn at any time, instead of limiting yourself to learning only when you expect to learn. Mistakes are especially useful as learning experiences. Experiences surround you not only in the form of personal ones, but in the form of experiences you read about, hear about, and see.

Learning By Experimenting Mentally

Experiments don't have to be done in the real world. They can be done in your mind.

You read earlier the story about how the setting sun prompted Nikola Tesla to figure out how to design an electric motor powered by alternating current electricity. Following that experience, for the next several months, Tesla conducted experiments in his mind to figure out the details of his imagined motor. But he *did not build* a single electric motor during that time. A year later Tesla finally had access to what he needed to build the first alternating current electric motor. The very first motor he built worked just as he had imagined it would. On the first try! The entire development had taken place in his mind.

It might seem that doing experiments in your mind would be unreliable. Yet, *to the degree your understanding matches reality*, testing ideas in your mind provides the same results as actually trying the ideas.

The big advantage of experimenting mentally is that it saves lots of time. It takes only *seconds* instead of hours, days, or even years to test new ideas.

To assure you that Tesla was not the only creative person to develop ideas mentally, consider this quote from the composer Wolfgang Amadeus Mozart: "The committing to paper is done quickly enough for everything is ... already finished; and it rarely differs on paper from what it was in my imagination."

To conduct experiments mentally, you already must have developed an understanding of reality inside your head that matches outside reality. Tesla did this by spending countless hours studying electricity and magnetism and building and playing with real devices, which included direct current electric motors. Mozart did this by spending countless hours playing and composing music. Everyone, not just creative geniuses, has the ability to conduct experiments mentally. However, very importantly, it's limited to the areas the person understands very clearly. Tesla couldn't have composed great operas and Mozart couldn't have invented an electric motor.

Although you might not clearly understand opera, electricity, and magnetism, there are plenty of areas you do understand clearly. To emphasize this point and demonstrate how mental experimenting is done, let's do some mental experiments that involve things you're familiar with, namely money, numbers, stores, banks, and people. Imagine that you want to design an electronic *money device* that could be used as a substitute for paper currency and coins. Obviously the money device shouldn't simply store numbers that represent an amount of money. If it did, and you lost it, whoever found it would become richer and you would become poorer. So, how can this flaw be eliminated? Imagine that the money device includes a set of pushbutton keys for entering a secret code. The device would work only if the correct keys were pressed. Would this modification eliminate the flaw? To answer this question, conduct an experiment in your mind. *Imagine* a person picking up your lost money device. Of course, this simple mental experiment reveals that the person couldn't use your money device because heshe wouldn't know the needed secret code.

Notice that in this mental experiment there is only a vague or hazy image of someone finding and trying to use the lost money device. Also, notice that the image probably includes some specifics about the person, such as hisher gender and what heshe's wearing. Thus, in some ways your image is vague and in some ways it's specific.

Although this experiment reveals that someone else couldn't readily access the money in your lost money device, neither could you because the device is gone. This makes it clear that the device isn't something that should somehow contain money. Instead, the device should store some kind of authorization code. When you buy something at a store, the store would send the authorization code to your bank along with a request to transfer the appropriate amount of money to their account. Whenever the bank receives the correct authorization code, the bank would transfer the money as if it had been authorized by you. (Note that this is what a bank check amounts to.)

Notice that the steps in refining the money device involve imagining how the money device would work if it were actually built and used. Also, notice that the results of these experiments are the same as if you actually did what you imagined. The results match because you understand how people, money, banks, and stores operate. Now, compare the time it's taken to develop this idea mentally with the hundreds or thousands of hours it would take to actually try these experiments. Trivial? That's exactly the point. It's relatively easy to experiment mentally when the experiments involve something you understand well.

Nikola Tesla understood electronics, magnetism, and mechanics as well as most people understand money and human behavior. That's why he was able to conduct seemingly challenging experiments in his mind.

In contrast, no one can conduct realistic mental experiments concerning complex systems, such as the human body and the economy, because those systems aren't clearly understood. In such areas, experiments must actually be done because no one (including doctors and economists) fully understand those complex systems.

So far we've considered experiments that involve things that can be directly seen or heard, such as motors, people, money, and music. Now, let's consider something that can't be seen: a new molecule. Specifically, let's consider creating a new chemical — whose unseen molecular structure determines the chemical's characteristics. This requires using *visual representations*, which are explained in the *Sketching Visual Representations* section in Chapter 6, *Thinking In Alternate Ways*. Recall that, roughly, visual representations are pictures of what can't be seen. For instance, time can't be seen, yet it's represented visually by a calendar. For chemical substances, the molecular structure is usually pictured as interconnected spheres, where each sphere is an atom, and a group of connected spheres is a molecule. Here are the steps for combining mental experimenting with visual representations:

1. *Identify what already exists that's similar to what you want to create.* When creating a new chemical, this amounts to identifying chemicals that have characteristics similar to the characteristics you want in the new chemical.

2. *Translate what already exists into visual representations.* This step amounts to imagining the molecular structure of those existing chemicals.

3. *Identify the features of the visual representations that account for the desired characteristics.* This amounts to understanding how the molecular structures of the existing chemicals account for the characteristics of those chemicals.

4. *Conduct mental experiments to create a new, different, visual representation that has the desired characteristics.* This is where the mental experimenting is done. A new molecular structure is imagined that would have the desired characteristics.

5. *Translate the new visual representation into something real.* This is when the laboratory work is done, using chemicals, test tubes, heaters, etc.

Notice that the designing — in step 4 — takes place in the mind, not in physical reality. By the time the chemical is actually created, the chemical already exists in the mind.

The key to using visual representations in mental experiments is to become so familiar with the nature of the visual representation that the visual representation has a reality of it's own. In chemistry, this amounts to learning visual representations such as chemical notations and the periodic table of elements.

To clarify this concept of a visual representation having its own reality, consider the two illustrations on the next page. They represent two stacks of wooden blocks. Which stack(s) would stay as pictured and which one(s) would fall down?

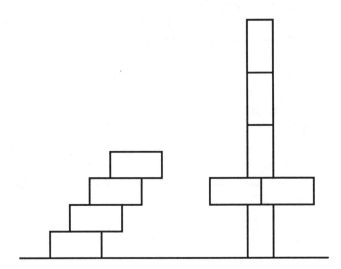

Suppose you aren't sure. You could spend time stacking dominoes to learn what falls and what doesn't. After playing with lots of specific stacks, you could look at illustrations of other stacks you've never tried and correctly predict which ones would fall.

This stacking example illustrates what's meant by a visual representation taking on a reality of it's own. It also illustrates that the key to establishing the *reality* of visual representations is to use *specific instances* when *learning* a new kind of visual representation.

When you do mental experiments, be open to *considering* (but not necessarily doing) anything. In short, be playful! This is how learning occurs in areas that aren't already well understood.

◄SUMMARY►

To the extent you study, play with, and understand objects and actions in the real world, outside your mind, you will be able to accurately represent them inside your mind. Then, for the areas you fully understand, you can quickly conduct mental experiments to test your new ideas.

For creating what can't be seen directly, combine mental experimenting with imagining visual representations. Make sure you thoroughly understand the connections between the representations and the reality they represent.

Identifying The Root Of A Problem

Identifying the root of a problem can reveal overlooked solutions.

How can painters who wear glasses keep paint from splattering onto their glasses? One simple way is to create adhesive pieces of clear plastic that can be stuck onto the glasses' lenses before painting and peeled off after painting. This is a creative and, perhaps, practical solution. But notice that it deals with the problem where it's most visible. In contrast, the paint splattering off the paint roller as it turns is less visible, yet this is the root of the problem. Stopping the splatter at the roller would not only eliminate the problem of splattered glasses, but the problem of splattered clothes, skin, and floors as well.

The best place to solve a problem is at its root. But the root of a problem isn't always as easy to identify as in the painting example.

Consider the problem of a person regularly taking mind-altering drugs such as cocaine or heroin. It might seem that the source of the problem is the source of the drugs, but this isn't the case. If it were, the person's problem would completely disappear if the supply of cocaine or heroin were cut off. Instead, cutting off the supply of these drugs is likely to prompt the person to find other drugs to use. If all illegal drugs were cut off, the person would turn to legal drugs such as alcohol. If *all* mind-altering drugs were cut off, the problem would likely shift to another kind of obsessive behavior.

This example illustrates that it can be useful to ask, "If this change were made, would the problem completely disappear or would it simply be transformed into a different problem with different symptoms?"

Continuing with the example of a person's drug use, what is the root of the problem? In one sense it's the person's *desire* to take drugs. This is verified by the fact that a person without any desire to take drugs can be surrounded by a supply of them and not take any. But eliminating a person's desire to take drugs requires reaching yet further to the root of the problem. We must ask, "Why does the person take drugs?" Here are some common reasons:

- The person takes drugs to escape misery. The misery can take a variety of forms, such as: living in poverty, having no hope of getting a good-paying job, losing expensive possessions because of a dramatic reduction in income, and being in an unhappy relationship. In such cases drugs enable the person to escape to a fantasy world where the misery is gone, or at least reduced.

- The person satisfies hisher social needs by associating with drug users and talking about drug-related topics.
- The person's income comes from selling drugs, and taking drugs fits naturally into this profession.
- The person uses drugs to avoid chores, jobs, and other responsibilities.

Does identifying the root of a person's drug problem help solve the problem? Yes. Notice that alternatives such as these appear almost automatically:

- Eliminate, or at least reduce, the misery — either directly or indirectly. For instance, if the person is living in poverty, changes can be made to provide an opportunity for the person to learn job skills that, in turn, make it possible to get a job that pays decently.
- Teach social skills, such as interpersonal communication and letting go of anger, that make healthy relationships possible.
- Teach, through association with role models, ways to escape misery that don't have the disadvantages of drugs. Examples include: making music, playing sports, playing games, learning skills, creating pottery, drawing pictures, dancing, gardening, and storytelling. Besides offering ways to escape the misery, creative activities provide enjoyment to balance the misery.

Of course, none of these solutions is easy to accomplish. If they were, drug addiction wouldn't be as common as it is. But notice that getting to the root of the problem reveals many alternatives beyond the original idea of stopping the drug supply.

▶ If you can't translate your understanding of the root of a problem into something specific that can be *done*, you haven't yet clearly identified the root of the problem.

▶ Often, people who must approve a change that would solve a problem at the root, aren't willing to approve the change. Yet, it's worth identifying the root of a problem because making the root change becomes your final goal. You can make progress in the direction of that final goal using the tools explained in the *Considering Indirect Approaches* section in Chapter 3, *Reconsidering Your*

Goals. Or, you can consider making the root change to be a separate problem with a separate solution.

◀SUMMARY▶

It's not easy to clarify what the root of a problem really is, but doing so can reveal overlooked alternatives. If making the needed change is outside your immediate influence, you can pursue indirect approaches that head in the direction of solving the problem at its root.

Eliminating Inconsistencies

How can you know whether you're making the right decisions in designing your solution? A very useful guideline is *consistency* or, more specifically, a *lack of inconsistencies*.

You're probably wondering, "What's consistency?" Imagine getting a pile of jigsaw puzzle pieces without knowing what the final picture is supposed to look like. If you're able to fit all the pieces together and the resulting picture *makes sense*, you know you've done it right — even though you can't verify its correctness by seeing that it matches a picture on the top of a box.

When Dmitry Mendeleyev searched for a way to make sense of the seemingly random characteristics of chemical elements, he found one scheme that fit their characteristics exceedingly well. It had so few inconsistencies that instead of concluding that his scheme was incorrect, he assumed that a few of the atomic weights measured by reputable chemists were in error! One of the values that Mendeleyev thought was incorrect was the atomic weight of the element gallium, which had been discovered and weighed by a French chemist named Lecoq. Lecoq initially objected to Mendeleyev's suggestion that he repeat his measurement of the element's weight. Eventually Lecoq repeated the measurement and discovered that not only was the original weight incorrect, but the correct value matched what Mendeleyev had predicted. The pattern that Mendeleyev saw was so consistent that it even enabled him to predict the future discovery of additional elements and to predict their atomic weights and chemical characteristics. He did make some minor mistakes, but, overall, his predictions were surprisingly accurate. The scheme Mendeleyev created is now called the periodic table of elements.

If you're able to design a solution such that almost everything fits together in a consistent way, then question whether the few inconsistencies are really at odds with what you're designing. Such minor inconsistencies frequently turn out to be based on incorrect assumptions.

Another example of eliminating inconsistencies appears in the *Using The Tools Together* section in Chapter 11, *Using The Creative Problem Solver's Tools*. It involves the characteristics of spoken sounds.

◀SUMMARY▶

Consistency provides an extremely useful guideline in designing what's new. More specifically, the presence of *inconsistency* indicates there's room for further improvement. When all the pieces fit together nicely, you've created a well-designed solution.

Comprehending Complexity

Shortcuts in trying to understand something that's complex usually lead to ineffective solutions and, surprisingly, to unnecessarily complicated solutions.

Many problems remain unsolved because they involve complexities that go beyond current levels of understanding. For instance, there are many human diseases for which cures are unknown because people, including doctors, don't yet understand the human body in all its complexity. When a problem goes beyond currently understood levels of complexity, it's common to use a trial-and-error approach to solving the problem. But, the trial-and-error approach isn't as effective as reaching a clearer understanding that makes solutions evident.

Let's consider something that's complex, but within an intelligent person's ability to understand: voting. In an effort to avoid the complexities that are inherent in voting, choices are usually limited to choosing between "Yes" and "No" or choosing between two candidates. Limiting choices to two alternatives simplifies the voting process in several ways, but it complicates the decision-making process for voters who prefer other choices besides the two that are offered. If many voters would prefer additional options on a ballot, it makes sense to offer such options because the point of voting is to find out what voters prefer. But adding more options causes complexities, so voting is usually limited to only two options.

A common suggestion for allowing more than two options is to have each voter mark one option and declare the option that gets the most votes as the winning option. But, as you learned in the *Imagining Exaggerated Specific Cases To Determine Effects* section (in Chapter 5, *Refining Your Ideas*), the outcome of this approach isn't fair. Specifically, the addition of a third candidate weakens the chances of winning for the candidate whose views are most similar to the third candidate, and this can make the outcome significantly different from what the voters prefer.

Another common suggestion is to have a run-off round of voting. In this case, the first round of voting determines which two options are most popular and the run-off vote determines the winner. This ensures a majority win in the run-off election (except in the case of a tie). Does this approach produce fair results? Only if the voting is done on candidates (rather than issues) and there are only three candidates in the first round of voting. If more than three candidates compete, the outcome isn't necessarily fair. (To find out why, imagine that one candidate is everyone's second preference, but no one's first preference.)

Suppose that voting is done between four candidates. Is there a fair way to determine an outcome? Yes. Let's suppose the names of the four candidates are Steve, Jennifer, Manuel, and René. In order to have a fair outcome, each voter must indicate the relative preference of the four candidates. For example, one voter might indicate Steve as her first choice, Jennifer as her second choice, and René as her third choice. There's no need for the voter to indicate her last choice because it's obviously Manuel. Based on each person's vote, a tally can be made in which the relative ordering of each possible combination of two candidates is considered. Visually, this amounts to putting a check mark in the appropriate places in the table at the top of the next page.

The middle column is needed for voters who indicate, for example, that their first choice is Manuel and their second choice is René, but don't indicate a third choice. In this case, the voter regards both Steve and Jennifer as equally acceptable or unacceptable. Let's suppose that after everyone's vote is counted and the counts are divided by the number of voters to produce percentages, the table looks like the one at the bottom of the next page.

First name ↓	Second name ↓	First name preferred over second name	Equal preference	Second name preferred over first name
Steve versus Manuel		✓		
Steve versus Jennifer		✓		
Steve versus René		✓		
Manuel versus Jennifer				✓
Manuel versus René				✓
Jennifer versus René		✓		

First name ↓	Second name ↓	First name preferred over second name	Equal preference	Second name preferred over first name
Steve versus Manuel		69%	0%	31%
Steve versus Jennifer		69%	0%	31%
Steve versus René		92%	0%	8%
Manuel versus Jennifer		38%	0%	62%
Manuel versus René		38%	8%	54%
Jennifer versus René		100%	0%	0%

(For more information about order-of-preference voting, see the interactive demonstration at: www.SolutionsCreative.com)

The bottom table summarizes, in numbers, the comparisons the voters have indicated. To fairly derive a winner based on these numbers is complex. But it's not beyond your capacity to understand if you understand mathematics and choose to spend the time understanding the following brief explanation. A computer would be programmed to accomplish what amounts to trying out every possible order-of-preference sequence. (If the four candidates were represented as A, B, C, and D, such sequences would include ABCD, ABDC, ACBD, ACDB, ADCB, ... DCBA, plus additional sequences in which two or more candidates are ranked at the same order of preference.) For each sequence, the cell (position in the table) from each horizontal row that applies to that sequence would be identified. The numbers in these cells, for one sequence, would be added together and divided by the number of vertical positions in the table (which is six in this case) to arrive at a number that indicates the popularity of each sequence. The sequence with the highest popularity number is the sequence that best represents the sequence the voters prefer. In this example the highest popularity number is 74% for the sequence: (1) Steve, (2) Jennifer, (3) René, and (4) Manuel. The candidate in the first position of this sequence, namely Steve, would be the winning candidate.

Complex, right? So complex that it requires a computer to calculate the result. But notice that this approach makes it possible for voters to indicate what they really prefer. This is an improvement over the usual approach of limiting choices to only two candidates. This approach enables the voter to say, in essence, "This is who I would really like to win, but since that isn't likely, this is the candidate I prefer over the other candidates." In contrast, traditional voting methods force a voter in this situation to make one of the following two choices:

- Vote for the candidate who has a chance of winning, even though this candidate isn't the one the voter prefers.
- Vote for the candidate the voter prefers, thereby weakening support for the candidate who is the most acceptable of the remaining choices.

Finally the point of this example can be seen. An understanding of complexity leads to a solution that's practical and, from some points of view (the voter's point of view in this case), isn't complex.

It's the explanation of the above voting scheme and the programming of the computer that's complex. The voting from the voter's point of view isn't complex. True, it's not as simple as current voting because more than one mark must be made. But voting is well within an average person's capacity to understand. To clarify this point, if voting were done using computer technology, such voting would amount to a voter answering the questions:

- Who is your first choice?
- If this candidate is eliminated because of a lack of popularity, who is your second choice?
- If both these candidates are eliminated because of a lack of popularity, who is your third choice?
- Your least favorite choice is ..., right?

Thus, voting can be made to be as simple as pointing to names on a screen. Notice that a voter doesn't need to understand the complexity of how the voters' preferences are combined to produce a single winner.

This example also illustrates another point. If there are only two candidates, the above complex calculations produce exactly the same numbers as a traditional voting approach. That is, the *popularity* numbers are simply the percentages of people voting for candidate A or candidate B, and the *sequence* that wins (AB or BA) is whichever has a popularity greater than fifty percent. This equivalence isn't a coincidence.

When something is fully understood, what commonly arises out of the complexity is something that gives the same results as a well-established approach — for the simple cases.

Until the complexities of voting are understood, there will be uncertainty about the fairness of voting for more than two options in a single ballot. Therefore, if you use the above voting approach in a small organization, such as a business or local organization, the issue of uncertainty would have to be addressed. One way to do this would be to have a run-off election between the two most popular candidates. If voters don't change their preferences between elections, the outcome will be the same as choosing the most popular candidate. It's crucial to understand that the above voting scheme applies only to voting for *candidates*. It is *not* appropriate for choosing *issues*. Why? In addition to the complexities already explained, voting for issues requires special consideration for the option of making no change. There are yet other complexities about voting beyond those explained here, so don't assume this example is a tutorial in the principles of fair voting. It simply points to the advantage of understanding complexity and the possibilities for improved ways of voting.

◄SUMMARY►

To the degree you clearly understand a complex situation, new solutions can appear. Ironically, those solutions can be simple rather than complex. For simple cases, those solutions are usually equivalent to conventional solutions.

Understanding People

Problems and improvable situations almost always involve people, so an understanding of people is essential.

Mikhail Gorbachev, the former leader of the Soviet Union, was told by one of the designers of Soviet nuclear power plants that the power plants he (the designer) helped design were unsafe. When Gorbachev asked a group of scientists whether this was true, they claimed the plants were safe. Gorbachev then assigned each scientist to inspect one nuclear power plant and asked each of these scientists to make a statement about the safety of his assigned plant, staking his personal reputation on his statement. After the inspections, eleven of the scientists reported that "their" plant was unsafe and should be shut down. Gorbachev recognized that people in a group respond differently when they are accountable as individuals.

Of course, everyone understands people to some degree. So what's needed is to deepen this understanding.

An important part of fully understanding people is to understand feelings.

Everyone knows that anger and fear are both negative feelings. But not everyone consciously notices that anger is a reaction to something that *has already happened* and fear is a reaction to a mental image of something that *has not already happened*. Thus, anger is oriented toward the past and fear is oriented toward the future. To broaden this concept of time as an important dimension in feelings, the table on the next page illustrates the relevance of time as it applies to feelings. The horizontal dimension is time and the vertical dimension is the dimension of positive versus negative.

	Already happened (past)	Happening now (present)	Has not already happened (future)
Positive	Pleased, Proud	Joyful	Hopeful, Optimistic
Negative	Angry, Guilty	Bored	Afraid, Unhopeful

Incidentally, the fact that the words *angry* and *guilty* appear in the same rectangle doesn't mean that anger and guilt are equivalent. It simply means that they share the same *time* and *positive versus negative* characteristics.

▷   Simply being able to *think about* feelings isn't enough to fully understand another person. You must be able to imagine yourself *feeling* what you would feel if you were subjected to the experiences heshe has experienced. A prerequisite to sensing other people's feelings is to become very familiar with all your own feelings, including deep, but commonly ignored, feelings such as hurt, anger, and fear. Reaching advanced levels of understanding people requires experiencing the joy and advanced kinds of love that arise after letting go of anger, guilt, fear, and hurt.

▷   Another important skill for dealing with people-related problems is an understanding of how to "speak" and "listen" without words. Obviously, such non-verbal communication includes facial expressions. Less obviously, actions convey messages. Consider a man who impresses women by driving an expensive car and taking his dates to fancy restaurants. He shouldn't be surprised to discover, after he's married, that he has attracted a woman who loves to spend money.

▷   Of course, there are problems involving children. Fortunately, there's an excellent book that clarifies lots of misunderstandings about how to deal with children. It's *Helping Young Children Flourish* by Aletha Solter.

An effective way to learn about relating to people of all ages is to learn, in person, from someone who really understands people. Many such people are counselors and teach their understanding through this profession. However, keep in mind that not all counselors clearly understand people. Also, not all counselors who clearly understand people can convey their understanding to you.

Here are a few sample insights that can make it easier to create solutions to people-oriented problems:

- When someone hurts you, it's natural to assume that the person *knew* heshe shouldn't have done what caused the hurt. However, it's useful to realize that *if* the person had known of a way to accomplish what heshe *believed* heshe *deserved* in a way that *did not inflict the hurt,* heshe would have done it that way.

  This reveals a way to deal with someone who is considering doing what you don't want himher to do. You can suggest a realistic alternative that doesn't hurt you, yet enables the person to accomplish what heshe thinks heshe deserves.

- It's useful to identify the feeling that is at the *root* of what you're feeling, because the feeling you're aware of isn't necessarily the root feeling.

  For example, the root feeling behind *anger* is the feeling of being *hurt* because, after all, someone hurting you is what prompts you to become angry. If the anger is out of proportion to the hurt, then the extra anger is typically the unresolved anger from an earlier similar hurt.

- *Fear* acts as a warning to indicate that harm — which can be emotional, such as embarrassment, rather than physical — can occur in the feared situation.

  Avoiding the feared situation isn't the only alternative. You also could improve a skill, gather knowledge, or deepen an understanding that would prepare you to deal effectively with the event you fear.

Additional insights appear in the *Being Aware Of Hidden Goals* section (in Chapter 3, *Reconsidering Your Goals*) and the *Uncluttering Your Mind* section (in Chapter 6, *Thinking In Alternate Ways*).

If your interpersonal communication skills are weak, consider taking a class that teaches such skills. Or, you could read *Looking Out, Looking In: Interpersonal Communication* by Ronald Adler and Neil Towne, which is a textbook for such classes.

Of course, an understanding of people cannot fit into one section of a book. What you've read are simply samples of the kinds of things that, when understood, make solving people-related problems easier.

◄SUMMARY►

A crucial part of solving real-life problems is to understand people. To reach that understanding, spend time studying this fascinating subject! The resulting insights can make solutions much easier to see.

Exercise 1. What's the main difference between guilt and anger? (An answer appears on page 312.)

Exercise 2. Identify the vertical and horizontal dimensions in the following matrix. Be specific. (An answer appears on page 312.)

Anger	Fear
Sadness	Hopelessness

Exercise 3. Select someone you know well and identify three specific things this person does that annoy you. Then, being completely honest with yourself, identify ways in which you act somewhat similarly.

Learning From People Who Understand

If you're unable to make sense of something on your own, seek out a clearer understanding from someone who really *understands*.

Managers in an automobile manufacturing plant discovered that the windshields in one of their car models frequently leaked. After unsuccessfully attempting to determine the cause of the problem, the company hired consultants to help them. They too were unable to determine the cause of the leaking windshields. But they discovered that the windshields installed during one particular shift didn't leak. They watched the windshields being installed during that shift and saw that the windshields were installed differently. When they asked the employee in charge why the instructions weren't being followed, he said, "If we did it that way, they would leak."

When looking for someone who understands a problem, don't be too influenced by titles, awards, academic achievements, attire, outward appearances, and how much money the person earns or charges. A more important consideration is how much *experience* the person has in dealing with situations similar to your situation. More broadly, what counts is whether the person clearly understands the problem you're trying to solve.

Where did Clarence Birdseye, who created a successful frozen foods business, learn how to quick-freeze vegetables? From Eskimos in Labrador. Few people have more experience with freezing than Eskimos.

When you've found a real expert, talk to them with a desire to more completely understand what isn't yet clear. This is very different from simply looking to them for advice — which, anyway, couldn't possibly take into account the many factors that only you're aware of. If the person you're talking to gives you advice, ask them to explain the reasoning behind their suggestions.

For many years, anthropologists and scientists tried to figure out how the huge stone statues on Easter Island could have been erected without the benefit of modern machinery. Various techniques were speculated, but no one could be sure how it was done. Finally, someone asked one of the natives living on the island if he knew. The native not only knew, but offered to demonstrate the process, and later did so. (Levers were used to pry the statue up a little bit at a time, and stones were used to keep it at the new angle of incline. When the angle was steep enough, the statue slid into the hole.) When asked why he hadn't told anyone before, he replied, "No one asked me."

Experts can provide valuable knowledge or insights, but they won't magically come knocking on your door. You must go to them to learn. However, personally asking questions of experts isn't the only way to learn from them. Many of the best experts have written books, magazine articles, and journal articles to share their knowledge and insights with you. Increasingly, audio and video tapes are also being used to share understanding. But, as with people, you must seek them out. So, consider reaching for a reference book, going to a bookstore or library, or perhaps looking through a videotape catalog for an expert teacher.

When looking for knowledge written by an expert, look for the same qualities as when looking for an expert to talk to. Read a few randomly picked sentences. Do you find clarifications, examples, and explanations that intrigue and entice you? Good. Or, do you find opinions, criticisms, rules, and instructions without supporting explanations? If so, unless you know the author to be a true expert, look elsewhere.

◄SUMMARY►

If you're unable to make sense of something on your own, seek out a book or person who clearly understands and can help you more clearly understand.

Exercise 1. Who would you go to for clarification or advice in the following situations? Look beyond what might seem to be obvious answers.

- Learning how to deal with allergies.
- Identifying which parts of a new child's toy will break first, and how soon that will happen.
- Identifying the best teachers in an elementary school.

Doing Your Own Thinking

In problem solving, if everyone else believes something, don't automatically believe it if it doesn't make sense to you. You're the person who suffers the consequences if you trust what's incorrect.

When Wilbur and Orville Wright were designing the shape of the cross-section of their airplane wing (the *airfoil*), they initially depended on tables of numbers printed in a book by a highly regarded glider expert. But, after doing careful experiments, they discovered that the printed information was incorrect. Thus, part of their success was due to designing their own airfoil shapes.

Interestingly, incorrect notions about airfoils still persist today because people tend to believe whatever they read in books. More than one would-be inventor has designed an innovative airplane wing based on the principle of airplane lift that's printed in countless science books. That principle states that an airplane wing provides lift because the air flows over the curved upper surface faster than the air flows beneath the flat lower surface, and that faster air flow results in a lower pressure over the top. When you first heard that explanation, did it make sense to you? Probably not. And for a good reason: it isn't correct! Accordingly, inventors who have believed this explanation have failed to design successful innovative wing designs.

Myth: Air flows farther over top; must flow faster; faster flow results in less pressure

In case you're interested in how an airplane wing really works, here's a more accurate explanation: The forward motion of an inclined wing exposes the bottom of the wing to high impact with the air in its path. The air hitting the wing's bottom deflects downward and, in reaction, the wing is pushed upward.

Air cannot quickly reach the top of the wing, so air pushes down on the top with less pressure than usual.

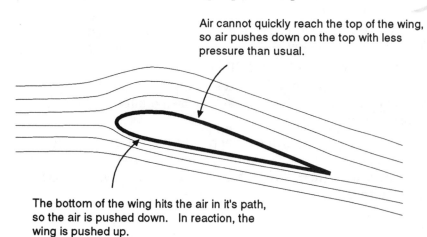

The bottom of the wing hits the air in it's path, so the air is pushed down. In reaction, the wing is pushed up.

Additional lift occurs because most of the air flowing over the top doesn't have time to get next to the top and push down with as much pressure as when the wing isn't moving. The upper side of the wing is curved (instead of flat) to allow the air above the wing to move into the space above the wing in a smooth flow instead of turbulently, which would vibrate the wing and increase friction. The wing's front edge is rounded so that the forward-most point of the wing, which determines the separation point for the air flowing around it, changes slightly when the wing's angle changes. In other words, the curved front edge enables the same airfoil shape to work at different angles.

This airfoil example illustrates the importance of not automatically believing something that doesn't make sense, if the only reason for believing it is that everyone else believes it. However, be careful not to misunderstand this suggestion as a recommendation to *disbelieve* what is popular or *disbelieve* what doesn't make sense. There's a major difference between *not believing* and *disbelieving*. *Not believing* consists of *being aware of the possibility* that something is untrue, whereas *disbelieving* consists of *believing* that something is *untrue*. To explain this subtle, but important, point another way, there are three, not two, possible cases for a belief:

- You know it's true and it fits with everything else you know to be true.

- You know it's not true. It conflicts with something you know to be true.

- You don't know whether it's true or not true. In some ways it's supported, and in other ways it's contradicted, by what you know to be true.

When you think a belief is true but don't know this with certainty, regard it as an *assumption*. You learned at the beginning of this chapter how to deal with assumptions.

Incidentally, the kinds of beliefs being discussed here are ones that can be tested. Beliefs that can't be tested fall into the realm of philosophy and religion.

A common way of letting other people do your thinking for you is to reject a creative idea simply because, "Surely someone else would have thought of it if it were worthwhile." Maybe this is true. Maybe it isn't.

Sometimes, people believe an idea because of who presents the idea. Sigmund Freud, a physician, dramatically advanced health care by popularizing the realization that traumatic childhood experiences commonly account for illnesses, such as hysteria and neuroses, which were previously thought to be caused by physical and biochemical problems. In addition, Freud also created theories about what typically goes on in the mind of young females. Many people trusted the correctness of such theories because Freud was regarded as an expert in understanding people. Yet, Freud himself said, "The great question ... which I have not been able to answer ... is *What does a woman want?*" Just because someone's understanding is very clear in many areas doesn't mean that it's clear in all related areas.

It's impossible to know what knowledge is true based only on who said it. So, always ask yourself, "Does this make sense?" If it makes sense, but conflicts with what you already believe, depend on experiments and experiences to reveal what's true.

Reality, not people's beliefs, is what determines what succeeds and fails. But, be careful not to confuse *simulations* of reality with reality itself. There are computer programs that are designed to predict the actions of complex systems, such as the atmosphere (weather) and economics. But beware! Such software makes use of simplifications, invalidated assumptions, and "empirically derived parameters" (which is a fancy term for "fudge factors"). Although it might appear that you're relying on the perfect accuracy of a computer to make predictions, you're actually relying on other people's *beliefs*. Computers simply do what programmers, who are people, tell them to do.

Having encouraged you to do your own thinking, a good place to start is to question the validity of everything written in this book! I haven't intentionally mislead you, but I'm likely to later discover some explanations written here that are ambiguous or misleading – or possibly incorrect. In advance, I apologize. But if you've learned to do your own thinking, you won't run into resulting problems because you'll be questioning whatever doesn't make sense.

◄SUMMARY►

Seek to clearly understand in ways that make sense to you. As you do, don't be intimidated if your understanding differs from what other people believe. Find out, through experimentation, which, if either, understanding is correct. Many creative solutions lie hidden behind believed, but invalid, "understandings".

Exercise 1. There's a tendency to limit choices of health care services to only the ones paid for by health insurance policies. What other services also prevent or cure health problems?

Noticing What You Normally Don't

Looking beyond what most people focus on can lead, in a natural way, to creative alternatives.

Consider what happens when someone tends to talk more than the other people in a conversation. It's easy to assume that such a person likes to dominate conversations. Although this might be true, there's another factor involved. Notice that a dominant talker typically starts talking after only a brief moment of silence. In contrast, a less talkative person waits longer before speaking up. This suggests an alternative to the usual approach of saying, "You talk too much." An alternative would be to say, "I like to wait for one or two seconds of silence before assuming that someone's stopped talking. Since you don't wait that long, I end up not saying much."

This example illustrates that looking beyond what most people focus on can lead to creative alternatives. But, don't simply notice what *other people* fail to notice. That's relatively easy. It's much harder, yet more useful, to notice what *you* normally overlook.

To become more observant, allow what you see and hear to come into your mind. This sounds simple, but it's harder to do than what comes naturally, which is to *compare* what's already in your mind with what's happening outside. If you find yourself thinking "Yes, just as I expected", then you're *comparing* instead of *observing*.

◄SUMMARY►

When a problem arises without an apparent solution, there's usually something you're failing to notice. What is it?

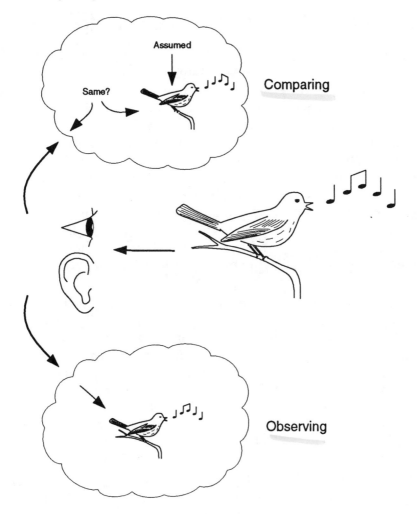

Exercise 1. Listen to some familiar music. But, instead of anticipating what comes next or thinking "Yes, this is how it goes", notice new aspects of the music. Of course, notice the music's rhythm and melody, but also listen for other aspects of the music. What's the last thing you notice?

Investing Effort To Reach Insights

▶ Contrary to some people's belief, insights don't arrive only by lying around waiting for them to pop into the mind.

➤ Consider the classic story of Archimedes. He was so excited by an important insight that he suddenly interrupted his bath and supposedly ran naked through the streets shouting "Eureka!", which is Greek for "I've found it!" What he found was the solution to the problem his king had hired him to solve, namely to determine whether the craftsmen who had made a golden crown for the king had put all the supplied gold into the crown — and none of the gold into their pockets. The drama and excitement of Archimedes' moment of insight draws so much attention to this one event that his long hours of effort seeking to understand weight and density seem insignificant in comparison. Yet that thinking effort is what made his moment of insight possible.

Furthermore, most people focus most of their attention on the *event* that triggered Archimedes' insight. Specifically, he saw that water overflowed a bath (a pool by our standards) as he or someone else got into the bath. Yet, this event alone wasn't enough. Anyone else who lacked his clear understanding of weight and density couldn't have translated the overflowing water into an effective way to measure the density of the king's golden crown. Archimedes had to spend several seconds or minutes understanding the implications of the water overflow before it was appropriate to run through the streets yelling "Eureka!"

▶ You now know that insights must be both preceded and followed by effort and thinking. Therefore, the insights you're hoping for won't arrive if your only focus is on the insights themselves.

It's true that sometimes a creative solution or innovation is created entirely by luck. However, this happens far less often than it might appear. More often, accidental creative ideas arrive after effort is invested trying to accomplish something else. Although the effort produced something unexpected, effort still preceded the accidental creative result.

▶ This need to focus effort on something specific can cause problems if your goal is simply to "be creative" or if your goal is to invent something of value without caring what you create. In these cases there's no focus except, perhaps, to impress people or earn money. Therefore, you need a *specific goal*. This requirement is clearly portrayed in the popular saying, "Necessity is the mother of invention." So, if you aren't aware of any particular goal, choose at least one specific problem to solve. In other words, choose your "necessity". Make sure it's a goal you're willing to put effort into achieving, because this is what it will take: effort. The insights will be a *by-product* of the effort.

To be fair, there are ways to prompt random creative ideas. But the results of using such techniques are typically unimpressive and of less value than what is created through effort.

Louis Pasteur remarked, "Chance favors only the mind which is prepared."

◀SUMMARY▶

To think creatively you must invest lots of *effort* to accomplish something specific. It requires curiosity, diligence, and a willingness to continue asking the question, "What isn't yet completely clear?"

Considering Your Goals Some More

In Chapter 3, *Reconsidering Your Goals,* you learned ways to clarify and refine your goals so that your goals include effective solutions you might otherwise overlook. Here are more ways to clarify and refine your goals. They involve more subtlety than the ones you learned earlier, but they're well worth learning.

Solving The Whole Problem

A useful strategy for solving a large problem is to break it down into separate small problems. As you focus on solving each small problem, don't lose sight of the whole problem.

Apparently one manufacturer of radio-controlled toy cars initially blocked out a superior solution because of such tunnel vision. One of their radio-controlled cars had two functions: (1) making the car go (or not go); and (2) steering (turning left or right or not turning). The initial design of the toy car was based on putting a motor in the back to *power* the *rear* wheels. This was the traditional way to power both real and toy cars, so it seemed appropriate. The design of the turning mechanism remained as a separate problem. The solution was clever. It used an electrically activated *brake* on each *front* wheel. (If the left front wheel was slowed down by the brake, the car turned left. Conversely for the right. If neither wheel was slowed down, the car traveled straight.) An illustration of the design appears on the next page.

A later design of the radio-controlled car was simpler, cheaper, and faster. A motor was used to *power* each *front* wheel *independently.* If both motors were on, the car traveled straight. If only one motor was on, the car turned according to which motor was on. This solution was even more clever because both the power and the turning were handled by the same devices (two motors). (It was cheaper because toy motors are standard devices whereas toy brakes must be specially manufactured. The car was faster on turns

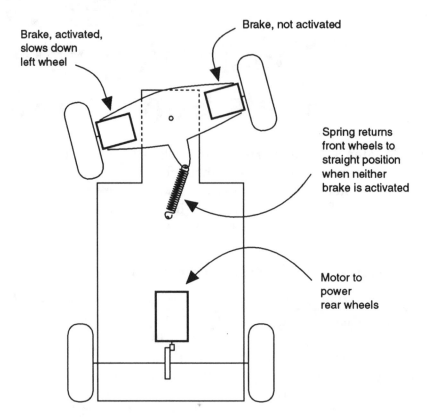

Brake, activated, slows down left wheel

Brake, not activated

Spring returns front wheels to straight position when neither brake is activated

Motor to power rear wheels

because there was no extra drag.) This second design is illustrated on the next page.

This toy car example illustrates that early commitments in choosing how to solve a problem can block creative ideas. When you realize you're about to reject an idea because it conflicts with a solution you've already chosen for another part of the problem, step back and view the whole problem.

Below are three common tendencies in choosing how to subdivide a problem. The first two were illustrated in the toy car example.

- The *easiest* parts of the problem are isolated and solutions are immediately assigned.
- The *hardest* part of the problem is initially put aside to be solved later.
- The parts of the problem you can *easily identify* are dealt with first and the less obvious parts are postponed or ignored.

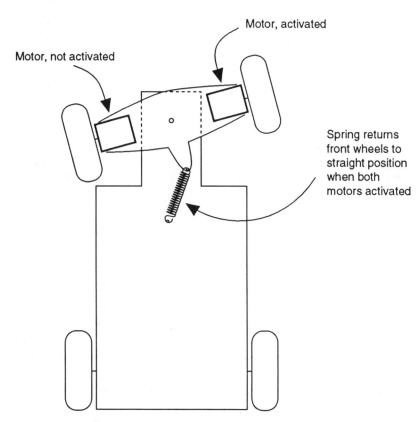

Motor, activated

Motor, not activated

Spring returns front wheels to straight position when both motors activated

Separating a problem into individual parts is *not* what limits creativity. What limits creativity is isolating the parts of the problem from one another in your mind.

If you work in an organization, such as a corporation or government agency, you might be asked to solve a problem that's actually a portion of a larger problem. If you create a solution to the whole problem that requires cooperation outside your designated territory, what can you do if other people in the organization reject your suggestion? Here are some alternatives:

- Regard the problem of talking people into adopting your solution as a separate problem with a separate solution.

- Say nothing more and wait to see if an idea similar to yours is implemented later.

- Make sure your "solution" doesn't simply shift the problem to a different area. If it does, it isn't a solution because a solution eliminates a problem from all areas.

- Recognize that an effective solution to the problem exists, but the people making decisions are choosing not to solve it.
- Appreciate getting an opportunity to practice your creative problem solving skills. Such practice will make it easier to solve other problems later.

◀SUMMARY▶

Subdividing a problem creates *artificial* boundaries. Creative solutions often cross those boundaries in unexpected ways. Keep the whole problem in mind as you focus on solving any part of it.

Creating Tools

Creating a tool can open up new possibilities.

Leopold Mannes and Leopold Godowsky were achieving promising results in their efforts to develop practical color photography, so Eastman Kodak Company hired them to continue their development efforts. Because Mannes and Godowsky were also professional singers, workers at Kodak weren't too surprised to hear them singing in the darkroom. What the workers didn't realize was that Mannes and Godowsky used the timing of the songs to measure the timing of their chemical reactions. This timing method was an essential tool in the days before darkroom timers and darkroom *safety lights* were invented. Eventually, the two men succeeded in inventing practical color photography.

One way to accomplish what otherwise seems impossible is to create a new tool. The tool, in itself, isn't the solution you're looking for. It's what the tool enables you to accomplish that's important.

Isaac Newton spent countless hours creating a new mathematical tool that he called "fluctions". It's equivalent to what we now call calculus. Initially he used it to account for the time it takes for the moon to move around the earth. Later, Newton used his fluctions to mathematically prove Edmund Halley's suspicion that the planets are attracted to the sun by a force that is reciprocal to the square of their distance from the sun. Specifically, Newton's calculations matched what had already been observed, namely, that planets orbit the sun in elliptical paths. Newton then learned that the same mathematical principle also applies to comets and that they move in either elliptical (for returning comets) or hyperbolic (for one-time comets) paths around the Sun. The match between observed facts and Newton's simple mathematical principle confirmed that the same force that attracts an apple to the ground attracts planets, stars, and comets to one another. Is the effort to create a tool worth it? Newton's creation of fluctions illustrates that a tool that's useful in one situation (namely accounting for the motion of the moon around the earth) can be useful in other situations (such as accounting for the motion of planets and comets around the sun and the motion of an apple falling to the ground). So, even though no use for the tool is expected after solving the current problem, the tool is likely to prove useful later in other situations.

Is there something you could create that would make a project easier to accomplish, even though you might discard it when you've finished working on the project?

◄SUMMARY►

A tool is like a bridge. It's worth creating to get someone somewhere, but it has little value otherwise. Yet, like a bridge, it can be worth leaving intact after it has served its purpose.

Considering Flexibility Instead Of Standardization

Standardization has become so popular, because of its usefulness in manufacturing, that its opposites — flexibility and diversity — are often neglected.

Of course, standardization offers considerable advantages in some situations. Imagine the impossibility of safe driving if each person could choose which side of the road to drive on. Or, imagine that flashlight and radio batteries came in hundreds of different sizes and electrical characteristics instead of the few standardized ones (*D*, *C*, *AA*, *9-volt*, etc.) now in use.

However, standardization isn't always the best approach, especially when people or nature is involved.

In agriculture, seeds are usually bred as if a few kinds of seeds can meet the needs of all farmers. Seed growers usually standardize both the desired qualities — such as largeness, machine pickability, and appearance — and the anticipated growing conditions — such as climate and the type of irrigation, soil, fertilization, and pest control. The result is that the seeds match the growing conditions of only some farms and don't grow as intended on other farms. Innovative seed companies have begun to offer a greater variety of seeds to match specific climates and farming practices that aren't average. This makes it possible for farmers to choose seeds that match their farm's conditions. As an added long-term benefit, diversity in plant types makes it harder for a new pest to evolve that's well adapted to wiping out one of the standardized kinds of plants.

Whenever the words *best* or *optimize* appear, recognize that multiple choices that fit differing needs — instead of a single standard that fits an average need — might be better.

Neither standardization nor flexibility is the *best* approach. Each should be considered for its advantages and disadvantages.

◄SUMMARY►

Flexibility and diversity can offer significant advantages, especially when people and nature, rather than just objects, are involved.

Exercise 1. Real estate developers who build large apartment complexes typically use the same floor layout, or the mirrored image of it, in every building. What advantages does this standardization offer? Who benefits by this advantage? What disadvantages are there to having all the apartments nearly alike? What advantages could be gained by taking a different approach? Who would benefit?

Chapter 10

Taking Action

A good idea in your head doesn't do anyone any good. When you've created a solution you really like, you must act.

Unfortunately, simply revealing your solution isn't enough. People rarely welcome new ideas, even ones that later turn out to be highly acclaimed. Fortunately, there are ways to overcome criticism and resistance — provided your idea really offers significant benefits. These are the tools you'll learn in this chapter.

Deciding Whether You're Ready To Act On Your Idea

Before taking action, you must ask yourself, "Am I ready to act on my idea?" The answer isn't necessarily "Yes" simply because you've come up with a creative idea and have refined it into something practical.

In choosing whether to act, it makes a difference whether people are now suffering due to hurt or pain. The suffering might be in the form of physical suffering as in the case of disease, or psychological suffering as in the case of children being separated from their parents. Suffering, as the word is used here, amounts to more than annoyance. For instance, managers of a business whose profits have recently fallen aren't actually suffering. If your creative idea is an innovation rather than broadly being a solution to a problem, the existing annoyance probably doesn't amount to suffering.

If you're uncertain about whether to implement your solution and people aren't suffering, do *not* implement your solution. The risk isn't worthwhile, especially if your solution has some undesirable side effects. As an example, using the existing alphabet for English is annoying because people need to memorize special spellings for many words and need a dictionary or knowledgeable person to learn how to pronounce or spell new words. However, few people would tolerate the effort of learning a new fully phonetic alphabet, in spite of the advantages it could offer.

If suffering is going on, a solution that ends the suffering might be acceptable even if the solution has undesirable side effects — if those side effects are significantly less severe than the suffering. Such situations involve risk, so make use of what you learned in the *Understanding The Dimensions Of Risk* section in Chapter 7, *Thinking Dimensionally*. Specifically, for each possible outcome, identify how much would be gained, how much would be lost, and the probability of each outcome. In rating possible losses, take into account the acceptability of possible losses. For instance, health hazards to consumers who use a new food product aren't acceptable, whereas losing money and having to lay off employees is, by comparison, more acceptable.

Before making your final decision as to whether you're ready to implement your solution, ask yourself the questions listed below. However, don't answer the questions with words. Instead, pay attention to the *gut-level reaction* that arises the moment you read the question. This is the same kind of reaction that's explained in the *Developing And Using Your Intuitive Judgment* section in Chapter 6, *Thinking In Alternate Ways*. Now, with your potential solution clearly in mind, check your reaction to the following questions:

- Does it solve the problem?
- Does it eliminate the problem or just eliminate the symptoms?
- Does it solve the problem permanently or just temporarily?
- Does it eliminate the problem or just shift the problem to another area?
- Does it solve the whole problem or just part of the problem?
- Is the solution simple or is it complex?
- Does this solution benefit nearly everyone involved or only a select few?
- Are there disadvantages for the people who are supposed to benefit?
- What are the undesirable consequences of implementing this solution?
- Are you willing to accept responsibility for these negative consequences?

- Is there something about the solution you hope no one will ever find out?
- Do you have any reservations or doubts about the above answers?

If you have no reservations, you're ready to take action! Go for it!

On the other hand, if you have some reservations and people aren't currently suffering, you're not ready to implement your idea.

If you have reservations about a solution to a problem in which suffering will continue if nothing is done, then you must make a decision and accept the consequences.

If you've heard that risk is a normal part of creative efforts, keep in mind that this connection mainly refers to financial risk. There might be some uncertainty about whether you will profit from your creative idea, but there shouldn't be uncertainty about whether your idea will create improvement.

If you have some uncertainty about whether your idea will create improvement, allow for the possibility that you're uncertain because neither choice — implementing or not implementing your idea — really deals appropriately with the problem. In spite of your efforts, you might not have yet created a solution to the problem.

A wise decision is easier to the extent you clearly understand the situation you want to improve. To the extent you don't clearly understand, there's uncertainty and risk. It might appear that you can bypass the need for clear understanding by using intuitive judgment to help make your decision, but this belief overlooks the importance of a clear understanding at an unconscious level.

It's easy to think you're ready to take action when, in fact, you're not. It might be that you've simply gotten stuck. Perhaps you've identified all the possible alternatives imaginable and have chosen the best one. But the process of creative problem solving is more than a process of creating lots of choices and then choosing one of them. It's a matter of creating an effective solution.

If you've gotten stuck, here are suggestions for getting unstuck:

- Seek to understand the situation more clearly, as explained in Chapter 8, *Understanding Clearly*. Do this to prompt an over-looked, but very important, insight.
- Apply the tools in Chapter 3, *Reconsidering Your Goals*.

- Consider that the alternatives you've collected might contain all the *elements* of a good solution, and that you can create that better solution by extracting and combining the best elements of your alternatives. This tool is explained in the *Choosing By Elimination With Extraction* section in Chapter 4, *Exploring Your Many Alternatives*. In turn, it makes use of the tools explained in the *Combining Ideas* section (also in Chapter 4) and the *Incorporating Advantageous Aspects Of Other Ideas* section in Chapter 5, *Refining Your Ideas*.

- Access your subconscious thoughts as explained in the *Using Subconscious Thinking To Provide Insights* section (in Chapter 6, *Thinking In Alternate Ways*), to find out if your "subconscious mind" has already figured out what your conscious mind hasn't yet figured out.

- Put the problem aside and come back to it later with a fresh mind.

In the remainder of this chapter you'll learn how to overcome other people's resistance to new solutions, but none of the tools can overcome a deficiency in the solution.

◄SUMMARY►

If you have any reservations about what you're thinking about implementing, don't implement it; you aren't yet done with the creative process. However, if your solution would end suffering and wouldn't add new suffering, it might be worth the risk. If you've created a solution that you have no reservations about, you're ready to take action!

Handling Criticism

Criticism is inevitable whether it's justified or not, so expect your creative solutions to be criticized.

History is filled with examples of innovations that have initially been heavily criticized and later become very much appreciated. Consider these examples:

- Many established chemists strongly opposed Dmitry Mendeleyev's periodic table of elements when he first introduced it.

- The first steamboat in the United States, built by Robert Fulton, was called "Fulton's folly".

- Outrage was a common initial response to translating the Bible into languages that people could read.
- It took 56 years after Dom Perignon invented champagne (in 1714) for the French to decide they liked it.
- Fannie Farmer's *Boston Cooking School Cook Book* was initially controversial because the recipes used quantities such as one cup instead of one handful.
- Eastman Kodak Company rejected Edwin Land's idea for an instant camera. So, Land started his own business, Polaroid, which became a major competitor to Kodak.

The list could go on and on, but you get the point. Typically, criticisms of your idea will persist until your creative idea has demonstrated its value. As Mark Twain said, "The man with an original idea is a crank until the idea succeeds."

Why do people resist change? Here are some common reasons:

- A change introduces the risk of things getting worse, instead of better.
- Making a change always requires mental effort and usually requires physical effort.
- Some people aren't bothered by the current situation. Usually, a problem has to become quite annoying before people are interested in making a change.

Now that you're prepared to expect criticism, how can you handle it? The secret is to realize that there are different kinds of criticism, each of which is best handled differently.

Consider the recent innovation of printing Universal Product Code (UPC) labels on grocery items. This innovation eliminates the need to put price tags on the items. The stripes of the UPC code represent, to a computer, a number that's different for each kind of item. For instance, hypothetically, item number 1119435048 might be a 16 ounce can of green beans from the Pick-a-Bean company. Notice that the item's price isn't included in the code. When people first heard that the UPC bar code eliminated the need for price tags, many people assumed that the code included the item's price. Therefore, a common criticism was, "That's no good because the price can't easily be changed." This is an example of a criticism that's *not valid*. Not only is the item's price not printed on the label, but the price, which is stored in an on-site computer, can be changed faster than someone can take an item off the shelf and get it to the checkout counter.

When someone criticizes a creative idea you suggest and the criticism is *not valid,* recognize that there's no evidence of a need to change the idea itself — although you might want to improve how you explain your idea.

Suppose that, instead of the above scheme, the original plan for Universal Product Codes had been to put the item's price into the bar code. Many people would have appropriately criticized this idea by saying, "That's no good because the price can't easily be changed." This would have been a *valid* criticism.

When someone criticizes your creative solution and the criticism is *valid,* you should improve your solution. Specifically, refine your idea to eliminate the flaw or weakness that's been appropriately criticized.

If someone responds to your idea with "I don't like it" or "It won't work", notice that the feedback is *judgmental* (relating to opinion). Judgmental criticism conveys an opinion of badness (in contrast to goodness), but alone doesn't provide information that indicates whether the judgment is valid.

An example of judgmental criticism would be someone saying "It won't work" to the UPC bar code innovation in its early stages. This opinion would have failed to provide enough information to determine whether the person saw a genuine flaw.

To deal with a judgmental criticism such as "It won't work!", ask the critic "What part of the idea won't work?" or "Why won't it work?" Do so with a genuine desire to determine whether they've seen something you've overlooked. Based on the critic's reply, you will hopefully be able to determine whether their criticism is valid or not. For example, if the critic says "It won't work when too many people are involved" and you realize that, indeed, it won't work in that case, the critic has revealed a flaw worth eliminating.

Ironically, of all the different kinds of criticism, the most useful kind is the one that's hardest to accept: *specific valid* criticism. Such feedback reveals you haven't yet finished refining your solution, and this is disappointing to realize. Yet, such criticisms are the most useful because they reveal flaws or weaknesses that would later create new problems to resolve.

A critic, when asked to be more specific about hisher judgmental criticism, often won't be able to do so. The critic might say something like, "I just know it won't work." In such situations, accept that the person is either unable or unwilling to offer you useful insights.

Here's a summary of the three kinds of criticisms explained so far:

Type of criticism	Characteristics of criticism	Appropriate response
Valid	The criticism includes enough information to indicate that, indeed, there's a flaw or weakness in the idea.	Refine the idea to eliminate the flaw or weakness, but without losing it's advantages.
Not valid	Your idea clearly doesn't have the disadvantage the critic claims it does. Apparently, the critic doesn't completely understand the idea.	Improve your ability to explain the idea to avoid future misunderstandings.
Judgmental	The reaction to the idea is negative, but there isn't enough information to indicate whether the negative reaction is valid or not.	Ask the critic for more specific information in hopes of learning whether hisher criticism is valid.

Valid, invalid, and judgmental criticisms aren't the only kinds of criticisms you'll hear. Someone might say, "You're a foolish person" or "Gosh you're stupid!" Notice that these are criticisms of you, not your idea. The integrity of your idea remains unshaken. If such criticism shakes your personal integrity, you might want to boost your self-confidence.

A comment that can arise in the early stages of trying to solve a problem is, "It can't be done." Don't worry. Simply translate this sentence into what it really means, which is, "It hasn't been done yet."

When you suggest an idea and are told "We've already tried that", ask the person what has already been tried. What's been tried might be similar to, yet significantly different from, what you have in mind. If you're sure that your idea will work even though their attempt failed, point out the feature in your idea that will make the difference.

Occasionally, someone will compliment your idea! When they do, notice whether it's judgmental or specific. If their compliment is specific, such as "I like the fact that a thief won't even notice that he's leaving evidence", then keep this compliment in mind when you consider changing your idea to remove other flaws. On the other hand, if the compliment is judgmental, such as "Hey, I like that idea!", then smile, appreciate the good feeling, and remember this appreciation for later when you find yourself in the midst of invalid and judgmental criticisms.

Now that you're armed with strategies for handling criticism, ask for opinions from people whose judgment is usually reliable. However, don't ask for feedback when an idea is still fresh and therefore fragile. Nor should you postpone asking for feedback until after you've committed yourself to implementing a creative idea exactly as planned. Instead, ask for opinions from friends or associates while you're still willing to make changes, but after you've built up some confidence in your idea.

Your goal in seeking opinions should be to get help seeing flaws you've overlooked. To accomplish this goal, focus on what the criticism or complement reveals — instead of simply focusing on whether the reaction is positive or negative.

◄SUMMARY►

Your creative solutions will be criticized whether they deserve criticism or not. What matters isn't how enthusiastically your creative solutions are welcomed, but, rather, do they work? The table in this section summarizes how to deal with valid, invalid, and judgmental criticism. Valid criticisms, although hardest to accept, are the most valuable — if you act on them by further refining your solution.

Exercise 1. Here are some sample ideas and criticisms. For each one, determine which kind of criticism it is and how you would handle the criticism. Allow for the fact that realistic criticisms don't necessarily fit neatly into only one of the categories explained above.

Idea being suggested	*Criticism*
"There are two parts to this idea...."	"The second part of your idea is based on a theory that has recently been disproved."
"First, we could .... Then, we could .... Finally, as the seventh step, we could ...."	"It's too complicated."
"Let's base people's taxes on the spin of a roulette wheel."	"Gambling doesn't belong in government activities."

Persuading By Benefitting Others

When promoting your creative solution, focus on how your idea will benefit your listener.

In the early stages of developing the (direct current) electric motor, Michael Faraday went to the Prime Minister of Great Britain, William Gladstone, to ask for development money. After a demonstration of Faraday's crude electric motor, the Prime Minister asked, "What good is that?" Faraday replied, "Someday you will be able to tax it!" He got the money. Notice that Faraday didn't explain how electric motors would ease the burden of laborers or make money for himself. Instead, he explained how the person he was talking to, the Prime Minister, would benefit.

Sales people learn that an effective alternative to being pushy is to point out how the customer would benefit by buying the product. Similarly, when you're trying to convince someone to adopt a solution you've created, emphasize how the person you're talking to will benefit by adopting your idea. However, make sure your listener would really benefit.

One of Thomas Edison's early inventions was a mechanism for recording the votes of Congressmen. It took 45 minutes for Congress to vote by roll call and Edison's invention would dramatically reduce that delay, so he was confident he could sell his invention to Congress. He was surprised to learn that the members of Congress liked the lengthy voting process because it enabled them to trade votes during voting. Edison vowed that he would never make another invention that wasn't wanted.

Usually, innovative ideas aren't appreciated as much as the innovator expects. Here are three reasons for the lack of appreciation:

- Other people don't share the innovator's confidence that the solution or innovation will actually work.
- The innovator fails to listen to people to find out what they want and don't want.
- The innovator overlooks advantages of leaving things as they are.

As an example of overlooking an advantage of leaving things as they are, suppose someone suggests a way to completely eliminate inflation. Eliminating inflation sounds desirable, yet inflation motivates people to put money in banks where, in addition to earning interest, the money is available for loans to buy houses and start businesses. If inflation didn't exist, many people would keep their money in currency, which would take money out of circulation and place heavy demands on the printing of currency.

If, after explaining how your listener will benefit by adopting your innovation, heshe resists your idea, reconsider. This suggestion doesn't mean you should give up. It simply means you should make sure your idea really does offer benefits — that people really want.

◄SUMMARY►

When you try to persuade someone to adopt your creative idea, point out how the person you're talking to will benefit by adopting it. But, make sure you know what people want, and don't overlook advantages that existing conventions offer.

Exercise 1. Landlords commonly hear pleas such as "I've looked at lots of places, I really like this place, and I need to move soon!", but less often hear evidence of responsibility and other characteristics they're looking for. If you were trying to talk a reluctant landlord into renting to you, what would you say?

Creating Implementation Ideas

In addition to using your creative skills to create a solution, use your creative skills to create ways to overcome people's resistance to accepting your solution.

When shopping carts first appeared in grocery stores, customers were reluctant to use them. No one wanted to be the only person in a store using a cart. One grocer cleverly overcame this resistance by hiring people to walk up and down the aisles with the carts, pretending to shop. Seeing that other people were using the carts, his customers used them too. After a while, he no longer needed to hire the cart pushers.

When you meet resistance, consider the problem of convincing people to adopt your idea as a separate problem with a separate, and perhaps creative, solution. For instance, after designing a new work schedule, you could come up with a creative way to talk your boss into accepting it.

Sometimes, the key to implementing a creative solution is to come up with a creative way to explain the solution. President Franklin D. Roosevelt used this approach to convince U.S. politicians and citizens to support his Lend-Lease Act. He compared the legislation to a person loaning a garden hose to a neighbor to help the neighbor put out a fire in the neighbor's house. This simple analogy made it easy for people to understand that the Lend-Lease Act allowed the United States to aid Great Britain's fight against Hitler's Germany without violating treaties that prohibited direct participation in the war.

◄SUMMARY►

When you find people resisting one of your solutions, look for creative ways to overcome their resistance. In other words, regard their resistance as a separate problem with a separate solution.

Implementing A Complete Solution

In the *Solving The Whole Problem* section (in Chapter 9, *Considering Your Goals Some More*) you learned the value of creating a solution to the whole *problem*. Now, it's important to recognize the value of implementing a whole *solution*.

Consider public education. It's clear that the inadequate quality of public education can be improved by not waiting for mediocre or unenthusiastic teachers to retire before finding better teachers. Yet simply ending the tenure system that protects teachers from being laid off doesn't solve the problem. Most of the reason job security, in the form of tenure, is emphasized by teacher's labor unions is because extending a teacher's career is a way to compensate for the low wages teachers earn. Eliminating tenure systems that protect mediocre teachers from losing their jobs cannot be done alone. A way to increase wages for competent teachers must also be created as part of the solution to improving public education.

Sometimes a problem can only be solved by implementing a collection of changes as a package. Attempting to make only some of the needed changes can fail to solve the problem.

◄SUMMARY►

Attempts to implement only one part of a complete solution, without also implementing the other parts of the solution, can fail to solve a problem.

Persevering, With Flexibility

If you've created a solution to a problem, don't just think, "Wow! My wonderful idea could dramatically eliminate that problem!" This is your cue to take action.

While working at Detroit Electric Company, Henry Ford worked on his own time developing an internal combustion engine for a motorized vehicle. Ford attended a company dinner at which the already successful Thomas Edison was a guest of honor. Edison overheard Ford explaining his personal project to people nearby and, because Edison was hard of hearing, Ford was soon seated next to Edison. After Ford had answered Edison's questions, Edison slammed his fist on the table and said, "Young man, that's the thing! You have it — the self-contained unit carrying its own fuel with it! Keep at it!" Ford later credited Edison's encouragement as inspiring him to pursue what eventually became the affordable assembly-line-manufactured *Model T* automobile.

People who are skilled in thinking aren't necessarily skilled in acting, so you might need to learn some skills for taking action.

A creative problem solver needs to achieve a balance between perfectionism and boldness. Perfectionists spend lots of time thinking about the possible negative consequences of their actions. This enables them to predict future criticism or punishment and avoid it by improving their planned actions. This refinement skill is valuable because the resulting ideas tend to be nearly flawless. However, a complete perfectionist doesn't act on a plan until the plan is completely flawless (perfect), which it never is. In contrast, bold people often attempt to implement ideas without carefully refining them. They do so because they know that the more attempts they make, the more successes they'll have. This courage is inspiring. However, along with more successes, their haste brings more failures.

Imitate a perfectionist's *refinement skills* and a bold person's *courage*. But *don't imitate* the perfectionist's *preoccupation with perfection* or the bold person's *haste*.

Creative solutions are seldom adopted quickly, so you must have patience. If the idea is truly worthwhile it will be adopted eventually. Yet, along with being patient, also be persistent. People won't adopt an idea that no one promotes.

It takes a strong belief in the value of what you've created to motivate you through the rough parts of implementing your ideas. To inspire yourself to take action and persist in the presence of obstacles, imagine people using your solution and genuinely appreciating it. Make this image real in your mind. At the same time, be careful that your belief in your creation doesn't blind you to its flaws.

If you find yourself pushing against an obstacle that isn't budging, try something different. Don't waste your effort trying the same thing again. Trying the same thing harder might work, but why not use your creative problem solving skills to find an easier path? If you find yourself wondering whether the problem you're attacking is too big, consider breaking the problem down into smaller steps and try taking one step at a time. These suggestions simply amount to applying the tools explained in Chapter 3, *Reconsidering Your Goals*.

If lots of people object to what you're trying to do, reread the *Handling Criticism* section earlier in this chapter. Specifically, realize that objections like "It can't be done" and "It will never work" can be largely ignored. But, if people tell you "I wouldn't buy it if it only cost five cents!" or "You've overlooked the damage it will do to the fish that use that river", then reconsider what you've created. You might need to make changes in your solution.

In taking action, you might find yourself fearing failure, fearing mistakes, fearing success (yes, this happens!), and fearing criticism. Don't let such fears stop you. Such fears probably indicate there are some skills you lack. Consider learning those skills to prepare yourself to handle the situations you now fear. Otherwise, learn how to avoid feared situations. But push forward!

There are two types of fear that should concern you: a fear that your solution won't work, or a fear that it might have some bad side effects. If either of these fears arise, you need to do more refining and testing before you're ready to take action.

To the degree you're confident of your idea's worth, take action and don't give up! Let your enthusiasm for what you've created motivate you!

◄SUMMARY►

In taking action, imitate a bold person's courage, but not his/her haste, and imitate a perfectionist's refinement skills, but not his/her preoccupation with perfection. If obstacles — other than a poorly-designed solution — stand in your way, learn the skills you lack, or apply the tools in Chapter 3, *Reconsidering Your Goals*.

To implement what you've created, you must *do* something. Your muscles and heart must take over from your brain. If you've already created a useful solution, the time to begin moving is *now*!

Chapter 11

Using The Creative Problem Solver's Tools

This chapter answers these and other questions about using the creative problem solver's tools:

- *Which tools are the most important to learn?*
- *How are the tools used together to solve a problem?*
- *Can the tools be used to avoid problems before the problems arrive?*
- *Can I use the tools to invent something and become rich?*
- *How can the tools be used in group situations?*
- *How can the tools be taught to children and adults?*

Practicing Using The Tools

Tools are worthless if they just sit in a toolbox. To get these tools out of the toolbox — which amounts to transforming the explained *techniques* into mental *skills* — you must *use* them.

Which tools should you focus on learning? Start with the tools that interest you the most. Later, progress to tools that you don't feel comfortable with. If, instead, you focus on perfecting the use of only a few tools, you won't be fully learning creative problem solving. Excellence in using some tools doesn't compensate for weaknesses in using other tools. This is analogous to automobile driving in which someone with poor car-driving skills cannot reduce the chances of getting into an accident by becoming an excellent storyteller or earning lots of money to put in the bank. In both driving and creative problem solving, your weakest skills limit what you can accomplish.

All the tools appear in the *Radial Outline Of The Creative Problem Solver's Tools* (pages 315-321). Consider marking with a pencil the tools you want to focus on learning next. Asterisks already identify which tools are especially useful but challenging to learn.

One approach to learning the tools is to choose a tool at the end of a day and look for opportunities throughout the following day to apply that tool. On other days, practice applying other tools.

Another approach is to choose a problem you want to solve and look through the tools in the *Radial Outline Of The Creative Problem Solver's Tools* (pages 315-321) to identify tools that seem promising. Choose one of the promising tools, read the examples and important points in the section that describes that tool, then figure out how to apply it to your chosen problem. After you've used this approach many times, choose to learn tools you've previously neglected.

As chiropractors you'll often have to remind
your patients to use good posture.

In choosing a problem to solve, don't start with a big problem ◀❶ or a desire to create a major innovation. That's like trying to play a two-handed Mozart composition the first time you sit down to play the piano.

Practice on problems you're especially interested in solving. ◀❶ Otherwise, you'll lose interest and mistakenly conclude that it's difficult to learn to solve problems. By analogy, realize how difficult it would have been to learn to read if, as a child, you only read dull stories that other people insisted you read. Your reading skills improved faster when you read stories or information you were especially interested in.

Because a book is unable to serve the same role that a teacher ◀❶ serves, consider working together with someone else who is also interested in learning these tools. A learning companion can enhance your progress far beyond what reading and thinking alone can accomplish. A person, unlike a book, can encourage you to invest the time it takes to create solutions, and can challenge you to develop tools you're weak in using.

As you learn to solve problems creatively, be creative in how ◀❶ you learn these skills. Do *not* regard *The Creative Problem Solver's Toolbox* as the final authority on how to solve problems creatively. The final authority is reality itself. Do whatever works and makes sense. Do your own thinking, instead of trying to make this book do your thinking for you.

For some final words about practicing, let's turn to the master innovator Leonardo da Vinci. He wrote, "Iron rusts from disuse; water loses its purity from stagnation and in cold weather becomes frozen; even so does inaction sap the vigors of the mind."

◀SUMMARY▶

To transform the tools in this toolbox into useful mental skills, you must practice using them. Use the *Radial Outline Of The Creative Problem Solver's Tools* (pages 315-321) as a checklist. Consider joining with someone else to learn the tools together. Be creative in how you learn to increase your creativity.

Using The Tools Together

Now that you've seen how to use each tool in isolation, it's time to see the tools used together to create a solution to a single problem.

The sample problem to be solved in this section is to increase the percentage of English-speaking people in the United States who can read and write English. Stating this problem in reverse, there are many people who speak and understand spoken English, yet can't read or write English. For brevity, this problem is called the illiteracy problem, even though the word illiteracy has other meanings besides the meaning used here.

As you read the example, keep in mind the following points:

- The discussion about illiteracy is abbreviated and incomplete, so misunderstandings about what's said here are likely. To avoid getting distracted by these misunderstandings, keep in mind that the creative problem solving process, not the illiteracy problem, is what's of primary importance in this example.

- Although the example is explained as a step-by-step sequence, no particular sequence is being followed. A very different sequence of steps could still lead to the same results.

- The solutions suggested at the end aren't the only ways to solve the illiteracy problem. Other effective solutions are also possible.

Section titles appear at the end of each paragraph to identify the sections that explain the tools used in the paragraph. To determine a section's page number, refer to the *Sections* entries in the index.

Let's begin the illiteracy example with the obvious idea of spending more government money on teaching illiterate people to read and write. This approach would reduce illiteracy, but it would cut off funds needed to deal with other problems, or it would require an increase in taxes. This idea will be kept in mind as a possible alternative even though it has major disadvantages. (Relevant sections: *Starting Anywhere; Following Strategies, Not Steps Or Rules; Looking For Merit In Crude Ideas; Evaluating Throughout The Creative Process; Finding Flaws And Weaknesses Early.*)

Now, let's look beneath the surface and ask, "Why are people illiterate?" One answer is that reading and writing are challenging skills that take lots of effort to develop. This prompts us to realize that there are two general approaches:

- Making reading and writing easier
- Increasing the effort of illiterate people to learn to read and write

(Relevant sections: *Looking For Fresh Perspectives; Understanding Why And How; Identifying The Root Of A Problem; Identifying Categories Before Specific Alternatives.*)

At this point we have in mind an outline of alternatives that could be represented on paper as shown here. (Relevant section: *Expanding A Radial Outline Of Alternatives.*)

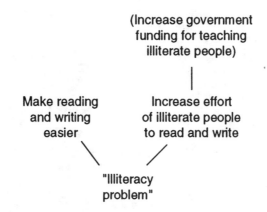

Let's explore the approach of making reading and writing easier. People learning to read are often confused by the fact that a single sound can be spelled in many ways. For instance, the *SH* sound is spelled differently in the following words: **shy,** *sugar, tissue, nation, emulsion, fascism, special, oceanic,* and *machine.* Another confusion is that the same letter can represent more than one sound. For instance, the letter *A* represents different sounds in the following words: *was, mat, fade, any, ball,* and *homage.* The complexity of these multiple associations between sounds and spellings is represented visually for vowels in the diagram on the next page. Each line indicates that at least one word uses the spelling at one end of the line to represent the sound at the other end. The associations are the ones listed in the *English Spelling and Sound Correspondences* section of *Webster's Ninth New Collegiate*

Dictionary. (Relevant sections: *Identifying The Root Of A Problem; Understanding Why And How; Finding Flaws And Weaknesses Early; Sketching Visual Representations; Learning From People Who Understand.*)

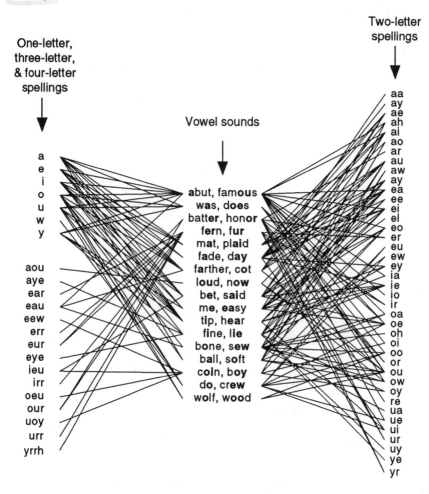

Interestingly, the lack of consistency between sounds and spellings is greater for vowels than consonants. This is because all modern-day alphabets, including the English (*Roman*) alphabet, evolved from the alphabet created by early Phoenicians, and that alphabet represented only consonants. Early Greeks adopted the Phoenician alphabet (about 800 BC). Because the Greeks had fewer consonant sounds, they used some of the extra Phoenician letters to represent vowels. Other steps were involved in the evolution of the Roman alphabet that's used to represent English, but there are still fewer vowel letters than vowel sounds. This is why each vowel letter in English represents both a *long* and *short* vowel sound. (Relevant sections: *Letting Curiosity Motivate Your Learning; Understanding Why And How.*)

Thinking idealistically, we can imagine creating an alphabet that doesn't have the limitations of the English alphabet. In such an ideal alphabet, each letter would represent only one sound, and each sound would be represented by only one possible symbol. These limitations make it possible to know how to pronounce a word when you see it written, and how to spell a word you already know how to pronounce. Notice that the requirement of allowing only one symbol for each different sound also eliminates the

Those Phoenicians have more consonants than we do, so we've got some letters left over. What shall we do with them?

confusion of using upper case and lower case letters, such as *g* versus *G* and *r* versus *R*, that aren't simply different sizes of the same shape. (Relevant sections: *Heading In The Direction Of An Ideal Solution; Creating Non-Objects; Pursuing Final, Rather Than Intermediate, Goals; Eliminating Inconsistencies; Noticing What You Normally Don't.*)

Would such an ideal alphabet help solve the illiteracy problem? Yes. It would make learning to read and write much easier. This advantage, plus curiosity, motivates us to wonder what an ideal alphabet would look like. For now, we ignore the obvious disadvantage that making a transition to a new alphabet would be extremely troublesome. (Relevant sections: *Learning By Experimenting Mentally; Looking For Merit In Crude Ideas; Letting Curiosity Motivate Your Learning; Heading In The Direction Of An Ideal Solution; Retaining Advantages And Eliminating Disadvantages; Providing A Bridge From The Old To The New.*)

We consult an expert in the field of language by looking in *The Cambridge Encyclopedia of Language* by David Crystal. We learn that an alphabet that fits our design requirements already exists. It's called the *International Phonetic Alphabet*. This alphabet can be used in many different languages, including German, French, Spanish, and Chinese. This universal phonetic alphabet would make the learning of foreign languages — including English for non-English speakers — easier, so we revise our ideal goal to include coverage of all languages. (Relevant sections: *Learning From People Who Understand; Incorporating Advantageous Aspects Of Other Ideas; Reconsidering Your Goals At Any Time; Heading In The Direction Of An Ideal Solution.*)

In spite of the advantages offered by the International Phonetic Alphabet, it has disadvantages. One disadvantage is that there are many different kinds of symbols to memorize. To remove this disadvantage we can extract an advantage from another alphabet: the *Shaw alphabet*. (The Shaw alphabet was named after George Bernard Shaw, but he didn't design it. It was created by several people after his death, as requested in his will.) The Shaw alphabet uses similar symbols for similar sounds. As an example of similar sounds, notice that the sound of *F* in *fine* and the sound of *V* in *vine* are similar because the *F* sound is the *V* sound without moving the vocal chords. In the Shaw alphabet, the symbols for these two sounds are inverted (upside-down) versions of one another. Similarly, the symbols in the Shaw alphabet that represent the sounds of the bold letters in each of the following word pairs are inverted versions of one another: p*eep* and *bib*, *to* and *do*, *kick* and *goat*, *thigh* and *they*, *so* and *zoo*, *sure* and *measure*, and *church* and *judge*. Representing similar sounds using similar symbols would make learning an alphabet easier, and that would reduce illiteracy, so we'll adopt the idea of representing similar sounds similarly. Although we're adopting this idea from the Shaw alphabet, we're not adopting the idea of regarding inverted symbols as similar because the mind doesn't quickly recognize inversions as similar. (Relevant sections: *Doing Your Own Thinking; Finding Flaws And Weaknesses Early; Learning From People Who Understand; Combining Ideas; Incorporating Advantageous Aspects Of Other Ideas; Choosing By Elimination With Extraction; Extracting Useful Concepts From Anywhere; Eliminating Inconsistencies; Thinking Visually.*)

Notice that the difference between the sounds *F* and *V* is a dimension. This same dimension also accounts for the difference between *K* and *G* (as in *goat*). Sounds such as *V* and *G* involve vibrating the vocal chords; they are called *voiced*. Sounds such as *F* and *K* are made with the vocal chords silent; they are called *unvoiced*. Therefore, this dimension is called voiced versus unvoiced. The presence of this dimension prompts us to identify other dimensions of vocal sounds. (Relevant sections: *Thinking Dimensionally; Recognizing Four General Dimensions; Noticing What You Normally Don't; Letting Curiosity Motivate Your Learning.*)

A well known dimension of vocal sound is volume. Volume is important in knowing how to pronounce words, such as rhinoceros, that have more than one syllable. In such words, some syllables are accented by being spoken more loudly than others. If a method of writing included a way of indicating which syllables to accent, a person first encountering a word in written form wouldn't need to look in a dictionary or ask someone in order to find out which syllables to accent. The fact that the International Phonetic Alphabet offers this advantage suggests support for the ideal we're pursuing. (Relevant section: *Recognizing Physical Dimensions.*)

Another dimension of vocal sound is pitch. In English, questions end with a rising pitch and statements end with a falling pitch. In Chinese, pronouncing a word with the wrong pitch amounts to saying a completely different word with a completely different meaning. For these reasons, representing pitch is important. (Relevant sections: *Recognizing Physical Dimensions; Letting Curiosity Motivate Your Learning; Evaluating Throughout The Creative Process.*)

The distinction between consonants and vowels is a dimension. Specifically, vowel sounds are made with the mouth open, and consonant sounds are made with the mouth partly or completely closed. However, this dimension characterizes how a sound is made instead of how it sounds, so this dimension isn't useful here. Notice that the presence of familiar names, *consonant* and *vowel*, make this dimension tempting to consider as significant. Adding support to the decision to disregard this dimension is the observation that a ventriloquist makes both consonant and vowel sounds using the same lip formation. (Relevant sections: *Eliminating Inconsistencies; Recognizing Dimensional Independence; Differentiating Appropriately; Avoiding Crucial Assumptions; Avoiding Oversimplified Associative Thinking; Choosing By Elimination With Extraction; Thinking Wordlessly; Learning From Experiences; Imagining Exaggerated Specific Cases To Determine Effects.*)

Yet another dimension of vocal sound is exemplified by the difference between *J* in *just* and *S* in *measure*. The *J* is a sudden change from no sound to sound. In contrast, the *S* in *measure* is a continuous sound that can continue for a full breath. This dimension can be called continuous versus momentary. (Relevant sections: *Noticing What You Normally Don't; Recognizing Physical Dimensions; Recognizing Different Ways To Categorize Thinking.*)

The *voiced versus unvoiced* and *continuous versus momentary* dimensions are independent of one another because a letter's categorization according to one of these dimensions doesn't indicate anything about how it's categorized according to the other dimension. Therefore, it's possible to draw the matrix below that shows how English letters fit these dimensions. Letters that fit into more than one category — because they have more than one pronunciation — aren't shown. (Relevant sections: *Recognizing Dimensional Independence; Sketching Visual Representations; Representing Dimensions Visually.*)

	A, E, I, L, M, N, O, R, U, V, W, Z, NG	B, D, G, J
Voiced	A, E, I, L, M, N, O, R, U, V, W, Z, NG	B, D, G, J
Unvoiced	F, H, S, SH	K, P, T, CH
	Continuous	Momentary

Besides revealing a clearer understanding of vocal sounds, this matrix suggests the possibility that sounds can be written using specific marks to represent specific dimensions. For example, as an alternative in this category, horizontal lines could indicate continuous sound characteristics and a vertical line could indicate the momentary, suddenly increasing version of the same sound. The height of the lines above a base line could indicate the pitch, as done in musical notation. The size of another mark could indicate the relative volume. (Relevant sections: *Sketching Visual Representations; Identifying Categories Before Specific Alternatives; Recognizing Dimensional Independence; Extracting Useful Concepts From Anywhere.*)

Notice that what we're now imagining isn't an alphabet. Instead, it's a method of representing the dimensions of vocal sounds. Notice that this idea arose by thinking more and more idealistically. (Relevant sections: *Reconsidering Your Goals At Any Time; Reconsidering Your Starting Point; Heading In The Direction Of An Ideal Solution.*)

Although this ideal kind of writing system will be possible in the distant future, it's not currently a practical solution. Part of its impracticality is that, currently, there isn't a way to provide a bridge between that writing system and the existing English alphabet. (Relevant sections: *Finding Flaws And Weaknesses Early; Providing A Bridge From The Old To The New.*)

Yet another obstacle is that all the dimensions of vocal sounds haven't yet been identified. This lack of understanding makes it impossible to design a dimension-based writing system at this time. The vocal dimensions explained above are the ones that are easy to identify. Other vocal dimensions are much more difficult to identify. (Relevant sections: *Understanding Clearly; Admitting To Yourself You Don't Know; Thinking Dimensionally; Comprehending Complexity.*)

Most efforts to identify the remaining vocal dimensions focus on the way the mouth, lips, tongue, and vocal chords create sounds. But the dimensions that need to be identified are the dimensions of the *sounds*, not the way the sounds are produced. This distinction can be understood in terms of the sounds *M* and *N*. These two sounds are similar, yet they're made using very different lip and tongue positions. (Relevant sections: *Doing Your Own Thinking; Eliminating Inconsistencies; Imagining Exaggerated Specific Cases To Determine Effects.*)

When the dimensions of vocal *sounds* are named and quantified (expressed in numbers), it will become possible to design a fully phonetic writing system. Thus, identifying the dimensions of vocal sounds is the first step toward one approach to dramatically reducing the illiteracy problem. (Relevant sections: *Considering Indirect Approaches; Creating Supporting Enhancements.*)

Scientists and business executives might be tempted to rush to identify vocal dimensions and then create a writing system based on what they come up with. Yet this approach is not the only (nor the wisest) approach. What's needed first is a way to try out an understanding of vocal sound dimensions. (Relevant sections: *Finding Flaws And Weaknesses Early; Anticipating Possible Negative Consequences; Admitting To Yourself You Don't Know; Providing A Bridge From The Old To The New; Understanding Experimenting.*)

Writing isn't the only way people communicate with one another. People who can't hear or can't speak communicate through sign language. (Relevant sections: *Noticing What You Normally Don't; Learning From Experiences.*)

Currently, there are two popular forms of sign language in the United States:

- *American Sign Language*, in which there's a unique hand sign for each concept. For instance, there's a specific gesture that involves moving both hands that represents the concept *important.*

- Finger spelling, in which there's a unique hand sign for each letter of the alphabet. For instance, to convey the word *important*, the signs for each of the following letters would be used: *I M P O R T A N T.*

(Relevant sections: *Letting Curiosity Motivate Your Learning; Learning From People Who Understand.*)

Another possibility for communicating with hand signs is to use unique gestures for each sound being represented. This amounts to creating a new kind of sign language: a phonetic sign language. (Relevant sections: *Doing Your Own Thinking; Retaining Advantages And Eliminating Disadvantages; Incorporating Advantageous Aspects Of Other Ideas; Combining Ideas; Choosing By Elimination With Extraction; Expanding A Radial Outline Of Alternatives; Creating Non-Objects.*)

Here are some advantages a phonetic sign language would offer:

- A phonetic sign language would be *faster to use* than finger spelling because there's a more direct – and consistent – association between sounds and signs. (Relevant sections: *Looking For Merit In Crude Ideas; Simplifying; Eliminating Inconsistencies.*)

- For people who can hear, a phonetic sign language would be *easier to learn* than American Sign Language. Learning American Sign Language requires memorizing thousands of signs. In contrast, learning a well-designed phonetic sign language would require learning only a few signing elements. (Relevant section: *Looking For Merit In Crude Ideas; Thinking Dimensionally.*)

- A phonetic sign language would be useful for *un*handicapped people in situations where speaking isn't practical, such as underwater, on opposite sides of a window, across a noisy room, and in a quiet auditorium. (Relevant section: *Looking For Merit In Crude Ideas; Avoiding Crucial Assumptions; Learning From Experiences; Noticing What You Normally Don't; Looking For Fresh Perspectives.*)

- If many *un*handicapped people learned a phonetic sign language, handicapped people could communicate with many more people. (Relevant sections: *Looking For Merit In Crude Ideas; Imagining Exaggerated Specific Cases To Determine Effects; Learning By Experimenting Mentally.*)

For solving the illiteracy problem, the most important benefit is that designing a phonetic sign language would amount to an experiment for testing researchers' understanding of vocal dimensions. Developing that understanding is needed before it will be possible to create a well-designed, fully phonetic, writing system. (Relevant sections: *Looking For Merit In Crude Ideas; Finding Flaws And Weaknesses Early; Understanding Experimenting; Considering Indirect Approaches.*)

The basis of a phonetic sign language would be to visually represent nearly every sound that can be made by the human voice. This includes being able to represent changes in volume, changes in pitch, mispronunciations, drawls, foreign accents, and the sounds in all spoken languages. Success in designing a phonetic sign language would be based on a clear understanding of vocal sound dimensions and wisely choosing how to represent those dimensions using finger, hand, and arm positions. (Relevant sections:

Eliminating Inconsistencies; Thinking Dimensionally; Understanding Clearly; Recognizing Different Ways To Categorize Thinking.)

In a phonetic sign language, the *motion* of fingers, hands, and arms would indicate changes from one vocal sound to another. Consider the sound of the letter *I* in *kite*. This sound is a smooth transition from a sound that's somewhat similar to the sound of *O* in *cot*, changing to the *E* in *me*. Therefore, the sound of *I* in *kite* would be represented by first making a gesture that indicates the first part of the *I* sound and then, with a smooth transition, changing the gesture to the second part of the *I* sound. This reveals that as a hand sign changes from one position to another, the intermediate positions also represent valid sounds. (Relevant sections: *Imagining Exaggerated Specific Cases To Determine Effects; Noticing What You Normally Don't; Eliminating Inconsistencies.*)

There's another advantage to allowing gestures to slowly change from one sound to the next: the gestures can represent singing! This leads to the realization that a fully phonetic writing system could be used to represent the words of a song on sheet music. In turn, this leads to the realization that the duration of a sound is another independent vocal dimension. (Relevant sections: *Following Multiple Ideas; Sketching Visual Representations; Recognizing Four General Dimensions.*)

Here's a summary of inconsistencies between spoken sounds and gestures that a phonetic sign language would need to avoid:

- One sign representing two different sounds.
- Two different signs representing the same sound.
- A characteristic of vocal sounds that can't be represented.
- Not being able to represent a smooth transition from one sound to another sound as a smooth transition from one sign to another sign.

(Relevant section: *Eliminating Inconsistencies.*)

Another benefit of a phonetic sign language would be that a computerized device could be built to translate hand signs of a non-speaking person into vocal sounds that unhandicapped people could hear. Conversely, a different computerized device could translate spoken sounds into an on-screen visual display of hand signs for use by a deaf person. (Relevant sections: *Looking For Merit In Crude Ideas; Creating Supporting Enhancements; Inventing*, which is a later section in this chapter.)

Such translation devices could be used to test the design of the phonetic sign language. Someone could speak into a device that translates sounds into hand signs, and those hand signs could be translated back into sounds by a separate device. A lack of differences between the spoken and re-created sounds would indicate a well-designed phonetic sign language. A similar test could verify that phonetic hand signs can be translated into sounds that are translated back into the same hand signs. In the process of ensuring these consistencies, a clearer understanding of vocal dimensions would emerge, and that understanding would lead to a better design of the sign language. (Relevant sections: *Finding Flaws And Weaknesses Early; Understanding Experimenting; Eliminating Inconsistencies.*)

In turn, a well designed phonetic sign language would make it possible to design a moderately successful written language. But such a writing system would most likely be used to write languages other than English. More likely, the writing system would be adopted for a spoken language for which there is currently a high rate of illiteracy, or a language that's currently difficult to learn to write. (Although *written* Chinese is very difficult to learn to write, *spoken* Chinese is many separate languages, not a single language.) Only much later, at least hundreds of years from now, is there a chance that English might be commonly written using a fully phonetic writing system. (Relevant sections: *Creating Supporting Enhancements; Understanding People; Handling Criticism; Making Categorical Dimensions Realistic; Considering Indirect Approaches.*)

In the meantime, a fully phonetic writing system would be used by some people the way shorthand is used: it's typically read by only one or two people. A fully phonetic writing system would also be useful to people learning to speak a foreign language because it could represent sounds that can't be represented in the person's native-language writing system. (Relevant sections: *Reconsidering Your Starting Point; Reconsidering Your Goals At Any Time; Providing A Bridge From The Old To The New.*)

A major consequence of identifying and quantifying vocal dimensions would be that vocal sounds could be stored electronically in less storage space (as measured in bits or bytes) than the space required using current storage methods. Among other uses, this advantage would reduce the cost, and improve the functionality, of voice mail systems currently used in large offices. (Relevant sections: *Understanding Clearly; Simplifying; Looking For Merit In*

Crude Ideas; Creating Implementation Ideas; Combining Ideas; Identifying Categories Before Specific Alternatives.)

Storing spoken sounds using vocal sound dimensions would also make practical *speaking books,* in which the entire text of a book would be available to a listener while heshe does activities such as driving, cooking, and exercising. In contrast to using audio cassettes, any part of the book could be accessed immediately. A sentence or paragraph could be repeated at the press of a button. And, the reading speed could be increased or decreased. Although spoken books wouldn't improve the listener's ability to read, listening to many well-written books could improve the listener's ability to write well-worded sentences. (Of course, spelling, capitalization, and punctuation skills wouldn't improve.) Listening to books parallels part of what it takes to learn to write well: reading lots of well-written books. (Relevant sections: *Learning From Experiences; Inventing; Creating Implementation Ideas; Considering Pulling Instead Of Pushing; Looking For Merit In Crude Ideas.*)

A variation of the innovation of a spoken book would be an electronic "book" that speaks syllables and words as they are pointed to — by someone learning to read. This approach bypasses the need to start learning to read by reading boring, simple books. This application certainly offers advantages for making it easier for some adults to learn to read. (Relevant sections: *Combining Ideas; Expanding A Radial Outline Of Alternatives; Considering Pulling Instead Of Pushing; Inventing; Understanding Why And How; Looking For Merit In Crude Ideas.*)

Speech recognition, which is the ability of electronic equipment to understand a person's voice, is a long-anticipated future innovation. Speech recognition would make it possible to control a VCR by talking, and to dial a telephone by speaking the digits into the telephone. Combined with a fully phonetic writing system, speech recognition would make it possible to "type" words into a computer by speaking the words. (Relevant sections: *Learning From People Who Understand; Combining Ideas.*)

Unfortunately, along with benefits, speech recognition will have some negative consequences. Ironically, one of the many negative consequences of speech recognition could be higher rates of illiteracy due to people being able to do through speaking what now requires writing. To appreciate this possibility, consider that television and radio have reduced people's motivation to learn to read and write, compared to the past when information could be widely distributed only in printed form. (Relevant sections: *Anticipating Possible Negative Consequences; Imagining Exaggerated Specific Cases To Determine Effects.*)

In imagining a radial outline of the alternatives considered so far, it's obvious that most of the focus has been within the category of making reading and writing easier to learn. So, now we'll briefly look elsewhere in the outline. (Relevant sections: *Expanding A Radial Outline Of Alternatives.*)

A different approach to dealing with the illiteracy problem would be to increase people's intrinsic (internal) motivation to learn to read and write. Within this category is the alternative of creating non-fiction books that offer the following benefits:

- Teach skills that are especially useful
- Lack unnecessary new terminology
- Contain interesting examples

(Relevant sections: *Expanding A Radial Outline Of Alternatives; Identifying Categories Before Specific Alternatives; Understanding People; Understanding Why And How.*)

The outline of alternatives now appears as shown on the next page. (Relevant section: *Expanding A Radial Outline Of Alternatives.*)

What's the solution to the problem of English-speaking people not being able to read or write? There is no quick-fix solution because there are so many inconsistencies between letters and spoken sounds. For slight gains in years ahead, one approach is to create and call attention to books that are especially worth reading. Another approach is to create electronic "books" that display syllables and words as they are spoken (with the reader setting the pace). For long-term gains, the first step is to identify and quantify the independent dimensions of vocal sounds. As part of that first step, it would be useful to create a phonetic sign language. Besides being used by both unhandicapped and handicapped people, the design and use of the phonetic sign language would refine our understanding of vocal sound dimensions. (Relevant sections: *Understanding Why And How; Following Multiple Ideas; Thinking Dimensionally; Creating Supporting Enhancements; Considering Indirect Approaches; Providing A Bridge From The Old To The New.*)

Eventually, fully identifying the independent dimensions of vocal sounds will make possible a fully phonetic writing system

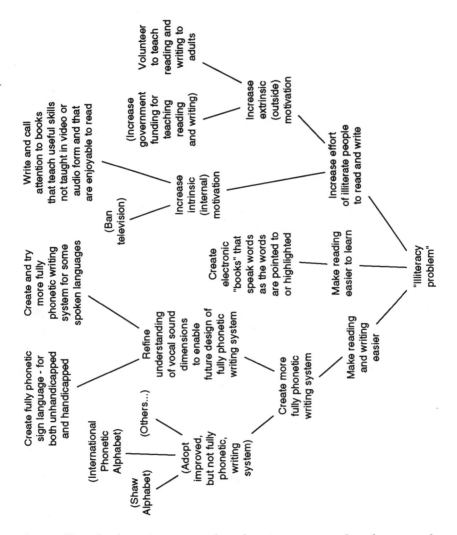

that will make learning to read and write so easy that few people will be illiterate. It probably wouldn't be widely used for English for at least a thousand years (or a few hundred years at the earliest). But other benefits will be possible in the meantime. When it's finally adopted, electronic communication will enable people to choose whether their display screen shows text written in traditional or fully phonetic form. (Relevant sections: *Identifying The Root Of A Problem; Simplifying; Solving The Whole Problem; Creating Non-Objects; Heading In The Direction Of An Ideal Solution; Understanding People; Providing A Bridge From The Old To The New; Considering Flexibility Instead Of Standardization.*)

What will motivate people to adopt a fully phonetic writing system? The information that's now available only in books and newspapers will increasingly become available in spoken form, further reducing people's motivation to learn to read. Of course, television is likely to continue to provide all the information that many people care to learn. If current public education practices remain the same, literate people might feel compelled to reduce illiteracy by offering a simpler form of written English, namely English written using a fully phonetic writing system. Once adopted, schools would no longer need to teach spelling, capitalization, or punctuation, and this would make school time available for teaching increasingly important higher-level thinking skills such as: writing well, speaking well, solving real-life problems (creatively, of course), understanding technology, and understanding dimensions (both numerical and non-numerical). In short, the problem of illiteracy could easily get worse before it gets better. (Relevant sections: *Imagining Exaggerated Specific Cases To Determine Effects; Anticipating Possible Negative Consequences; Preventing Problems,* which is the next section in this chapter; *Simplifying; Looking For Merit In Crude Ideas; Understanding Clearly; Understanding People.*)

Even though this example is lengthy, it doesn't completely cover the subject of reducing illiteracy. A complete discussion could easily fill a book. So, here are clarifications to avoid some possible misunderstandings:

- What's described above are scenarios, not predictions. Ultimately, it's not possible to predict how — or if — the illiteracy problem will be solved.

- A fully phonetic writing system isn't a replacement for any language. It only changes the way the spoken language is visually represented (on paper or on a screen).

- A fully phonetic writing system will never reach common use in English until — and unless — it can coexist with the way English is now written. This means no one will ever have to stop using the form of reading and writing they grew up learning.

- The example is incomplete. (As just one instance, the momentary versus continuous dimension would be expanded into a three-category dimension of initial versus continuous versus terminal. This expansion is needed to account for the difference in the sounds made by the letter *D* in the word *did*.)

Challenging problems that won't be solved for many years, such as the above illiteracy problem, are useful as practice problems, even if no clear solution emerges. The practice gained makes it easier to solve smaller problems.

In closing, remember that this illiteracy example serves to illustrate how the creative problem solver's tools can be used together to create possible solutions to a real problem.

◄SUMMARY►

Although most of this book's examples illustrate the application of only one of the creative problem solver's tools at a time, normally the tools are used together, as illustrated in this section's example. The tools are applied as they are needed, not in any particular sequence.

Preventing Problems

The creative problem solver's tools can not only be used to solve a problem that you're already confronting. The tools can be used to prevent the arrival of problems that are now heading your way.

Imagine walking through a crowded room by walking in straight lines and changing direction each time you bump into someone. Of course this would be foolish. Yet this is similar to what some people do in everyday life. They wait until they bump into a problem before they begin to solve it. Then they wait until they bump into the next problem before they begin to solve that one.

Of course, walking through a crowded room is best done by looking ahead to see if someone's in your way and changing your direction before you bump into the person. Similarly, life is more wisely handled by looking ahead to see if you're heading in the direction of a problem and solving the problem before the full force of it hits you. This simple, yet frequently overlooked, strategy is expressed in the proverb that says, "If we don't change direction, we're likely to end up where we're headed."

The key to recognizing an approaching problem is to see links between what you're doing now and what will happen as an undesirable consequence. This is a more advanced version of a skill that children learn as a part of growing up. For instance, a child learns that the consequence of continuing to tease a cat after it has begun to hiss is getting scratched. Until the child learns this connection, the scratch comes as a surprise.

Connections between what someone does now and what will likely happen later aren't always obvious, especially in these cases:

- The consequence arrives *delayed,* long after the action.
- The consequence is *invisible.*
- The consequence is *physically distant,* and therefore not normally seen.
- The consequence is *indirectly,* rather than directly, connected to current actions.
- The consequence arises *through the behavior of other people.* Yet, if a negative consequence occurs, you still suffer even if "It's their fault."
- The consequence arises because a *large number* of individual *small contributions* add together to become a large problem.

An impending problem that exhibits all these characteristics is the release of gases that break down the ozone layer of the earth's atmosphere. Specifically:

- *Delayed:* It takes a decade or two for the gases to reach the ozone layer after they have been released from the earth's surface.
- *Invisible:* The ozone layer cannot be seen with the eyes, so losing it wouldn't be directly noticeable. Also, increased high-energy radiation reaching the earth's surface cannot be seen with the eyes. Also, ozone-depleting gases escaping from refrigerators and air conditioners are invisible.
- *Distant:* Most of the people who will suffer from skin cancer and other undesirable consequences are in other cities and countries.
- *Indirect:* The choice to contribute ozone-depleting gases into the air is made when you buy something, such as a refrigerator or air conditioner, that contains the chemicals. The actual release of the chemicals occurs when appliance repair people don't trap the escaping chemicals, or when waste disposal people crush the refrigerator, air conditioner, or air conditioned automobile.

- *Other people involved*: The people who physically dispose of the products aren't the same people who manufacture or use the products. The people who choose which gases to put into products aren't the same people who use or dispose of the products.

- *Countless seemingly insignificant contributions*: Each person individually accounts for only a small amount of the released gas, but the total quantity of released ozone-depleting gas is very substantial.

(Incidentally, an additional important factor in the ozone-loss problem is that *each* ozone-depleting molecule breaks down hundreds, and perhaps thousands, of ozone molecules.)

Seeing non-obvious connections is a very useful skill which, like all skills, must be practiced. But many people don't have much practice in seeing connections between actions and non-obvious consequences. Why? Because traditions, customs, rules, and laws tell people not to do most things that cause seemingly unrelated problems. For instance, restrooms in restaurants have signs to remind employees to wash their hands before returning to work because the invisible, delayed, and distant consequences of infecting food aren't obvious. With so many traditions and rules telling us not to do what would lead to undesirable results, it's easy to assume that there's no need to look ahead. Just follow the rules, right?

Practice looking for the connections that rules (and laws and traditions) are based on. But, instead of looking for rules that seem to be unjustified, as rebellious people do, try to understand *why* each rule was created. This practice develops the thinking skill that makes it easier to see future problems that don't have rules to prevent them.

In your life, what problems are heading your way now?

◄SUMMARY►

One of the most creative solutions possible is to prevent a problem. It's creative because, alas, it's not the usual way to solve a problem. The key to preventing problems is to become aware of easily overlooked connections between *actions* and *consequences*.

Inventing

Chapters 2 through 10 explain *how to* invent because all the
creative problem solver's tools can be used to invent. This
section covers the *value* of inventing.

As a reminder, *inventions* are *innovations* that involve objects
and substances. Another way to define inventions is as whatever
can be patented. Because a patent provides a legal monopoly on
making and selling an invention, you might wonder, "Can an
invention make me rich?"

One woman invented a significantly improved baby carrier that
holds the baby in front of the parent. When she applied for a patent,
the patent office claimed that her idea was already covered by
existing patents, including one for a brassiere. By paying lots of
money for a patent attorney and investing lots of personal time, she
was eventually able to get a patent. Getting the patent turned out
to be just the first of several obstacles. As is common, it took considerable effort for this inventor to find a manufacturer willing to buy
a license to manufacture and sell the new baby carrier. When she
found such a company, she figured the hardest part was done.
Unfortunately, the manufacturer insisted on altering her design.
Despite her objections, they manufactured and sold baby carriers
that way for many months before one of the company managers
finally tried carrying a friend's baby in one of the carriers. It didn't
work well. Ironically, the company complained to the inventor.
Her reply was, "That's what I've been trying to tell you." Most
inventors never get as far as this inventor did. Few can afford the
patent attorney fees and patent filing fees. Even fewer can afford to
set up a business to manufacture the product, which this inventor
eventually did. How much money does it take? This inventor and
her family had to mortgage their house to get the needed money.
The entire experience was summed up in her husband's reaction
when she told him she felt an idea coming for another great invention. He said, "Get it out of your mind! I don't want to deal with
another one!"

The satisfaction of creating something new that other people
will appreciate, and the acclaim that's typically given to inventors
in history books, can strengthen a belief that profits will arise by
sharing the idea. Sometimes this happens, but not always, and not
always for the reason expected.

Before you blindly get involved in trying to profit from an invention, there are two points worth learning about patenting:

- Profits are earned by making and selling a product without competition. The lack of competition is maintained by taking to court any person or business that infringes on your patent. If a business buys your patent rights, the money they give you is based on their expectations of future profits from making and selling a product without competition.

  Notice that simply getting a patent doesn't earn you any money. In fact, it costs money to get a patent.

- A patent is essentially a statement from the patent office that says, in effect, "We, the patent office, received an application for such-and-such an idea from so-and-so on such-and-such a date and, based on a search of existing patents, did not find any patents for the same idea."

  The patent office *does not* take any action against people who infringe on patents. It's up to the patent owner to hire an attorney and take an infringing business to court to sue for damages.

  As an added complication, a product you're making and selling might infringe on someone else's patent. This can happen because a single product can be covered by many different patents, some of which you might not own.

In other words, after you invent something, you must invest additional effort and money to profit from the invention.

The Wright Brothers sued the infringers of their airplane patent, paying lots of money for legal fees and spending years in court. Wilbur Wright died before their most important infringement case was settled — in their favor.

In spite of these obstacles, individual inventors sometimes become wealthy. However, that doesn't always happen for the reason you might expect.

Robert McCormick invented the reaper and his son, Cyrus McCormick, patented the reaper, sold reapers, and became rich. However, much of Cyrus' wealth came from offering a new way to pay for his reapers, what we now call monthly payments, and from setting up a network of dealers. In other words, marketing innovations were an important ingredient in his financial success.

Yes, some individual inventors do earn money for their invention. But, are they being rewarded for the hard work of creating
and refining the idea or for the hard work of surmounting legal,
financial, and marketing obstacles?

In addition to the obstacles already mentioned, here are more
challenges facing the individual inventor:

- You are not alone in your quest to invent. On February 14, 1876,
  Alexander Graham Bell applied for a patent on his invention of
  the telephone. Within hours Elisha Grey also arrived at the
  patent office to patent his invention of the telephone.

- Typically, businesses won't even consider your invention until
  you sign a contract that says they're not obligated to pay for
  your idea. This contract protects them from being unjustly sued
  for copying your invention, in case they're already developing
  a similar invention.

- Often, even a wonderful invention is unappreciated when it's
  first offered. Surprisingly, few people regarded the Wright
  Brothers' flying machine as having any value, except as a toy.

- The more valuable your invention, the more time, effort, and
  money competitors will invest to develop *legal* ways to bypass
  or undermine your patent.

- A patent establishes a legal monopoly only within the country
  issuing the patent.

These are only some of the challenges an individual inventor faces
by trying to profit from an invention. There are others, but you get
the point. Future changes in the legal system might someday make
it easier for individuals to share useful ideas and be recognized and,
perhaps, rewarded for their inventions. In the meantime, the
existing obstacles amount to an extra challenge, beyond the challenge of inventing itself.

If you want to seek profit through inventing, go for it! It can be
done! But don't blindly assume that the world is anxiously waiting
to financially reward you for your creative efforts.

For information about how to obtain a patent, plus suggestions
for profiting from your invention, I recommend David Pressman's
book *Patent It Yourself*.

Fortunately, making a profit isn't the only reason to invent.
Inventing can be an enjoyable activity that you can pursue for your
own individual benefit. For instance, you can make a new toy for

your kids or make something that fixes a problem around the house. If you confine what you make to personal use at home, the legal problems concerning patents don't apply.

▶ When inventing for the fun of it, there's yet another advantage besides benefiting from the invention itself. The effort spent in inventing provides an excellent way to practice the skills of creative problem solving.

▶ Inventing simple physical things is especially valuable as an activity for children because it provides practice in applying basic creative problem solving skills involving objects a child can see, touch, and understand. Incidentally, it was through simple inventing as a child that I learned some of the tools explained in this book.

◄SUMMARY►

There are many opportunities to invent things for personal use. Enjoy the satisfaction of creating what doesn't yet exist (as far as you know) and seeing it work.

If you're confident that you've created something that offers lots of value to many people and you have an entrepreneurial spirit, consider braving the financial, legal, and marketing obstacles to earn a profit from your invention.

Exercise 1. Design a pair of eyeglasses, or an adaptation to existing eyeglasses, that enables a color-blind person to determine the color of an object. (Hint: Make sure you understand how the eyes sense color.)

Conducting Group Problem Solving Sessions

Getting together with other people to come up with creative ideas can produce more and better ideas than working alone. And, with the right orientation, it's lots of fun!

▶ A group problem solving session (sometimes called a *brainstorming* session) can be conducted *formally* or *informally*. The formal kind is commonly done in business and government organizations, whereas the informal kind can be done spontaneously among a group of friends. Within the formal category is the new practice of using computer networks to connect participants who aren't in the same room at the same time. Most of what's written in this section applies to all these kinds of group sessions.

The main reason that group thinking can prompt ideas that wouldn't arise otherwise is that the participants bring together a diversity of thinking habits. The advantage of a diversity of thinking habits was explained in the *Imagining What Someone Else Might Suggest* section in Chapter 6, *Thinking In Alternate Ways*. Another advantage of group thinking is that the available pool of knowledge and experience is richer than that of any one person.

The biggest obstacle in a group can be a lack of cooperation. The remainder of this section explains ways to overcome, or at least minimize, a lack of cooperation.

A significant lack of cooperation arises if anyone in the group criticizes imperfect ideas. Creative ideas are easy targets for criticism because they arrive in a crude and impractical form, full of flaws and weaknesses. If a critic is present, everyone in the group becomes less willing to share their imperfect, creative ideas.

Instead of responding to flawed ideas with criticism, ideas should be recognized for their *advantages* and *disadvantages*. The advantages and disadvantages should be handled separately, just as you do for your own ideas. Specifically, crude and impractical ideas can be refined by modifying them in ways that retain their advantages and eliminate their disadvantages. Or, useful concepts can be extracted from impractical ideas and combined with other, more promising, ideas. But, combining advantages and disadvantages into a single judgment of badness (or goodness) fails to accomplish anything useful in a creative problem solving session.

If someone is repeatedly unable to resist criticizing, consider not inviting that critic to future creative problem solving sessions.

If someone criticizes one of your ideas, you can diplomatically remind the person that rough ideas can frequently be transformed into better ideas or used as a stimulus to prompt better ideas. For example, you might say:

- "It's true the idea as I've presented it is impractical, but if there were a way to make it practical, wouldn't it solve the problem?"
- "Yes, the idea's impractical, but I'm presenting it in hopes that it might prompt someone to think of a related, but better idea."

In a formal group problem solving session, there's usually a facilitator who can establish a rule to ban criticism. If this approach is used, anyone can say "Hey, no criticizing" whenever it's appropriate. However, this approach has some limitations because criticisms are similar to pointing out weaknesses, which is sometimes needed as a part of refining an idea. For example, suppose someone says, "This idea has the weakness of not working when large numbers of people are involved. How can we refine this idea to remove this weakness?" Does the first of these two sentences amount to a criticism? Perhaps. But does this person's suggestion need to be censored as a criticism? No.

In formal sessions, the tendency for people to criticize can be reduced by a facilitator "warming up" the group with an exercise that's similar to the exercise at the end of the *Looking For Merit In Crude Ideas* section in Chapter 2, *Welcoming New Ideas*. Specifically, the facilitator can suggest a silly and foolish idea as a solution to an unrelated problem and ask everyone to identify advantages of the flawed idea. After hearing everyone make positive comments about an idea that's obviously flawed, the participants will be more willing to reveal their ideas, expecting not to be criticized.

If the threat of criticism is fully removed, not only does everyone feel free to share their ideas, but no one feels a need to preface their ideas with words like, "I know this is going to sound stupid, and it probably won't work, but suppose we ...."

There's another kind of problem that can arise in a group session: participants trying to claim credit for the best solution. In a group session, ideas become mixed, so it's usually misleading to identify a single person as the source of a good idea.

A group of five people were asked to invent a vapor-proof closure for space suits. During the group session one of them suggested using an insect to pull a thread through holes in each side of the closure. Most people would readily reject this idea as impractical, foolish, stupid, and worthless. Fortunately, the people in this group were wise enough not to toss it out. The insect idea prompted someone else to think of the idea of using steel wire in the shape of a spring to be rotated in order to thread the wire through holes in each side of the closure. It was obvious that rotating the coiled wire one turn for each pair of openings would take too much time to be practical. But, someone else realized that two coiled springs could be meshed together lengthwise and a stiff wire could be inserted into the overlapped opening to join the coiled wires together, as shown below. This became the basis for a new closure device. (The dialog for this example appears in both William Gordon's book *SYNECTICS: The Development of Creative Capacity* and James Adams' book *Conceptual Blockbusting*.) In this example, which person deserves the credit for inventing the new vapor-proof closure for space suits? The person who suggested an insect threading the closure? The person who suggested using a coiled wire? Or, the person who suggested using two coiled wires and inserting a stiff wire where they overlap?

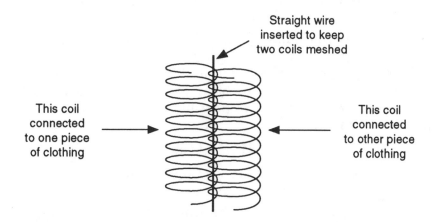

Straight wire
inserted to keep
two coils meshed

This coil
connected
to one piece
of clothing

This coil
connected
to other piece
of clothing

Just as in soccer or basketball, the *whole team* deserves the credit for success. A group's final solution will usually be a combination of elements from the suggestions of several people, so credit cannot usually be given to only one person.

A related problem occurs when someone says that "his" or "her" idea shouldn't be combined with other ideas. The unspoken goal is to keep the idea well-defined so that the person can proudly proclaim it as "mine!" if the idea is chosen as the best alternative. Ultimately, such egocentric tactics can usually be dealt with by reminding the person that the group's goal is to solve the problem, not to create heroes or heroines. Participants who are unwilling to respect this priority can expect not to be invited to future group sessions.

More could be said about the dynamics of welcoming and refining creative ideas in a group context, but the dynamics are very similar to what's involved in welcoming and refining your own ideas. So, if you're seriously interested in improving the dynamics of a group session, reread (or read) the following chapters of this book with an emphasis on seeing how the creative problem solver's tools can be applied in group situations:

- *Welcoming New Ideas*
- *Reconsidering Your Goals*
- *Exploring Your Many Alternatives*
- *Refining Your Ideas*
- *Considering Your Goals Some More*

As you read these chapters, replace the image of an individual learning to be creative with the image of a group of people seeking to be creative. The same principles apply.

Many books, including *Conceptual Blockbusting* by James Adams and *The Creative Edge: Fostering Innovation Where You Work* by William Miller, describe specific strategies for overcoming the blocks to creativity in group problem solving sessions. Such books are worth reading if you're responsible for promoting creativity within an organization.

◄SUMMARY►

To fully appreciate the value of group thinking, give it a try! It's both productive and fun when done in a spirit of cooperation.

Criticism, which dampens the group's creative spirit, can be reduced by judging ideas according to advantages and disadvantages instead of goodness and badness. Attempts to claim ownership of ideas disregard the mixing of ideas that occurs in group thinking.

Encouraging Children
To Solve Problems Creatively

▶ Whenever the opportunity arises, encourage children to solve problems creatively.

Young children don't need to be taught how to *think* creatively. They're naturally creative. Watch kids of about two to seven years of age at play and you'll see them imagining an airplane where you see only boxes, and they'll play "school" using an imaginary blackboard and imaginary desks. Creativity and imagination come naturally. But children are soon taught to stop thinking creatively. They hear, "Now that's a silly idea" or "But that wouldn't work." Adults judge kids' ideas according to adult standards and the kids' ideas are usually flawed.

If a young boy comes up with the idea of using a laser beam to zap mosquitoes he can't know that such an idea is impractical due to the difficulty of detecting mosquitoes and accurately aiming a laser beam, not to mention the high cost of the electric bill. Yet, the underlying idea is creative (if he didn't learn it from somewhere else). When you hear children's creative ideas, you can encourage their creative thinking by saying something like, "That's a clever idea" or "I like the basic idea, but it has some disadvantages." Such comments separate the creative part from the impracticality and make it clear that creative thinking is valued. However, don't mistake this recommendation to mean that lots of praise is needed; undeserved praise undermines the value of deserved praise.

Looking back on my own experiences, I now see that I preserved my creative thinking by keeping my ideas to myself. I quickly learned that sharing a creative idea led to criticism. Fortunately I realized I didn't have to stop thinking creatively, I only had to stop revealing my creative ideas. As my understanding of the world improved, my ideas became more practical.

In addition to encouragement, kids need more opportunities to practice solving *real* problems. It might seem that homework problems provide children with lots of problem solving practice, but most school problems have already been solved countless times using well-established techniques. The table on the next two pages dramatically conveys the differences between school problems and real-life problems. With these differences in mind, typical school problems might be more accurately called exercises, drills, tasks, questions, and puzzles.

Recall from Chapter 1, *Opening The Toolbox*, that one of the reasons for including the word *creative* in the phrase *creative problem solving* is to emphasize that the word *problem* refers to real-life problems, not the kind of problems assigned in school.

School-assigned problems	Real-life problems
The problem has been solved many times before, by many people.	If the problem had already been solved, there wouldn't be a problem.
The motivation to solve the problem is low because no one suffers if the problem isn't solved.	The motivation to solve the problem is high because the undesirable situation continues until the problem is solved.
The goal is clearly stated.	You must identify and clarify your goals.
All the needed information is presented in the problem. That information is correct and relevant.	The readily available information can be incorrect, irrelevant, and misleading. Some of the needed information is usually missing.
Rules can be followed to reach the desired result.	There are no rules to follow.
Usually, there is only one right solution.	There are multiple solutions, none of which is obviously better than the others.
Someone nearby can tell you whether your solution is right or wrong. If there is more than one right solution, someone can tell you how good your solution is.	As far as you know, no one else knows whether your solution will work or whether it's the best solution.

School-assigned problems	Real-life problems
The solution is usually written down somewhere, such as at the back of a book.	A new solution must be created. If the solution already existed, there wouldn't be a problem.
The problem normally involves only objective factors that are definable and measurable.	The problem involves ambiguous information and people's preferences, interpretations, and feelings.
The fact that a problem exists is obvious. Often, it's even labeled with a number.	Sometimes the fact that a problem exists isn't apparent until someone discovers a solution.

It's ironic that the failure of schools to teach children how to solve real problems is leading businesses and government organizations to fund research efforts to "teach" computers how to simulate high-level thinking skills, such as problem solving. This effort is especially ironic because schools focus on teaching the skills that computers can do, such as memorizing facts, doing arithmetic, recognizing misspelled words, and identifying grammatical mistakes in writing. In one sense, these orientations amount to putting artificial intelligence into children and attempting to put real intelligence into computers.

What are the results of failing to give children practice in solving real problems? Business managers find it difficult and expensive to find and hire employees who can create solutions to previously unsolved problems. Even worse, children learn to depend on others to solve their problems for them, leaving them vulnerable to manipulation by people who promise to solve their problems. In a larger context, recall that Adolf Hitler rose to power based on his promise to solve Germany's many post-World War One problems.

So, if you spend lots of time around children, help them become creative problem solvers by doing for them what you do for yourself to facilitate creative problem solving skills:

- See the merit in their crude ideas.
- Express an interest in their suggestions for dealing with situations that don't have a right or wrong answer.
- Encourage them to create what doesn't yet exist, but which might work.
- Permit them to think idealistically as a starting point.
- Allow children to keep their creative ideas to themselves when they so choose.

◄SUMMARY►

Whenever you have the opportunity to do so, encourage children to create solutions to real problems. They're going to need creative problem solving skills as much as any generation ever has.

Exercise 1. If you provide opportunities for children to play, consider presenting them with a challenge of accomplishing something specific, simple, and physical that can be done in many ways — such as moving a round magnet from one side of a room to another. Express your enthusiasm for their ideas. Allow them to try out their ideas right away.

Teaching Creative Problem Solving

There is a growing need for people to teach *problem solving* and *creative problem solving* classes and seminars. This demand is the result of an increasing awareness in schools and businesses that children and adults need to know how to solve real-life problems, not just how to solve academic problems that have well-established correct answers.

If you have experience as a teacher, you might consider teaching such a class or seminar. If you're intimidated by thinking you have to be a creative genius who can come up with great solutions to any problem, relax. That's not necessary.

Teaching creative problem solving is different from teaching conventional subjects such as spelling, biology, and mathematics. Teachers of conventional subjects must be experts who know the correct answers to most questions about their subject. In contrast, a teacher of creative problem solving must be a *facilitator*. As a facilitator, you don't need to immediately answer the question, "How can this problem be solved?" But you do need to understand the skills of creative problem solving well enough to explain how to apply the skills to many different kinds of problems.

What other requirements are important for teaching creative problem solving?

- A contagious enthusiasm for creative problem solving.
- An ability to quickly see merit in students' creative ideas so that you'll greet their ideas with encouraging comments, such as "That's another possible approach" or "Who sees the advantage in Cynthia's idea?" This makes it less likely that you'll say something like, "Well, that idea won't work, but nice try."
- A low level of anger and irritability so that the tone of voice matches the words being spoken. A critical tone of voice can convey criticism even when no critical words are spoken.
- High self-esteem. This stops you from competing with students to come up with clever and practical ideas before they do.
- A diverse range of interests. This diversity broadens the kinds of problems you choose as examples, and better matches the diversity in the kinds of problems students choose as practice problems.

Your primary role as facilitator is to provide opportunities to practice specific techniques of creative problem solving. In choosing exercises and problems to solve, make sure you choose ones that are of interest to the students. To ensure their interest, sometimes ask them to choose practice problems of personal interest. (Note that a problem of personal interest isn't necessarily a personal problem.)

In choosing what to teach, don't get distracted by focusing attention on terminology used to talk about creative problem solving. A knowledge of terminology isn't the same as an ability to solve problems. What the students need is to spend time *doing* creative problem solving and *practicing* creative problem solving skills in exercises.

If grades must be given, avoid the temptation to use written tests that involve right and wrong answers. Such tests steer education away from higher-level thinking skills (such as creative problem solving) toward lower-level thinking skills (such as spelling and arithmetic) that can be programmed into a computer.

Be creative in how you test progress and assign grades. For example, as an assignment, you can ask each student to choose hisher own grade and justify the answer. (This is an application of what you hopefully learned in the *Learning From People Who Understand* section in Chapter 8, *Understanding Clearly*.) Or, you can ask the students on one occasion to create an outline of possible approaches to grading, and on another occasion ask them to refine one of the alternatives. And, in case you've forgotten what you learned in the *Considering Flexibility Instead Of Standardization* section (in Chapter 9, *Considering Your Goals Some More*), consider using different grading approaches for different students. If some of these suggestions seem inappropriate, recognize that:

- Standardized written tests would be less fair because they wouldn't test creative problem solving ability.

- Grades are an example of oversimplified one-dimensional thinking, as explained in the *Recognizing Dimensional Independence* section in Chapter 7, *Thinking Dimensionally*. A grade is a single dimension that attempts to combine these and other independent dimensions: attendance, ability to memorize, interest, effort, progress, the student's skill level at the end of the course, the teacher's ability to teach, and the degree of compatibility between how the teacher teaches and how the student learns most effectively.

It's useful to ask students to give comments and suggestions on written assignments from their classmates. Such peer-review assignments expose students to a useful diversity of ways of thinking.

If you teach students who voluntarily choose to be in the class, the students bring a degree of creativity with them into the classroom. This reduces the burden on you. You don't have to be exceptionally creative. As an added benefit, if you're at a loss for how to deal with a class-related problem, you can ask the students for suggestions.

◀SUMMARY▶

If you choose to teach a class or seminar in creative problem solving, remember that your role is as a facilitator, not an expert. Provide students with opportunities to practice creating solutions to problems. Resist the temptation to teach terminology or give tests that have right and wrong answers. Be creative in how you grade because a grade is a single dimension that attempts to combine multiple independent dimensions. In addition to teaching creative problem solving skills, use the skills in class. Good luck and enjoy!

Chapter 12

Closing The Toolbox

In closing, here are:

- Reminders of highlights
- Suggested additional reading
- Acknowledgments

Highlights

It's not possible to *summarize* what's in this book, but it's possible to list some highlights of what you've read:

- The word *problem*, as used in this book, applies to situations in which there is room for improvement — even if the situation wouldn't otherwise be called a *problem*.
- Use the creative problem solver's tools in any order. Don't mistake the order in which the tools are explained as an indication of the order in which the tools are used. There is no useful step-by-step sequence to follow when creating a solution.
- When a new idea pops into your mind, find the idea's merit. Also, expect the idea to need refinement.
- Refine an idea by removing the idea's disadvantages and keeping its advantages. Don't mistake creativity, cleverness, goodness, and badness as advantages or disadvantages.
- Outline your alternatives, either on paper or in your mind, with an emphasis on identifying new categories. Use the outline to identify overlooked alternatives, and to supply ideas that can be combined to create better ideas.
- When combining ideas, extract the best parts from each idea.
- Prune your collection of ideas by using the process of elimination with extraction. Specifically, before choosing not to pursue an idea, extract the idea's advantages and incorporate them into the remaining ideas.
- To prompt creative solutions, seek insights — which are fresh perspectives that reveal creative alternatives. To prompt useful fresh perspectives, think in alternate ways, seek a clearer

understanding of your goals, and seek a clearer understanding of the situation you want to improve.

- To think in alternate ways:
  - Don't limit your thinking to words and numbers.
  - Think in concepts. A concept can be regarded as a similarity in what's different. Collect useful concepts from anywhere.
  - Think visually. Sketch visual representations to stimulate visual thinking.
  - Develop your intuitive judgment. Facilitate recognition of intuitive judgments by letting go of mental clutter.
  - Think dimensionally. Specifically:
    - Recognize dimensions as possibilities for change.
    - Avoid oversimplifying dimensions as simplistically categorical.
    - Recognize that risk and many other common dimensions are multi-dimensional.
    - Identify combinations of two independent dimensions by drawing a matrix.
    - Differentiate appropriately. When treating things, or people, differently, choose the most appropriate differences, not the most obvious differences.
    - Recognize common dimensions, especially: time, direction, positive versus negative, and existence versus non-existence.
- To seek a clearer understanding of your goals:
  - Head in the direction of an ideal goal. However, don't confuse ideals with fantasies.
  - Pursue positive, rather than negative, goals.
  - Pursue final, rather than intermediate, goals. In pursuing final goals, consider indirect approaches. Especially useful indirect approaches are: redirection, amplification, leverage, and the step-by-step approach.
  - Break down a general goal into multiple specific goals, and prioritize the specific goals.
  - Reconsider your starting point.
  - Save effort by pulling instead of pushing.

- (To seek a clearer understanding of your goals, continued:)
  - Create non-object solutions, not just object-oriented solutions.
  - Be willing to reconsider your goals at any time, especially when you're about to disregard an alternative just because it doesn't fit within your stated goal.
- To seek a clearer understanding of the situation you want to improve:
  - Use curiosity to motivate yourself to learn more about the situation.
  - Learn through your experiences, and the experiences of other people.
  - Conduct mental experiments, using exaggerations to determine the effects of making changes.
  - Conduct safe experiments and learn whatever the results teach you. Recognize that experiments need not be done formally.
  - Avoid oversimplified associative thinking. Do so by understanding why and how things are associated with one another — instead of simply thinking of them as associated.
  - Understand people. Especially, become more clearly aware of your own feelings so that you can better understand other people's feelings and behavior.
- To fully refine a solution:
  - Repeatedly modify a solution to eliminate disadvantages, without losing any of the solution's advantages.
  - Look for disadvantages besides the ones that show up on their own. To prevent creating new problems, anticipate negative consequences.
  - Enhance a solution by incorporating advantages that appear in other ideas.
  - Simplify a solution, without confusing simplification with laziness or over-simplification.
  - Provide a bridge from the old to the new. Although the decision to make a change is usually abrupt, the change itself doesn't have to be abrupt.
  - If necessary, create supporting enhancements.

- When implementing a creative solution:
    - Make sure your solution will really work and doesn't have any unacceptable negative consequences.
    - Handle a criticism according to which kind it is. Respond to a specific valid criticism by removing the criticized disadvantage.
    - If necessary, regard implementing a solution as a separate problem with a separate solution.
    - Overcome a person's resistance to your solution by explaining how the person you're talking to would benefit by making the change.
    - Imitate a bold person's courage, but not hisher haste. Imitate a perfectionist's refinement skill, but not hisher preoccupation with perfection.
    - Be both patient and persistent.
- Transform the techniques of creative problem solving into thinking skills by spending time applying the tools to specific problems of interest to you.

May your creative problem solving skills lead you to greater opportunities and joy!

Sources Of Additional Information

The Creative Problem Solver's Toolbox is designed to serve not only as a book to be read from chapter to chapter but also as a reference book. Consider using it as such, making heavy use of the index and the *Radial Outline Of The Creative Problem Solver's Tools* (on pages 315-321). Because many of the examples in this book illustrate the use of more than one tool, additional examples of specific techniques can be found using the index entries listed under *Tools/techniques/skills, additional examples of.*

Sources of additional information about creative problem solving and innovation are listed below. Within each of the following categories, the items are listed roughly in order of my personal preference.

Books relating to solving people-related and personal problems:

- *Helping Young Children Flourish* by Aletha J. Solter, Ph.D. — Highly recommended. The underlying concepts apply to adults as well as children. Conveys wisdom about the importance of crying and laughing and presents insights about fears, love, challenges, learning, behavior, and social conflicts.

- *Looking Out, Looking In: Interpersonal Communication* by Ronald B. Adler and Neil Towne — An excellent textbook about the relevant issues concerning communication between individuals.

- *Focusing* by Eugene T. Gendlin, Ph.D. — Seemingly the only book that explains the process at the core of effective therapeutic counseling. The examples are worth reading.

- *What Color Is Your Parachute? A Practical Manual for Job-Hunters and Career-Changers* by Richard Nelson Bolles — Useful suggestions for planning job and career changes.

- *Using Your Brain – For A CHANGE* by Richard Bandler, edited by Connirae Andreas and Steve Andreas — Describes innovative techniques for making changes in mental habits and attitudes.

Books about visual thinking:

- *Experiences In Visual Thinking* by Robert McKim — A good how-to book about sketching creative ideas, seeing with a receptive mind, and learning to think visually.

- *Thinking With A Pencil* by Henning Nelms — A comprehensive explanation of techniques that make drawing and sketching easier. It's also intended to make sketching accessible as a tool for thinking and communicating.

- *Drawing On The Right Side Of The Brain* by Betty Edwards — Because a large part of the skill of drawing is *seeing*, this book emphasizes improving your ability to see. Of course, drawing techniques are also explained.

Books about other ways of thinking:

- *A Soprano On Her Head: Right-side-up reflections on life and other performances* by Eloise Ristad — Excellent! Describes innovative approaches to improving musical performance abilities by thinking in new ways. As the subtitle implies, the approaches also apply to improving skills in areas other than music.

- *The Intuitive Edge: Understanding and Developing Intuition* by Philip Goldberg — Filled with many examples of thinking in non-analytical ways. In *The Intuitive Edge*, the phrase *evaluative intuition* is roughly equivalent to the phrase *intuitive judgment* as used in *The Creative Problem Solver's Toolbox*.

- *Visualization: Directing The Movies Of Your Mind* by Adelaide Bry — Includes examples of the tool explained in the *Using Fantasy Visualization To Prompt Insights* section of *The Creative Problem Solver's Toolbox*.

- *Frames Of Mind: The Theory Of Multiple Intelligences* by Howard Gardner — Useful reading for someone who assumes there is only one way of thinking. The author's categories are, however, only one way of grouping the many different ways of thinking.

- *Roget's International Thesaurus* originally by Peter Mark Roget – The *Synopsis of Categories* at the beginning of this reference book is useful for prompting an understanding of some common dimensions and concepts. (Don't confuse this title with the similar title *Roget's Thesaurus*.)

Books that teach clear thinking:

- *How To Write, Speak, And Think More Effectively* by Rudolf Flesch — Excellent. Explains some very useful, but uncommon, techniques to improve clarity in thinking. (The chapters about clear thinking can also be found in *The Art Of Clear Thinking* by the same author.)

- *Information Anxiety: What to do when information doesn't tell you what you want to know* by Richard Saul Wurman — Clarifies the difference between information and understanding, and offers suggestions for dealing with large amounts of information.

Books and resources relating to social innovations:

- *Horace's School: Redesigning the American High School* by Theodore Sizer — Discusses some of the changes needed to improve the quality of public education at the high school level.

- *New Dimensions Radio,* which is broadcast by many public radio stations, hosted by Michael Toms — Interviews with social innovators in areas such as health, relationships, psychology, spirituality, and peace.

- *Megatrends: Ten new directions transforming our lives; Megatrends 2000;* and *Reinventing The Corporation: Transforming your job and your company for the new information society* by John Naisbitt and Patricia Aburdene — Three books by the same authors that describe social, economic, and business changes now taking place.

- *Legal Breakdown: 40 Ways to Fix Our Legal System* by the editors of Nolo Press — Recommends innovations to "make law fair, affordable, and open to all." Of special interest is the last suggestion: creating a *National Idea Registry* that would offer individuals an affordable alternative to the expensive patent system.

- *Marva Collins' Way* by Marva Collins and Civia Tamarkin — An account of one teacher's struggle to bring quality teaching into the classroom.

Book about helping children think creatively:

- *Growing Up Creative: Nurturing a Lifetime of Creativity* by Teresa M. Amabile — Explains how parents and teachers can promote creative thinking in children. Stresses the importance of intrinsic motivation (such as curiosity and personal interest) over extrinsic motivation (such as motivation from adults and rewards announced in advance).

Book about how innovations become popular:

- *Diffusion of Innovations* by Everett M. Rogers — A textbook that covers research findings about how innovations are adopted and why some useful ones aren't adopted. Includes interesting examples.

Great innovators (who created more than only inventions) whose biographies appear in various books:

- *Leonardo da Vinci* — Extremely creative and highly talented artist who also sketched ideas for many inventions. His paintings include the *Mona Lisa* and *The Last Supper*. His sketched inventions include an innovative clock, a spring-driven vehicle, an armored car, a parachute, a crude helicopter, and many other flying machines, to name only a few. Leonardo, from the town of Vinci, was born in 1452. Possibly the greatest creative thinker in history.

- *Isaac Newton* — One of the two men who, independently, created calculus. (Newton called it *fluctions*.) Not only did Newton use this mathematical tool to prove that the planets, moons, sun, and apples are attracted to one another by a force that varies according to distance, but he was the first person to properly account for the paths comets follow, why the axis of the earth changes slightly over many years, and why tides occur. Newton also advanced the understanding of optics and invented what was possibly the first reflecting telescope.

- *Albert Einstein* — Created an understanding of how light, mass, motion, time, distance, and gravity interact with one another in the form of the *specialized theory of relativity* and the *general theory of relativity*. He created the famous equation $E=mc^2$, which indicates how much energy is created when a substance is completely converted into energy. He explained the principle behind the *photoelectric effect*. A brilliant and creative thinker.

- *Benjamin Franklin* — Participated in creating political innovations embodied in the Declaration of Independence and the United States Constitution and promoted local innovations, including setting up an academy that later became the University of Pennsylvania. He invented bifocal glasses, the Franklin stove, and the lightning rod. He made scientific contributions, including proving the electrical nature of lightning.

- *Johann Sebastian Bach* — Extremely innovative in the music he composed. Also, he pioneered the use of thumbs in playing keyboard instruments (at a time when the thumbs were used only if they had to be used) and developed the tuning scheme used in today's keyboard instruments.

- *Walt Disney* — Pioneered and developed the technology and art of making quality animated cartoons, created perhaps the first family (as opposed to kiddie) amusement park, created many innovative movies, created lifelike moving and talking mechanical animals and people, and planned the future-oriented Epcot Center of Disney World.

- *Thomas Jefferson* — Composed the first draft of the innovative Declaration of Independence for the thirteen American colonies, planned the University of Virginia, created the library that became the basis for the Library of Congress, and designed the innovative architecture of his Monticello home.

Books about inventing:

- *Steven Caney's Invention Book* by Steven Caney — Written to inspire and help children to invent. The stories about the creation of familiar inventions such as drive-in movies and roller skates are enjoyable for readers of any age.

- *Patent It Yourself* by David Pressman — Written by a patent attorney, this book explains in detail the patent process and the process of marketing an invention. Highly recommended for anyone interested in obtaining a patent or profiting by inventing.

- *The Genius of China: 3,000 Years of Science, Discovery, and Invention* by Robert Temple — An account of numerous inventions created in China and copied in Europe many centuries later. They include the ship rudder, magnetic compass, parachute, paper, paper money, deep wells for natural gas, gunpowder, and the decimal system.

- *The Wall Chart of Science and Invention: The growth of human knowledge from pre-history to space travel* by Peter North — An illustrated time line of significant innovations in which different kinds of innovations are presented in parallel with one another. It can be read as a book or fastened to a wall.

- *Mothers Of Invention: From the Bra to the Bomb, Forgotten Women and Their Unforgettable Ideas* by Ethlie Ann Vare and Greg Ptacek — The stories behind inventions created by women. They include Catherine Littlefield Greene's participation in the invention of the cotton gin (Eli Whitney was visiting her when he built it), and Lady Mary Montagu's introduction of smallpox inoculations to Europe a century before Edward Jenner was credited for this innovation.

- *Eureka: An Illustrated History of Inventions from the Wheel to the Computer* edited by Edward de Bono — An encyclopedia of important inventions in transportation, communication, energy, materials, agriculture, food, clothing, building, health, tools, mental aids (such as language and mathematics), and other areas. The story of the invention of television is a good example of many people successively contributing to the development of what is often perceived as one invention.

- *The Flight of the Gossamer Condor* — A video program that visually documents the final stages of Paul MacCready's successful invention of the first human-powered aircraft. Filmed as it happened, this program conveys a realistic (although abbreviated) view of the trial, error, and rethinking approach that characterizes the innovation process.

Great inventors whose biographies appear in various books:

- *Nikola Tesla* — Exceptionally creative and productive inventor. Invented various kinds of alternating current (AC) electric motors, various kinds of high voltage transformers, devices for distributing AC electric power, choosing 60 cycles per second for AC electric power distribution in the United States, electric clock synchronized to AC frequency, various kinds of neon and fluorescent lamps, phosphorescent lamp, electron tube, radio tuning, radio antenna with ground connection, radio remote control, and many other inventions, only a few of which he patented. Some biographies of Tesla are wildly inaccurate. *Tesla: Man Out of Time* by Margaret Cheney is accurate concerning his personal life, but weak in correctly identifying his technical accomplishments. *The Prodigal Genius: The Life of Nikola Tesla* by John O'Neill is an accurate, but lengthy and slightly technical, biography of Tesla.

- *Wilbur and Orville Wright* — Pursued their dream of flying to the successful invention of the airplane. Their efforts to overcome countless technical and financial challenges exemplify creativity, teamwork, and the refinement process.

- *Paul MacCready* — Designed the first human-powered aircraft to fly a figure-eight pattern, the first human-powered aircraft to fly across the English Channel, a solar-powered aircraft that flew from Paris to England, a race-winning solar-powered car, and a battery-powered car with good acceleration and practical range.

- *Thomas Edison* — Invented the mechanical phonograph and the carbon microphone (which is still used in the traditional telephones of today). With the help of creative assistants, he invented numerous improvements in existing devices, including an improved filament for electric light bulbs. He patented over 1,100 of these inventions.

- *George Washington Carver* — Best known for his development of more than 300 products made from peanuts and more than 100 products made from sweet potatoes. Also, a talented artist, pianist, and vocalist.

- *Hypatia* — Invented a hydrometer (which measures fluid density) and a variation of a plane astrolabe (which was used in her day to track the motion of the sun, planets, and stars). She lived from 370 AD to 415 and taught science and mathematics in Alexandria, Egypt. She is one of the few bright and innovative women whose existence has been preserved through historical accounts, although this is largely due to her violent murder by monks. An account of her appears in *Hypatia's Heritage: A History of Women in Science from Antiquity through the Nineteenth Century* by Margaret Alic. A picture of her, based on the picture in that book, appears on the cover of *The Creative Problem Solver's Toolbox* as a reminder that women also innovate.

How-to books about creative problem solving, innovation, and creating:

- *A Kick In The Seat Of The Pants: Using Your Explorer, Artist, Judge, & Warrior To Be More Creative* by Roger von Oech — A nice overview of some popular creative problem solving techniques. Enjoyable and inspiring.

- *Wake Up Your Creative Genius* by Kurt Hanks and Jay A. Parry — A good overview of creative thinking techniques with an emphasis on inventing. Enjoyable to read.

- *The Universal Traveler: A soft-systems guide to creativity, problem solving, and the process of design* by Don Koberg and Jim Bagnall — A rich source of creative techniques, more comprehensive than most, but lacking concrete examples.

- *Conceptual Blockbusting: A Guide To Better Ideas* by James Adams — A very good description of blocks to creative thinking.

- *The Search For Solutions* by Horace Freeland Judson — A well-written book that tells the stories behind numerous creative discoveries and solutions. The photographs add interest.

- *The Creative Edge: Fostering Innovation Where You Work* by William C. Miller — Useful perspectives of innovation for people seeking to create innovations within the business environment.

- *Creating* by Robert Fritz — Explains the process of creating, which applies to creating anything from music and lifestyles to solutions and innovations. The summary at the back of the book is especially useful. The author, a professional musician, understands the creative process better than most authors who write about the subject.

- *Winning The Innovation Game* by Denis E. Waitley and Robert B. Tucker — Presents interesting stories of business innovations while explaining the basics of creative thinking.

Answers To Selected Exercises

Page 40, Exercise 2:

Have some students teach other students. This increases the number of people teaching without increasing the number of "teachers".

Page 47, Exercise 2:

Difficult but possible:

- A boundary between departments in an organization.
- A rule that employees arrive at work at 8 a.m. and leave at 5 p.m. – in some kinds of businesses for some kinds of employees.

Very unlikely:

- A rule that employees arrive at work at 8 a.m. and leave at 5 p.m. – for employees who serve walk-in customers in businesses that are open from 8 a.m. to 5 p.m.
- Removing a written law that prohibits littering.

Virtually impossible:

- Changing the number of hours in a day – whether by making the earth turn slower or faster, or by getting everyone to agree to a change in the definition of an hour.

Completely impossible:

- Creating electrical energy without getting it from some other form of energy.

Page 50, Exercise 1:

The final goal is to avoid getting seriously hurt by the attacker.

Page 83, Exercise 2:

Use a tripod. Use a gyroscope. Suspend the binoculars with elastic (such as rubber bands) to isolate its motion from the motion of a hand-held frame. Make the binoculars massive to resist jiggling motion. Design a handle that can be held more steadily. Support the binoculars against the chest instead of being held in the hands. Support them from the head instead of the hands.

Page 90, Exercise 2:

Define a universal *unit* of money, such as a "unidollar", that's never represented in coins or paper currency. A fixed amount, say 10 unidollars, could be defined as equal to an average cost of food, rent, and utilities for an "average" person for one day at a specified standard of living. This definition enables people from different countries to talk about quantities of money in a unit that's the same for all countries (and doesn't change over time). Actual exchanges of money would be done in whatever currency the buyer owns. A central bank would guarantee conversions to any other currency at current exchange rates.

Page 118, Exercise 1:

Eliminate the jars and turn each end of the clear plastic tubing upward. At each location, use the ruler to measure the vertical distance between the ground and the water level within the tube.

Page 127, Exercise 1:

Lakes or, more specifically, the bottoms of lakes.

Page 172, Exercise 2:

Ban store-bought guns but allow homemade guns. Homemade cardboard or wood guns are difficult to mistake for real ones. This suggestion appears in *Helping Young Children Flourish* by Aletha Solter.

Page 181. Exercise 2:

Lower levels of radioactivity reduce the *probability* of disease, but — with the specified assumptions — don't change the gain or loss dimensions.

Page 197. Exercise 1:

Horizontal dimension: Motivation is to avoid pain or discomfort (left side) versus motivation is to seek pleasure (right side).

One interpretation of the vertical dimension: Desirable but not easy (top) versus undesirable but easy (bottom).

Another interpretation of the vertical dimension: Long-term advantages but short-term disadvantages (top) versus short-term advantages but long-term disadvantages (bottom).

Page 203, Exercise 1:

The theater was a drive-in movie theater.

Page 230, Exercise 1:

The main difference is who did the action, the *self* or the other person. Specifically, guilt is a negative feeling about what the self did, whereas anger is a negative feeling about what someone (or something) else (outside of the self) did. Note that actions include speaking and inaction.

As a clarification, the self can feel guilty about what someone else does if the self regards the acting person as somehow representative of the self. For instance, they might both be members of the same group.

Page 230, Exercise 2:

All four feelings are negative reactions to actual or possible event(s). The horizontal dimension is time — past versus future — in terms of when the event(s) happened or might happen. The vertical dimension is the *arrival* of something *disliked* (top) versus the *loss* of something *liked* (bottom).

Thanks To Many People

First, and most important, I thank you, the reader, for taking an interest in creative problem solving and innovation. May your efforts lead to improvements in our lives.

Also, on behalf of appreciative readers, I thank the following people:

- All the students who took my classes in creative problem solving. Through their challenging questions and interesting comments, I learned a lot.

- The hundreds of people from whom I've personally learned ideas, insights, points of view, knowledge, and stories that have been incorporated into the material in this book. To list all their names would be impossible. If you happen to be someone I've met and you feel your name belongs here, this *Thank you* is for you.

- Housemates, close friends, relatives, and acquaintances who taught me useful alternate ways to view the world. Those views are an integral part of this book.

- The thousands of creators of books, magazine articles, classes, lectures, audio tapes, wall charts, public radio programs, public television programs, museums, and other sources whose stories, facts, and concepts have been incorporated into this book.

- Ted Wadman and Gregg Kleiner, of Terra Pacific Writing Corporation, who made the creating of this book possible.

- Anne Smith, Fran Turner, Ted Wadman, Amy Welsh, Bryan Dawley, Bea Cornely, Al Frank, Margaret Fobes, Marilyn Schwader, Julian Kilker, Chris Pyle, Carol Wenk, Norton Hathaway, and others who reviewed, commented on, and edited the manuscripts for this book.

- Ted Wadman, Frances Pepini, and numerous others who taught me how to write gooder.

- Jan Reed, the multi-talented artist who transformed my crude cartoon sketches into real cartoons.

- Jana Johnson, the highly talented artist who transformed an Einstein photograph and a profile drawing of Hypatia into impressive drawings. I failed to do justice to those drawings by electronically tracing them, making simplifications, and putting the results on the cover.

- Brad Johnson, the creative and skilled professional sign painter who created initial layout and lettering ideas for the front cover. (I created the cover artwork, so its imperfections are mine, not his.)

- The benefactors whose financial assistance and financial considerations made it possible to survive on minimal income while writing this book.

- Don Fobes, my brother, through whom I first learned important aspects of inventing.

- Gertrude Branthover, Jerome Henwood, and others who taught me how to clear out the cobwebs in my mind.

- Lottie Klock, the caregiver who taught me the joy of living.

- Margaret Fobes and George Fobes, my parents, who taught me far more than I used to realize, and who provided countless opportunities for me to learn yet more. I'm especially grateful that they gave me opportunities to think for myself instead of only teaching me to rely on others to think for me.

To all the above people, on behalf of readers who appreciate this book, *THANK YOU!*

Radial Outline Of
The Creative Problem Solver's Tools

The following six pages contain a radial outline of the tools explained in this book. (Details about radial outlines are explained starting on page 68.) The outline serves as all of the following:

- An overview showing how the tools in this book relate to one another.

- A checklist of the creative problem solver's tools.

- An index of the tools.

The illustration below indicates what the six-page outline would look like if it could fit onto a single page. The main topic, *Creative Problem Solver's Tools*, is the central item.

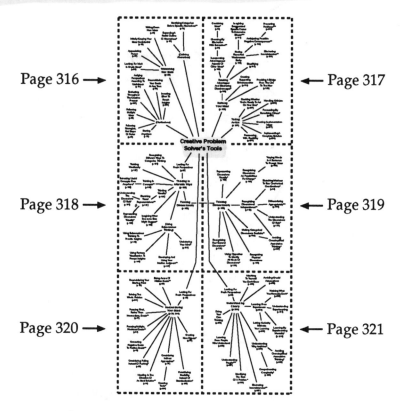

Page 316 → ← Page 317

Page 318 → ← Page 319

Page 320 → ← Page 321

A few of the tools appear more than once because they are closely related to more than one tool. The tools inter-relate in additional ways besides those shown.

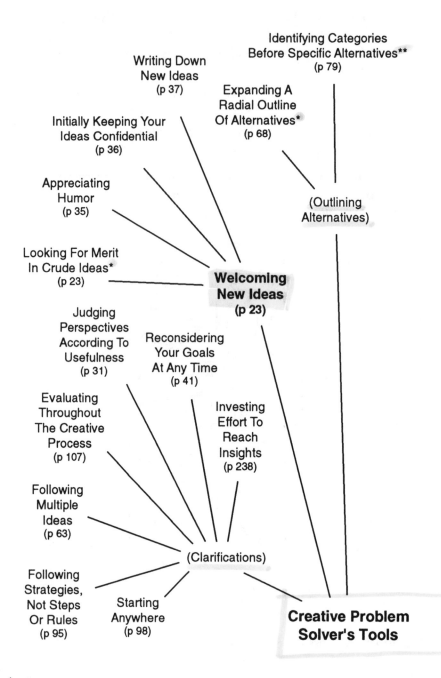

Identifying Categories
Before Specific Alternatives**
(p 79)

Writing Down
New Ideas
(p 37)

Expanding A
Radial Outline
Of Alternatives*
(p 68)

Initially Keeping Your
Ideas Confidential
(p 36)

Appreciating
Humor
(p 35)

(Outlining
Alternatives)

Looking For Merit
In Crude Ideas*
(p 23)

**Welcoming
New Ideas
(p 23)**

Judging
Perspectives
According To
Usefulness
(p 31)

Reconsidering
Your Goals
At Any Time
(p 41)

Evaluating
Throughout
The Creative
Process
(p 107)

Investing
Effort To
Reach
Insights
(p 238)

Following
Multiple
Ideas
(p 63)

Following
Strategies,
Not Steps
Or Rules
(p 95)

Starting
Anywhere
(p 98)

(Clarifications)

**Creative Problem
Solver's Tools**

* Especially important, but takes time to fully learn

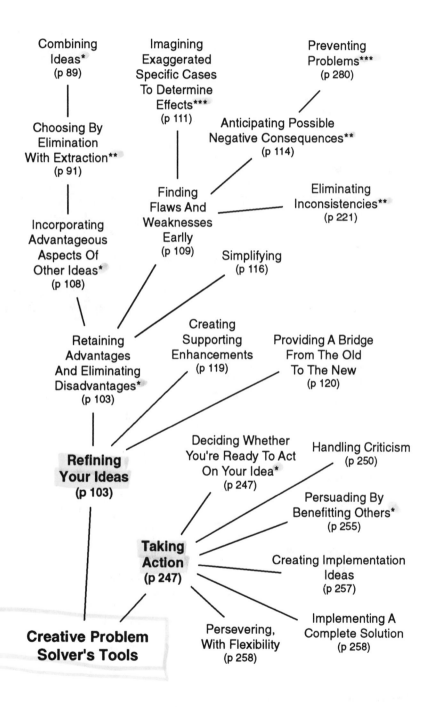

Combining
Ideas*
(p 89)

Imagining
Exaggerated
Specific Cases
To Determine
Effects***
(p 111)

Preventing
Problems***
(p 280)

Choosing By
Elimination
With Extraction**
(p 91)

Anticipating Possible
Negative Consequences**
(p 114)

Incorporating
Advantageous
Aspects Of
Other Ideas*
(p 108)

Finding
Flaws And
Weaknesses
Earlly
(p 109)

Eliminating
Inconsistencies**
(p 221)

Simplifying
(p 116)

Retaining
Advantages
And Eliminating
Disadvantages*
(p 103)

Creating
Supporting
Enhancements
(p 119)

Providing A Bridge
From The Old
To The New
(p 120)

**Refining
Your Ideas**
(p 103)

Deciding Whether
You're Ready To Act
On Your Idea*
(p 247)

Handling Criticism
(p 250)

Persuading By
Benefitting Others*
(p 255)

**Taking
Action**
(p 247)

Creating Implementation
Ideas
(p 257)

**Creative Problem
Solver's Tools**

Persevering,
With Flexibility
(p 258)

Implementing A
Complete Solution
(p 258)

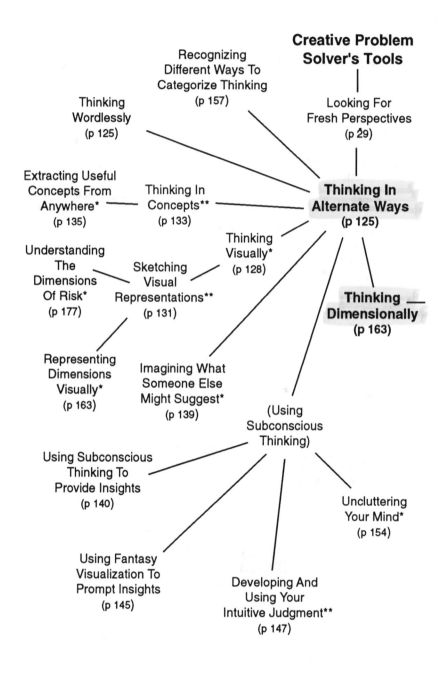

Recognizing
Different Ways To
Categorize Thinking
(p 157)

**Creative Problem
Solver's Tools**

Thinking
Wordlessly
(p 125)

Looking For
Fresh Perspectives
(p 29)

Extracting Useful
Concepts From
Anywhere*
(p 135)

Thinking In
Concepts**
(p 133)

**Thinking In
Alternate Ways
(p 125)**

Thinking
Visually*
(p 128)

Understanding
The
Dimensions
Of Risk*
(p 177)

Sketching
Visual
Representations**
(p 131)

**Thinking
Dimensionally
(p 163)**

Representing
Dimensions
Visually*
(p 163)

Imagining What
Someone Else
Might Suggest*
(p 139)

(Using
Subconscious
Thinking)

Using Subconscious
Thinking To
Provide Insights
(p 140)

Uncluttering
Your Mind*
(p 154)

Using Fantasy
Visualization To
Prompt Insights
(p 145)

Developing And
Using Your
Intuitive Judgment**
(p 147)

* Especially important, but takes time to fully learn

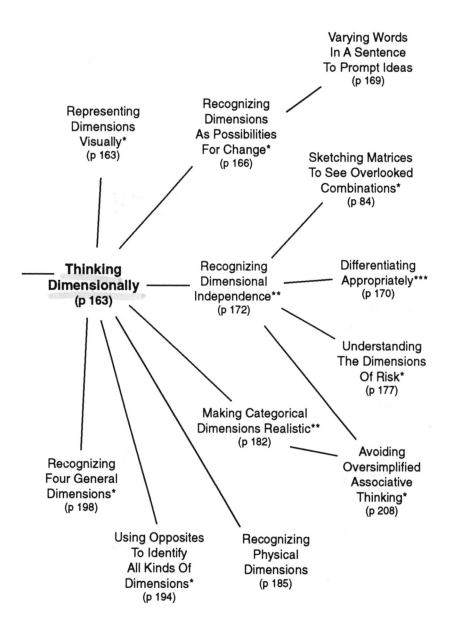

Varying Words
In A Sentence
To Prompt Ideas
(p 169)

Representing
Dimensions
Visually*
(p 163)

Recognizing
Dimensions
As Possibilities
For Change*
(p 166)

Sketching Matrices
To See Overlooked
Combinations*
(p 84)

**Thinking
Dimensionally
(p 163)**

Recognizing
Dimensional
Independence**
(p 172)

Differentiating
Appropriately***
(p 170)

Understanding
The Dimensions
Of Risk*
(p 177)

Making Categorical
Dimensions Realistic**
(p 182)

Recognizing
Four General
Dimensions*
(p 198)

Avoiding
Oversimplified
Associative
Thinking*
(p 208)

Using Opposites
To Identify
All Kinds Of
Dimensions*
(p 194)

Recognizing
Physical
Dimensions
(p 185)

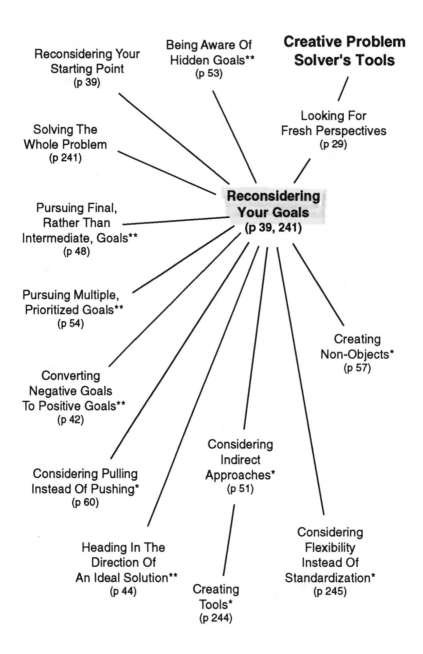

Reconsidering Your
Starting Point
(p 39)

Being Aware Of
Hidden Goals**
(p 53)

**Creative Problem
Solver's Tools**

Looking For
Fresh Perspectives
(p 29)

Solving The
Whole Problem
(p 241)

Pursuing Final,
Rather Than
Intermediate, Goals**
(p 48)

**Reconsidering
Your Goals**
(p 39, 241)

Pursuing Multiple,
Prioritized Goals**
(p 54)

Creating
Non-Objects*
(p 57)

Converting
Negative Goals
To Positive Goals**
(p 42)

Considering Pulling
Instead Of Pushing*
(p 60)

Considering
Indirect
Approaches*
(p 51)

Heading In The
Direction Of
An Ideal Solution**
(p 44)

Creating
Tools*
(p 244)

Considering
Flexibility
Instead Of
Standardization*
(p 245)

* Especially important, but takes time to fully learn

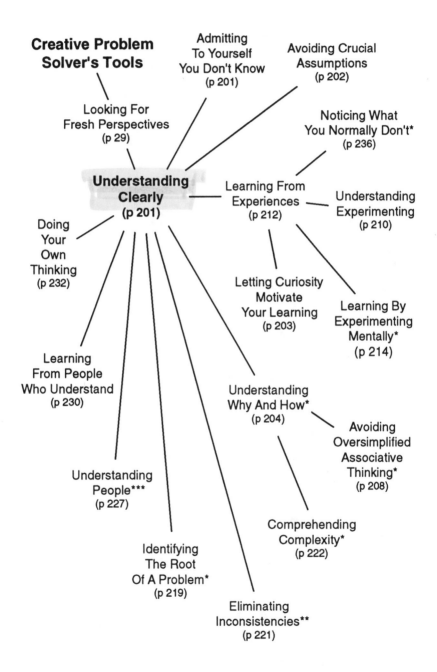

**Creative Problem
Solver's Tools**

Admitting
To Yourself
You Don't Know
(p 201)

Avoiding Crucial
Assumptions
(p 202)

Looking For
Fresh Perspectives
(p 29)

Noticing What
You Normally Don't*
(p 236)

**Understanding
Clearly
(p 201)**

Learning From
Experiences
(p 212)

Understanding
Experimenting
(p 210)

Doing
Your
Own
Thinking
(p 232)

Letting Curiosity
Motivate
Your Learning
(p 203)

Learning By
Experimenting
Mentally*
(p 214)

Learning
From People
Who Understand
(p 230)

Understanding
Why And How*
(p 204)

Avoiding
Oversimplified
Associative
Thinking*
(p 208)

Understanding
People***
(p 227)

Comprehending
Complexity*
(p 222)

Identifying
The Root
Of A Problem*
(p 219)

Eliminating
Inconsistencies**
(p 221)

Index

Page numbers are given in tenths. The number to the left of the decimal point is the page number. The digit (0-9) to the right of the decimal point indicates how far down the page, as indicated on the ruler to the right, to find the referenced paragraph.

.0

.1

.2

.3

.4

.5

.6

.7

.8

.9

Inventions, specific

Aircraft, human-powered
212.5-213.1

Airplane 36.8-36.9, 110.4-110.9,
284.6-284.7, 285.3-285.4

Audio cassette deck, reversing
116.8-117.2

Automobile 258.9-259.2

Automobile lift 91.4-93.9

Baby carrier 283.2-283.8

Boat, Leonardo's paddle-wheel
powered 128.8-129.0

Boat, steam-engine powered
250.9

Car, Leonardo's spring driven
128.8-129.0

Champagne 251.0

Chocolate chip cookie
166.6-166.9

Circular saw 108.3-108.5

Clock radio 89.1-89.2

Clock, Leonardo's innovative
128.8-129.0

Electric light filament 119.8-119.9

Electric motor, alternating
current 135.1-135.7,
153.2-153.6, 214.6-214.8

Electric motor, direct current
255.7-255.9

Elevator, energy efficient
107.1-107.3

Engines 14.9

Fork 36.7-36.8

Geodesic dome 203.6-203.8

Helicopter 204.6-205.2

Helicopter, Leonardo's
128.8-129.0

Key chain, beeping 80.6-81.8

Keyboard layout, Dvorak
44.1-44.5

Money device 215.4-216.5

Paper 136.3

Parachute, Leonardo's
128.8-129.0

Photocopiers 9.9-10.1

Photography 126.6-126.7

Inventions, specific (continued)

Photography, Polaroid
251.1-251.2

Photography, color 244.3-244.5

Printer, bidirectional computer
117.6-117.8

Radio, FM stereo 120.6-120.9

Radio-controlled car's turning
mechanism 241.4-243.5

Reaper 284.8-284.9

Roller skates 109.5-109.9

Sewing machine 140.4-140.8

Shopping carts 257.4-257.5

Skyscraper 108.6-108.8

Snorkel, Leonardo's diving
128.8-129.0

Tank, Leonardo's military
128.8-129.0

Telephone 14.8-14.9, 285.1-285.2

Telephone, carbon microphone
for 210.3-210.9

Typewriter 136.0

Vapor-proof closure for space
suit 288.8-289.6

Velcro fastener 136.2

Windshield wipers on glasses
40.5-40.6

J

Judgment, see *Evaluation and
judgment*

L

**Learning the tools explained in
this book** 261.6-263.5

N

Non- prefix 184.4-184.5

Not word 184.4-184.5

O

Outlines, radial 68.0-81.9,
186.9-189.9, 192.0-193.7,
315.0-321.9

P

Brief Book Description

The Creative Problem Solver's Toolbox describes more than sixty-five learnable thinking skills that enable you to create innovations or creatively solve problems of any kind. More than two hundred examples illustrate how to apply these skills to real-life situations. Behind-the-scene stories about well-known innovations such as the typewriter and basketball are included. Examples cover a wide variety of situations including solving business problems, raising children, improving relationships, looking for employment, inventing, and solving global problems.

About The Author

Richard Fobes (*Fobes* rhymes with *robes*) teaches Creative Problem Solving Skills workshops, and wrote a *Creative Problem Solving Tips* column for four years for the American Creativity Association's *Focus* publication. The material explained here he learned outside of classrooms, beginning in childhood. He holds a Bachelor of Science degree in Physics and studied atmospheric science as a graduate student. He has worked as a writer, interactive multimedia software designer, systems analyst, computer programmer, inventor, electronics technician, hardware store clerk, and dance instructor.

For information about how to order additional copies of this book:

www.SolutionsCreative.com
(author's web site)

1-800-954-8715
(voice message from author)

Solutions Through Innovation
PO Box 19003
Portland, OR 97280-0003